Professions and Professional Service Firms

Professions are increasingly linked with enterprise at a number of interrelated levels. By considering the relationship of professions to the enterprise contexts in which they work, this book reveals the dilemmas posed to professional groups, and the opportunities and constraints that can arise in their organisational frameworks.

Addressing both private and public sectors, this collection explores questions including: what are the implications for the culture, practices and identities of professions of working in enterprise contexts, including with increased globalisation? Are professions becoming more entrepreneurial in a knowledge economy? What are the tensions between professionalism and enterprise and how are these resolved? These are themes that are extremely important to professionals and their managers, especially with the rise of large-scale professional service firms serving corporate clients with truly global reach.

This cutting-edge collection will be of interest to researchers, educators and advanced students studying professional behaviour in fields such as business studies, management, organisational analysis, public administration, political science, social policy and sociology, as well as students on focused programmes of professional study in fields such as health, law and social care.

Mike Saks is Emeritus Professor at the University of Suffolk, UK. He has published more than fifteen edited and sole-authored books on professions, health, regulation, and research methods with leading publishers, including five volumes with Routledge, and many articles and book chapters on these subjects.

Daniel Muzio is Professor of Professions and Organisation at Newcastle University, UK. His research has been published in leading journals and he is a founding editor of the *Journal of Professions and Organization* and associate editor of *Gender, Work and Organization* and the *Journal of Management Studies*.

Routledge Advances in Management and Business Studies

For a full list of titles in this series, please visit www.routledge.com/series/SE0305

67 **Diversity in Multinational Corporations**
   Roxana D. Maiorescu and Brenda J. Wrigley

68 **Gender Equality in a Global Perspective**
   Edited by Anders Örtenblad, Raili Marling, and Snježana Vasiljević

69 **Turnaround Management and Bankruptcy**
   Edited by Jan Adriaanse and Jean-Pierre van der Rest

70 **Strategies, Leadership and Complexity in Crisis and Emergency Operations**
   Stig O. Johannessen

71 **Automotive Global Value Chain**
   The Rise of Mega Suppliers
   Wilson Kia Onn Wong

72 **Managing Social Purpose Driven Organizations**
   Looking at the Third Sector
   Wee Beng Geok

73 **Navigating Through Changing Times**
   Knowledge Work in Complex Environment
   Edited by Anne Eskola

74 **Transitions from Education to Work**
   Workforce Ready Challenges in the Asia Pacific
   Edited by Roslyn Cameron, Subas Dhakal and John Burgess

75 **Professions and Professional Service Firms**
   Private and Public Sector Enterprises in the Global Economy
   Edited by Mike Saks and Daniel Muzio

Professions and Professional Service Firms

Private and Public Sector Enterprises in the Global Economy

Edited by
Mike Saks and
Daniel Muzio

LONDON AND NEW YORK

First published 2018
by Routledge
2 Park Square, Milton Park, Abingdon, Oxon OX14 4RN

and by Routledge
711 Third Avenue, New York, NY 10017

Routledge is an imprint of the Taylor & Francis Group, an informa business

© 2018 selection and editorial matter, Mike Saks and Daniel Muzio; individual chapters, the contributors

The right of Mike Saks and Daniel Muzio to be identified as the authors of the editorial matter, and of the authors for their individual chapters, has been asserted in accordance with sections 77 and 78 of the Copyright, Designs and Patents Act 1988.

All rights reserved. No part of this book may be reprinted or reproduced or utilised in any form or by any electronic, mechanical, or other means, now known or hereafter invented, including photocopying and recording, or in any information storage or retrieval system, without permission in writing from the publishers.

Trademark notice: Product or corporate names may be trademarks or registered trademarks, and are used only for identification and explanation without intent to infringe.

British Library Cataloguing-in-Publication Data
A catalogue record for this book is available from the British Library

Library of Congress Cataloging-in-Publication Data
Names: Saks, Mike, editor. | Muzio, Daniel, editor.
Title: Professions and professional service firms : private and public sector enterprises in the global economy / [edited by] Mike Saks and Daniel Muzio.
Description: Abingdon, Oxon ; New York, NY : Routledge, 2018. | Includes bibliographical references and index.
Identifiers: LCCN 2017051364 (print) | LCCN 2017054525 (ebook) | ISBN 9781315560311 (eBook) | ISBN 9781138675957 (hardback : alk. paper)
Subjects: LCSH: Professional corporations–Management. | Professions. | Globalization.
Classification: LCC HD62.65 (ebook) | LCC HD62.65 .P75 2018 (print) | DDC 338.4–dc23
LC record available at https://lccn.loc.gov/2017051364

ISBN: 978-1-138-67595-7 (hbk)
ISBN: 978-1-315-56031-1 (ebk)

Typeset in Times New Roman
by Wearset Ltd, Boldon, Tyne and Wear

Contents

List of illustrations vii
Notes on contributors viii

1 Introduction: professions and professional service firms 1
   MIKE SAKS AND DANIEL MUZIO

PART I
Professions and enterprise in global perspective 7

2 Professions and entrepreneurship in international
   perspective 9
   KEVIN T. LEICHT

3 Professions and professional service firms in a global
   context: reframing narratives 26
   JOHN FLOOD

4 Professional strategies and enterprise in transnational
   projects 46
   JACOB HASSELBALCH AND LEONARD SEABROOKE

PART II
Changes in professionalism in an enterprise context 65

5 Professionalism as enterprise: service class politics and the
   redefinition of professionalism (with Postscript:
   Extinguishing professionalism?) 67
   GERARD HANLON

6 Enterprise, hybrid professionalism and the public sector 93
MIRKO NOORDEGRAAF

7 Entrepreneurship and professional service firms: the team, the firm, the ecosystem and the field 110
MARKUS REIHLEN, ANDREAS WERR AND CHRISTOPH SECKLER

PART III
Key issues related to professions and professional service firms 135

8 The implications for gender of work in professional service firms: the case of law and accountancy 137
HILARY SOMMERLAD AND LOUISE ASHLEY

9 Regulation and governance of the professions: institutional work and the demise of 'delegated' self-regulation of the accounting profession 157
MARY CANNING AND BRENDAN O'DWYER

10 The medical profession, enterprise and the public interest 177
MIKE SAKS

Index 194

Illustrations

Figures

7.1	Framework of an entrepreneurial ecosystem in professional services	119
9.1	Institutional work and governance change in the accounting profession	167

Tables

6.1	Responding to conflicts between organisational and professional logics	98
7.1	Opposing concepts – entrepreneurship versus professionalism	112

Box

9.1	Key events leading to regulatory change in the Irish accounting profession	160

Contributors

Louise Ashley, is Lecturer in Human Resource Management and Organisational Behaviour, Royal Holloway, University of London, and Visiting Fellow, Cass Business School, City University, UK.

Mary Canning is Associate Professor in Accounting, Quinn School of Business, University College Dublin, Belfield, Republic of Ireland.

John Flood is Professor of Law and Director of Law Futures Centre, Griffith University, Australia.

Gerard Hanlon is Professor of Organisational Sociology, School of Business and Management, Queen Mary University, UK.

Jacob Hasselbalch is a Postdoctoral Researcher, Department of Business and Politics, Copenhagen Business School, Denmark.

Kevin T. Leicht is Professor of Sociology, Department of Sociology, University of Illinois Urbana-Champaign, United States.

Daniel Muzio is Professor of Professions and Organisation at Newcastle University, UK, and holds visiting positions at Manchester Business School, Saïd Business School, Oxford University, and the University of Law, London, UK.

Mirko Noordegraaf is Professor of Public Management, Utrecht School of Governance, Utrecht University, The Netherlands.

Brendan O'Dwyer is Professor of Accounting, Faculty of Economics and Business, Amsterdam University, The Netherlands.

Markus Reihlen is Professor of Strategic Management, Institute of Management and Organisation, Faculty of Business and Economics, Leuphana University of Lüneburg, and International Research Fellow at the Saïd Business School, Oxford University, UK.

Mike Saks is Emeritus Professor at the University of Suffolk, UK, and Visiting Professor at the University of Lincoln, Royal Veterinary College, University of London, and Plymouth Marjon University, UK, and the University of Toronto, Canada.

Leonard Seabrooke is Professor of Business and Politics, Department of Business and Politics, Copenhagen Business School, Denmark.

Christoph Seckler, is Lecturer in Management and Organisation Studies, Leuphana University of Lüneberg, Germany, and Visiting Research Fellow at the Saïd Business School, Oxford University, UK.

Hilary Sommerlad is Professor of Law, School of Law, University of Leeds, UK.

Andreas Werr is Professor of Economics, Stockholm School of Economics, University of Stockholm, Sweden.

1 Introduction

Professions and professional service firms

Mike Saks and Daniel Muzio

The rationale for the book

This co-edited book aims to fill a significant gap on professions and professional service firms in the enterprise context in the literature. There are many texts on enterprises in the private and public sector, as defined in terms of business organisation – from the book by Carter and Jones-Evans (2006) on *Enterprise and Small Businesses* to that of Lam (2014) on *Enterprise Risk Management*. The relationship between professions and professional service firms and enterprise in the global economy, which is often seen to be in tension, is also frequently discussed in standard business studies books, albeit typically only in a few paragraphs. This is illustrated by the edited collection by Linstead, Fulop and Liley (2009) on *Management and Organization* and the text by Thompson and McHugh (2009) entitled *Work Organisations*. A key rationale for the edited collection presented here is that these areas have not been systematically brought together and addressed, except in articles in outlets such as the *Journal of Professions and Organization* (see, for example, Na Fu, Flood and Morris 2016; Pickering 2017) and dedicated profession-specific journals such as *Accounting, Organizations and Society* (see, for instance, Kurunmaki 2004; Lander, Koene and Linsson 2013). To be sure, such areas are also occasionally discussed in segmented book chapters, like the sole-authored text by Freidson (2001) on *Professionalism: The Third Logic* and the edited compilation by Dent, Bourgeault, Denis and Kuhlmann (2016) entitled *The Routledge Companion to the Professions and Professionalism* – but crucially they remain relatively at the periphery in terms of focus.

This current collection, however, synergistically focuses on professions working in enterprise contexts in both the public and private domains. This was a key part of the framework adopted for an International Sociological Association conference on professions and enterprise held at University Campus Suffolk in the United Kingdom in academic year 2012/13 – from which the idea for this volume originated. This conference was co-ordinated by one of the editors of this book who was the then President of the International Sociological Association Research Committee on Professional Groups. The level of interest generated on the theme on which it was based was very evident and forms a central aspect of the profile of the second editor, who has published widely and presented many papers on professions and professional service firms in the private and public sector. The attractiveness of the professions, professional service firm and enterprise theme has also been highlighted in the clustering of papers around this field in a global context at several subsequent conferences – including the annual, specially invited, Professions Fest at Edinburgh University and the Professional Service Firms Conference linked to the Saïd Business School at Oxford University – recently held at this latter venue and the School of Economics at Stockholm University. Both of the editors regularly attend such meetings and other related international conferences and are therefore very aware of the direction of development of the field. They are joined in this venture by a carefully selected group of thirteen contributors from eight different countries – spanning from Europe to Australia and North America – who are among the top writers globally on the themes it contains. At this point the specific contents of the book will now be outlined.

The contents of this volume

Professions are increasingly linked with enterprise at a number of interrelated levels in a fast-changing global socio-economic context. The content of this collection explores this shift, particularly in modern Western neo-liberal societies. In considering the relationship of professions to the enterprise contexts in which they work, it focuses on the dilemmas posed for professional groups – including the opportunities and constraints that can arise in the organisational frameworks in which they are based. This is best highlighted by examples of the questions the book addresses in the private and public sector: what are the implications for the culture, practices and identities of professions of working in enterprise contexts, including with increased globalisation? What role, in particular here, is played by professional service firms? What is the impact in terms of hybridisation of professional work and how is this managed? Are professions becoming more entrepreneurial in a knowledge economy placing ever greater importance on the creation, diffusion and transfer of knowledge? What are the tensions between professionalism and enterprise and how are these resolved? In addressing these and other related questions, this book has drawn largely on freshly commissioned, high standard work, reflecting both landmark and newly emerging issues in the area. The nine further thought-provoking constituent chapters of this book – following this Introduction – are organised into three parts, which are set out below.

The first part of this co-edited collection considers professions and enterprise in global perspective. It opens with a chapter by Leicht who considers the relationship between professions and entrepreneurialism. He notes that professions and professional knowledge have been criticised by post-modernists whose views challenge on various grounds the modernist quest for collective justice and community. Their critique has been amplified by neo-liberal political and economic ideologies that hold that unfettered markets can provide higher quality services at lower prices. Leicht argues, though, that this is contentious and professionals themselves can be entrepreneurial in an international context in championing the common good in such roles as risk managers, information interpreters, propagators of values and ideologies, and promoters of change. This is followed by a chapter by Flood who more discursively discusses how the global narrative about professions has been reconstituted theoretically and substantively with wider changes over time. These changes include the emergence of enterprise as a dominant logic, along with the development of professional service firms. They lead to contemplation about the future of professions in a world of increased technology and democracy. The theme of whether professions may no longer be such a dominant force in modern neo-liberal societies is taken up further by Hasselbalch and Seabrooke who raise the analysis to another level by examining how complex transnational projects involving enterprise can be addressed by professionals. A central part of the process involves transnational professionals adopting various types of knowledge and framing strategies to provide policy solutions – thereby creating markets for their own services, as well as giving managers of the organisations concerned more control.

The second part of the book examines changes in professionalism in an enterprise context. It begins with a seminal chapter by Hanlon that features his reprinted article from the 1990s which was among the first to consider the shifting relationship between professions and enterprise. More specifically, it examines the cleavage in the service class and the redefinition of professionalism in a more entrepreneurial culture – in which traditional values and priorities such as universal access, public services and social trusteeship have steadily been replaced by new commercial priorities emphasizing cost effectiveness, efficiency and the ability to add value. A brief Postscript by the author is added to reflect further significant interrelated changes in enterprise and professionalism in the global economy over the past two decades. The next chapter by Noordegraaf then explores trends related to enterprise, hybrid professionalism and the public sector. In examining the implications of the new era of enterprise for both classical and other professions in public arenas, he analyses schematically how the various conflicting institutional logics are mediated by the professional workers involved and explores the range of responses to such logics, including hybridisation. Finally, Reihlen, Werr and Seckler examine entrepreneurship in professional service firms. In addressing the question of how the growing number of such firms can act entrepreneurially in an enterprise context, this chapter reviews previous work on entrepreneurship in professional services covering three levels of analysis – the entrepreneurial team, the entrepreneurial firm, and the entrepreneurial ecosystem within which the creation and exploitation of entrepreneurial opportunities take place on a growing scale.

The third part of this volume looks at key issues related to professions and professional service firms. In their chapter Sommerlad and Ashley consider the implications of gender for work in professional service firms – focusing on law and accountancy in the Anglo-American context which have been most heavily defined by the existence of such firms. In examining through the lens of complexity theory how an increasingly commercial orientation, and the new models and practices this inspires, affect the work patterns and lived experiences of female professionals, the analysis centres on issues like long hours and career trajectories. Canning and O'Dwyer then consider regulation and governance in the professions with reference to the demise of 'delegated' self-regulation in the accountancy profession in the Irish context. This enables them in their chapter to provide important insights into the interplay between local and global patterns of professional regulation. Finally, Saks examines at a macro level the profession of medicine – which is not so directly linked to personal service firms, but is nonetheless highly significant in terms of the professional pecking order. In considering the activities of the medical profession in the United States and Britain, he argues that both have been affected in different ways by the relevant enterprise contexts in which they operate. In a climate that has become more critical of professions both theoretically and in terms of popular culture, he considers how far professional altruism claims can be seen as being preserved in serving the public interest or whether they are simply an ideological smokescreen to mask self-interests in enhancing income, status and power in a complex world, influenced increasingly by users of services and multinational corporations.

Conclusion

Understanding such themes of this co-edited book is very important to both professionals themselves and those managing at different levels in private and public enterprise environments in modern societies – not least with the rise of large-scale professional service firms serving corporate and other clients in the global economy. As such, the book should appeal to those actively involved in professional and managerial fields, as well as those studying on a range of related final stage vocational undergraduate and postgraduate programmes. It should also prove valuable to students engaged on purely academically driven higher-level courses and to lecturers and researchers in cognate fields in business, law and management schools, as well as those in the social sciences. This is accentuated by the fact that there are as yet no other texts specifically focused on the exploration of professions, professional service firms and enterprise in the private and public sector in a globalised context. Although there are numerous articles and book chapters mentioned at the outset that each cover some, usually quite a small, part of the ground – as well as parallel, but not directly competing, texts focused on areas like entrepreneurship like *A Handbook of Research on Entrepreneurship in Professional Services* edited by Reihlen and Werr (2012) – these do not provide the extensive overview available here. It is therefore hoped that this book can not only stimulate fascinating debates about the past, present and future role of professions and professional service firms in an enterprise environment, but also ensure that this area is coherently covered in one volume by drawing together the work of internationally well-known expert contributors in this field.

References

Carter, S. and Jones-Evans, D. (2006) *Enterprise and Small Businesses: Principles, Practice and Policy*, Harlow: Pearson Education Limited, 2nd edition.

Dent, M., Bourgeault, I., Dennis, J. and Kuhlmann, E. (eds) (2016) *The Routledge Companion on Professions and Professionalism*, Abingdon: Routledge.

Freidson, E. (2001) *Professionalism: The Third Logic*, Cambridge: Polity Press.

Kurunmaki, L. (2004) 'A hybrid profession: The acquisition of management accounting knowledge by medical professionals', *Accounting, Organizations and Society* 29, 327–47.

Lam, J. (2014) *Enterprise Risk Management: From Incentives to Controls*, Hoboken, NJ: John Wiley and Sons, 2nd edition.

Lander, M. W., Koene, B. A. S. and Linsson, S. N. (2013) 'Committed to professionalism: Organizational responses of mid-tier accounting firms to conflicting institutional logics', *Accounting, Organizations and Society* 38(2): 130–48.

Linstead, S., Fulop, L. and Liley, S. (eds) (2009) *Management and Organization: A Critical Text*, Basingstoke: Palgrave Macmillan, 2nd edition.

Na Fu, Flood, P. C. and Morris, T. (2016) 'Organizational ambidexterity and professional firm performance: The moderating role of organizational capital', *Journal of Professions and Organization* 3(1): 1–16.

Pickering, M. E. (2017) 'Strategic decision making in publicly traded professional service companies: An exploration of senior professional participation in acquisition decision processes', *Journal of Professions and Organization* 4(2): 179–202.

Reihlen, M. and Werr, A. (eds) (2012) *A Handbook of Research on Entrepreneurship in Professional Services*, Cheltenham: Edward Elgar.

Thompson, P. and McHugh, D. (2009) *Work Organisations*, Basingstoke: Palgrave Macmillan, 4th edition.

Part I
Professions and enterprise in global perspective

2 Professions and entrepreneurship in international perspective

Kevin T. Leicht

Introduction

Professional work and the professionals that do it have faced increasing pressure to submit to markets in order to reform overall service delivery and increase efficiency (see Hanlon 1999). The relatively new emphasis on market efficiency has occurred in tandem with several other cross-cutting developments – well-publicised financial scandals involving new entrepreneurial roles for professionals (exemplified by Enron and Parmalat) and the cultural shifts accompanying 'the end of expertise' (Nichols 2017) and its most recent manifestations, the Brexit vote and the election in the United States of Donald Trump. These trends are part of a wider trend towards growing radical reflexivity among consumers and cultural fragmentation associated with the spread of post-modernism, with the accompanying scepticism of grand narratives and the coercive component of expert claims. These cross-cutting trends leave individual consumers and clients adrift in a sea of contradiction – mistrustful of free markets, yet mistrustful of experts and their grand narratives. This existential dilemma provides several opportunities for revitalised professions to stand in the breach between the global and the personal. I will start this chapter with a look at recent developments then tie those developments to broader long-term trends that have changed the nature of professional work.

The end of expertise and the rise of post-modern reasoning

Recent cultural developments spell trouble for professional groups who occupy institutional niches based on expert claims. Most damaging is the appearance of a 'war on expertise' and the implications that this has for the future of professional expert knowledge. The most prominent recent version of this argument is by Nichols (2017). Nichols suggests that there is a campaign against established knowledge that is dangerous for democracies and their citizens. The traditional role of the expert (in our case synonymous with the professional) is to collect and interpret knowledge for citizens in specific areas. The traditional division of labour as Durkheim described it requires that people defer to professional judgements in specific areas of expertise. The combination of lots of different experts in lots of different areas (and the commitment of professionals to defer to others outside of their area of expertise) leads to an active dialogue where debates centre on factual knowledge and interpretation with citizen input. Surgeons are not legal experts. Middle East scholars don't make pronouncements on Japan. English scholars don't do accounting, and so on.

In Nichol's analysis this dynamic has fallen victim to a pseudo 'democratisation of knowledge' where everyone's opinion is of equal value regardless of what the conveyor actually knows. Any suggestion that there are factual, scientific, or logical errors in one's argument is met with a direct attack suggesting the critic is 'elitist', 'out of touch', or worse. This form of 'aggressive ignorance' denies that people who have studied a topic for years know anything of value that cannot be googled. Nichols points out that the forms of pseudo-expertise this flattened hierarchy has created are elusory and dangerous. Google will confirm any random opinion we have, no matter how fanciful. So-called 'citizen journalists' don't do very good journalism. Pontificators and pundits talk about everything from global warming to heart surgery and know next to nothing about any of it. Worse still, the so-called 'expert citizen' is never corrected when wrong and their opinions don't change, unlike professionals where there is a check-and-balance system in place that makes corrections (sometimes slowly). Nichols blames a wide swath of institutions in the public sphere for this problem, from colleges and universities that sell 'experiences' that assure that students are never challenged or corrected, to talking heads on news programmes, to the general narcissism of American millennials.

Two classic and recent examples of Nichols' argument about expertise – and the accompanying post-truth world it portends (Pippenger 2017; Rogers 2017) – are the United Kingdom vote in support of leaving the European Union (commonly known as Brexit) and the election of Donald Trump as President in the United States. Both spell trouble for democratic polities and professional expertise. The nuances of each case differ, but overall these are the same – globalisation has produced a 'democratic deficit' (Stiglitz 2013) where decisions about people's lives are surrendered to distant cities filled with people who are immigrants or otherwise viewed as 'other'. Many of these others (foreign and domestic) are skilled professionals who are viewed as out of touch with the 'real people' who view themselves as harmed by the prerogatives of experts and the policies they advocate. The politicians who populist voters champion are viewed as political outsiders, but more directly they are outside of the conventional corridors of expertise from which elected politicians and policy analysts come. In the case of Brexit, voters seemed to be expressing exasperation with globalisation and the idea that their lives needed to be tied to a group of 'unknown others', many with whom they shared little culturally. In the case of Donald Trump, we saw the revolt of so-called 'common people' against 'inaccessible and clueless elites' promoting globalisation and multiculturalism while paying no attention to the short-term havoc such changes cause. In both cases, campaigns were waged using blatant inaccuracies, if not outright lies, passed off as truth. The almost complete free pass granted by publics and supporters to these bogus claims has led many to conclude that we are entering a 'post-truth' world.

The implications for professional work based on logic, science, knowledge, and expertise is indeed threatening if these analysts are right. But this overall questioning of the value of expertise has a much longer tradition in the form of post-modernism, and the latest attacks on professional work and expertise are only the most recent manifestations.

Professional expertise and the challenge of post-modern scepticism

The relatively recent 'war on expertise' appears to be a recent manifestation of post-modern questioning of professional knowledge and its use (see Antonio 2000). Post-modern writers focus on modernity as a form of hegemonic domination of people, places, and cultures. This domination is coercive and tied to grand narratives of modernity, rationality, and science that are injurious to individual autonomy and diversity. Post-modernists at once speak of actual changes to social and culture life and political programmes designed to restore difference and diversity to a world that is being crushed by modernist rationality, collectivism and scientist tendencies (Bauman 1992, 1993; Gutmann 1994; Lyotard 1984; Nicholson 1996). At the most basic level post-modernism pairs a description of social life with a proscriptive programme for restoring locality, diversity, identity, and discourse. These emphases seem to fly in the face of the modernist quest for collective justice and community and have serious implications for professional work (Antonio 2000) for the following reasons:

1 Post-modernists charge that the political left's focus on social policy and the state suppresses cultural difference and dialogue, promotes environmental degradation, social exclusion, and homogenisation (Antonio 2000; Eagleton 1996; Jencks 1986; Lyotard 1984; Zizek 1997).
2 Writers argue that globalisation, multinational corporations and multinational finance capital have rendered ineffective any form of political action based on states and governments. The extreme cultural fragmentation produced by these forces leaves collective politics and action exhausted (Beck 1992; Bell 1976; Gamble 2014; Jameson 1984).
3 Culture is described as autonomous from traditional sociological categories and material auto-referential boundaries (see Baudrillard 1983). When combined with the cultural fragmentation listed above, this undermines the ability of people to grasp, assimilate, and take seriously systematic efforts to analyse or intervene in social life (the very interventions that professions are geared towards providing).
4 The principle of anti-universalism opposes the alleged homogenising forces of universalistic, grand theories of modernity and celebrates difference and local knowledge (see Bauman 1992, 1993; Lyotard 1984). Since professional work is intimately tied to grand narratives associated with rationality and science, this is particularly threatening.

5   The primacy of cultural politics over class materialist politics privileges the preservation of cultural difference over and against the homogenising tendencies of rational, scientific progress. Science and a scientific class of experts are viewed as imposing uniform solutions from above to the detriment of local difference and action (Beck, Giddens and Lash 1994).
6   The communications programme of modernity (Habermas 1984) with its corresponding emphasis on dialogue among different groups of people is viewed as coercive (Antonio 2000). Instead, all knowledge is delivered from a standpoint and these standpoints represent incompatible views that limit the possibility of common communication and community.

The epistemological and political critiques of the professions from a postmodern perspective are ominous for professional groups whose standing depends on common interpretations of community, rational action, and scientific claims. In particular, cultural fragmentation and difference undermine the ability of professional groups to speak for constituents and clients, other than themselves. The primacy of local action and the incompatibility of standpoints therefore render professional claims meaningless as a way of communication and action. The de-emphasis on the state and political action, and the view that such action is ultimately coercive and threatening, renders governing by professional elites and any conceptions of the collective good and professional governance highly problematic. In short, the cultural and social fragmentation described by postmodernists, combined with their normative political programme, renders professional claims, actions and prerogatives suspect at best and coercive and dehumanising at worst (Jencks 1986; Lyotard 1984).

Of course, there is quite serious cultural affinity between the deeper questioning of experts and expert narratives in post-modernism and the much more recent 'war on expertise' narrative. In both cases, elites are viewed as out of touch with common people and controlling them using knowledge that is of dubious value. The only way out of this conundrum is to 'democratise knowledge' and claim that one narrative is just as good as another. But as we will see this is not the only problem professional expertise has faced when it comes to making expert claims. The second set of complaints used strictly economic reasoning to arrive at largely the same conclusions, but recent scandals and economic crises have led analysts and clients to question this position as well.

The rising salience of markets and ideologies after the Keynesian crisis

In the last thirty years, the rise of neo-liberal political and economic ideologies has threatened the expert claims of professional groups and the logic of professional organisation as an alternative to and protector of client and public welfare. The 1970s and early 1980s brought inherent crises to prevailing post-war economic arrangements and a questioning of the role of professional expertise in wide areas of social and economic life. This historic change was triggered by the crisis of Keynesian economics in the mid-1970s and the implications this crisis presented for a post-industrial future dominated by technical and administrative expertise (Bell 1976; Leicht and Fennell 2008; Leicht and Lyman 2006). This change is reflected in the Western European context by the rise of New Public Management ideas in professional civil service bureaucracies (Bourgeault, Benoit and Hirschkorn 2009; Kuhlmann, Allsop and Saks 2009; Leicht et al. 2009).

The contemporary situation of management and the professions can be contrasted with the early to mid-1960s predictions regarding the spread of professional expertise and reliance on liberal-technocratic professionals in the new post-industrial developed world (see, for example, Bell 1976; Frank 1997; Frank, Meyer and Miyahara 1995). In this world of the future, professions and knowledge-based work roles develop in response to the demands of post-industrial capitalism. The process of filling these jobs and the larger societal adjustments that come with the demand for highly educated workers (educational expansion, credentialing, longer stretches of time in school, and mass higher education) create a professional elite that applies its specialised knowledge to a broad range of problems. Managers, and especially the professionalised manager envisioned by the Carnegie Commission and the post-war Eisenhower, Kennedy, and Johnson administrations, were an integral part of a post-war economy actively managed for the public good.

This view of a post-industrial world where knowledge experts would manage the economy in the name of full employment, low inflation and general prosperity was challenged by two developments: first, the crisis in Keynesian economics that resulted from the stagflation and economic stagnation of the 1970s; and, second, the subsequent inability of skill-based models to explain rising income and earnings inequality among professionals and between professionals and non-professional groups (see DiPrete, Eirich and Pittinsky 2010). These developments led to a broad-based questioning of the relationship between technological expertise and the general social welfare, while also leading to serious questioning of the ability and desirability of attempting to manage the economy (Stein 1995).

The new neo-liberal consensus (see Reich 2012; Stiglitz 2013) takes free markets and moves them from their place as part of the technical environment of organisations to an all-encompassing role in the institutional environment of organisations. The traditionally defined professions have always walked a tightrope between the institutional logic of professional practice centred on professional–client relationships, autonomy, collegiality, and professional ethics on the one hand, and a technical environment stressing market efficiency, technological change, and organisational innovation on the other (see Cummings 2011; Leicht and Lyman 2006; Malhotra, Morris and Hinings 2006).

With the perceived failure of Keynesian economics and its conception of rule by experts, neo-liberal economic ideologies have promoted markets as the dominant force in the institutional environment. The present challenge of neo-liberalism as an economic and political ideology has profound implications for the professions as coherent occupational entities that control task domains and exercise discretion over the performance of complex tasks for the benefit of clients and the larger society. Many of these challenges are clarified if we take the colloquialisms of traditional professional practice and contrast them with the new neo-liberal consensus concerning professional practice and expert labour (see Leicht and Fennell 2008):

1 *Traditional professional practice – Professionals know best*
Credentialing, extensive training, and extensive socialisation into the norms and practices of the profession are designed to create a self-governing 'community of equals' devoted to high-quality professional practice. Self-governance is viewed as a key mechanism for controlling quality and access to professional practice. The knowledge and ethical standing of the professional is all that stands between the customer (who cannot figure out what was best on their own) and a calamitous outcome created by choices between an infinite number of alternatives offered by those looking to make quick profits.
Neo-liberal consensus – Consumers know best
Any attempt to interfere with, regulate, or affect consumer choice costs consumers money. This means that any interference with service provision (such as licensing procedures, legally defined monopolies over task domains, competency tests, and other devices for restricting professional service provision) extracts costs that are rarely if ever justified. Consumers of services eventually will reward competent, scrupulous providers and punish incompetent, unscrupulous ones. All that is necessary is to let the market do its work with the dollars of the consuming public voting for best practices.

2 *Traditional professional practice – Professional activities are too important to be left to markets*
Since professions address the core values of most societies (for instance, health, justice, financial wellbeing and scientific discovery), market anarchy in these areas is viewed as the very thing the organisation of the professions (as conceived by Durkheim and the old institutionalists) is trying to avoid. Nobody's health and safety can be left to an 'invisible hand' that prices everything from car mufflers to carrots in grocery stores.
Neo-liberal consensus – Markets will determine what is right
The market is the locus of human perfection (see Giddens 1994). No expert can make, guide or direct choices in the ways that markets will. No authority can make the wise choices that markets can make. Let markets do their job and stay out of it.

3 *Traditional professional practice – Credentialing by colleges, universities and professional associations is the major assurance that quality will be maintained and the public interest protected*
Credentials and licenses were meant to assure consumers with little or no reliable information that practitioners had been vetted and their performances monitored. A customer might 'find' the right brain surgeon in the long run, but they might die first.

Neo-liberal consensus – No credentialing or licensing
These are simply attempts to collect monopoly rents. Consumers will naturally be led to choices that are best for them, and credentialing and licensing are just an attempt to extract windfall profits at the expense of consumers.

4   *Traditional professional practice – Codes of ethics balance the interests of specific clients and the interests of the institution as a whole (as in areas such as medicine, law, criminal justice and science).*
    The client right in front of you is not supposed to have exclusive say about what they want lest their actions harm their own interests and, indirectly, the interests of others interacting in the professional domain.
    Neo-liberal consensus – No codes of ethics
    Markets will naturally reward those who behave in the best interests of those who purchase professional services. Information about ethical and unethical practices can be sorted out in the wash and those practitioners who do what clients want them to do and who act in their best interests will win out in the end.

5   *Traditional professional practice – Price competition is a negative*
    This is because clients are not capable of evaluating the relationship between costs and quality. If practitioners are fully vetted via good credentialing and licensing practices, then the prices charged for services should be similar and price is eliminated from the competition for clients and business.
    Neo-liberal consensus – Price competition will lower fees and salaries
    Service delivery from a variety of professional groups, in a variety of settings, with a wide range of organisational arrangements will keep fees and salaries low and service delivery of the best quality.

In the case of the neo-liberal consensus, markets are normative and all other organisational arrangements are not (Leicht and Fennell 2008).

In European contexts, the 1970s and 1980s and the accompanying economic recessions and deindustrialisation led to a widespread questioning of the salience of European models of capitalism (Bourgeault, Benoit and Hirschkorn 2009; Esping-Anderson 1989; Fourcade 2006; Ironside and Seifert 2003; Leicht *et al.* 2009; Rifkin 2004). Since professional practice (and especially the delivery of health care and education) has much more extensive ties to the public sector in most European countries, the main response to this general crisis in confidence (for professional groups) was the rise of the New Public Management. While New Public Management is a label applied to a diverse set of reforms, ideas, and ideologies (Savoie 1995), the general thrust of New Public Management initiatives is to subject the provision of public service by professionals to market forces through disaggregation, competition, and incentivisation (see Dunleavy *et al.* 2005; Leicht *et al.* 2009), vis:

> *Disaggregation* – splitting up large public sector bureaucracies into much smaller units, flattening organisational hierarchies and constructing management information systems that facilitate non-bureaucratic forms of control.

Competition – separating purchasers and providers so that more activities can be subjected to competitive bidding and provision through multiple providers, both public and private. These competitive pressures are designed to replace hierarchical decision making as the arbiter of appropriate action in the name of efficiency.

Incentivisation – a general movement away from rewarding service providers in terms of diffuse public service or professional norms and moving towards specific performance incentives that are pecuniary and directly measurable. This impact has been especially serious for professional groups.
(See Dunleavy et al. 2005)

The specific manifestations of the New Public Management vary from place to place and affect a wide array of professional groups. Attempts to implement its concepts in the United Kingdom National Health Service in particular have been controversial (see Ironside and Roger 2003). As with attempts to bring market incentives to professional practice in the United States (see Scott et al. 2000), there are very few examples of successful implementation of New Public Management concepts in European professional health services (see especially Bottery 1996; Christiansen and Laegreid 1999; Dunleavy et al. 2005; Kaboolian 1998; Lynn 1998; Reschenthaler and Thompson 1996; Scott et al. 2000). The criticisms of it in these contexts revolve around the disarticulation between public service and revenue maximisation, and the inability to 'get prices right' in the provision of services and intermediate goods that are government-supported natural monopolies.

The crisis of Keynesian economics discussed earlier, and the economic reasoning that followed, was an expression of scepticism about the role that professional expertise plays and the championing of a new market-based, spontaneous order as a source of revived prosperity and growth for economies, communities, and individuals (Stein 1995). The deregulated, free market, globalised world that neo-liberals promoted came under serious attack as a result of the financial scandals of the mid-2000s and the 2008 Great Recession. These crises led not only to a further questioning of professional expertise but also a desire to re-regularise and reassert local control over people's lives.

Bumps on the road to market nirvana: Enron, Parmalat and the 2008 financial crisis

The financial scandals that hit the American and European business community in 2005 and 2006 (such as Enron, Tyco International, Royal Dutch Ahold and Parmalat) exposed many of the institutional and technical problems with deregulated financial systems, deregulated markets, and the deregulation of the interface between management consulting, accounting and law. These problems were then exposed in full force in the 2008 global financial crisis (see Leicht and Fitzgerald 2014). This crisis has and will have profound implications for management consulting, accounting, and law in particular, but it also has larger implications for citizen trust in markets as deliverers of advice and professional services.

In the 2005–2006 financial scandals the problems at each company were very similar. Top executives were paid through stock options. These options were supposed to tie the compensation of top officials to the financial performance of the company, but instead they provided a built-in incentive to report ever-rising profits to Wall Street and the larger financial community so that stock prices would rise. None of this would be problematic if professional groups (lawyers, accountants, and management consultants) exercised their professional prerogatives to independently monitor the legal and financial behaviour of the firms involved. But there were conflicts of interest that prevented this. In each case the tangled web of financial transactions unravelled to reveal systematic misrepresentations of the financial health of each firm, misrepresentations that were certified by accounting firms with substantial financial interests in the consulting income they were deriving from the firms they were auditing; law firms that were more content to look the other way as legal fees were regularly paid and audits were certified as legitimate; and Chief Executives and top managers who made millions from falsified corporate profits and backdated stock options.

However, this was just a precursor to the general financial collapse and the Great Recession in 2008 that began in the United States and spread to the rest of the world. In this case, accountants, financial analysts and lawyers were certifying financial instruments (mortgaged-backed securities) as sound when, in many cases, they had no idea how worthy the mortgages were in these securities, and most were rated 'AAA'. Worse still, the ability to sell off mortgages after they were issued increased the volume of mortgages written and lowered the financial oversight and fiduciary responsibility that mortgage lenders traditionally exercised. Loans were written for people with 'No Income/No Job/No Assets' (referred to as NIJAs) and then buried in a larger security that was certified as solid (see Leicht and Fitzgerald 2014). When investors started to question the underlying value of the mortgages in these securities, the asset-backed securities market collapsed and the mortgage market in the United States collapsed. The stock market quickly followed suit and the crisis spread to the financial markets in the rest of the developed world (Grusky, Western and Wimer 2011; Krugman 2009; Paradis 2009). The resulting financial collapse destroyed over $7 trillion in global wealth and led to a widespread questioning by elites, experts and citizens alike about the relative efficacy of unbridled free markets, a crisis in confidence to which we will return.

Discredited markets and sceptical clients: the existential dilemma

Antonio and others suggest that there is a remarkable affinity between neo-liberal, market-based challenges directed at professional and knowledge work and the epistemological and political critiques of expert knowledge from the post-modern perspective (Antonio 2000; Antonio and Bonanno 1996; Kumar

1995; Leicht 2016; Sanbonmatsu 2003). In both cases, the creation of collectives to promote the general welfare is construed as a ruse for private rent collection and control. The major difference between them is what is lost through that action (market efficiency or cultural distinctiveness). The critiques of the Keynesian welfare state, and its emphasis on expert labour as a guider of social progress, puts post-modernism in direct accordance with neo-liberal critiques of state intervention emanating from the political right. Both groups share this lack of confidence in professional expertise as a guidepost for the good society (Antonio 2000). Antonio (2000) further thinks that radical cultural movements of the political right have embraced post-modern critiques of modernity and demanded various types of cultural recognition and exclusion. This type of new right political ideology accuses modernity of technocratic cultural homogenisation that must be resisted in the name of animated cultural ideologies.

And there are other problems and contradictions. The 'war on expertise' and the embrace of post-modern reasoning is a revolt against distant professionals who do not share the cultural values of locals. But market fundamentalism and neo-liberalism do not represent good solutions to this problem even though both question the value of expertise as a means of championing 'consumer choice' and 'global citizen empowerment'. The deregulation and accompanying financial scandals led to a backlash against global, disembodied markets that paralleled the revolt against global, disembodied knowledge. The major problem here is that the individual consumer and client is left with no guidance when faced with critical life decisions about health, wellbeing, legal status, and an array of other conditions of life. Unbridled free markets produce financial ruin and professional malfeasance. Just criticising experts as distant, disembodied, and clueless does not provide positive guidance either. What consumers seem to want is embodied local control over decisions that are important to them. This is where re-imagined entrepreneurial professions can fill a niche that is very important institutionally. The professions have the ability to span this breach between globalised and impersonal social change and the life worlds of individual clients, a niche that is very consistent with the view of professions as a third-way alternative to markets and hierarchies (Freidson 2001).

Where do the professions go from here?

New would-be professionals face a dilemma that is only slightly better than the citizen/client they seek to serve. Clients do not like disembodied knowledge deliverers from distant places and they definitely do not like free markets that promise better times in the long run while wreaking havoc and destruction in the here-and-now. I would argue that a culturally decentred, anomic and marketised world needs professions as much or more than the culturally homogeneous, Fordist world did. The major shifts have been (and will be) in the rationales we use to justify professional work and the organisational forms used to deliver professional services. Here I will focus on a few themes mentioned by prior literature as a way forward for scholars of the professions and for professional and would-be professional groups.

Professions as risk managers in a risk society

One constructive possibility broadens the scope of professional practice by casting professionals as risk managers in a risk society (see Beck 1992; Beck, Giddens and Lash 1994). This perspective recognises (as critical and postmodern scholars do) that the cumulative result of the global commitment to hegemonic science, technology and rationalisation is a series of unintended consequences and externalities that need to be managed. This perspective also recognises the full-scale assault on individual life worlds that result from these commitments (Beck, Giddens and Lash 1994). Here professionals mediate and interpret the gap between an impersonal, rational, scientific and technologically-infused world fraught with manufactured risks and contradictions and the personal project of producing individual wellbeing. This mediation occurs in an environment where choices are abundant and contradictory, and every choice has a trade-off. The professional's claim to prestige and earnings lie as managers of this risk. The fact that the risks are manufactured by the same rationalist, hegemonic forces that provide training and an ideological rationale for professional work does not change the fundamental dynamic for consumers. Risks must be managed and those who can reduce risks for individuals in their personal life worlds will be rewarded regardless of the source of those risks.

This is another instance where pure and unfettered markets are an inferior individual choice. After all, an unqualified brain surgeon can kill us and the only people benefitting from this 'market signal' will be those who seek treatment after we are dead. In the financial world, we need management, accounting and financial advice from people who work with us to shelter us from the risk of globalised financial markets while allowing some of the benefits to trickle through. This new role for entrepreneurial professionals is especially salient in the United States where capitalist market forces are allowed to have the most sway. In more corporatist contexts, the state itself seeks to manage some of these risks, uses professional workers to aid them, and may only indirectly provide such advice to individual clients on an ongoing basis (see Krause 1995).

This is an area where individual consumers could use the classic liberal professions and the professionals they produce or (in a different context) bureaucratic professionals conferring the services of social citizenship (Krause 1995; Webb 1999). The inherent problem with combining the need for individualised advice with services from risk managers is to find a risk manager that does not also profit from the creative destruction and mayhem caused by neo-liberalism and cultural fragmentation. Corporate organisational forms put the need for profits (and more directly, immediate profits) ahead of the welfare of individual practitioners and the clients too. The direct fee-for service liberal professional may represent a profession, but the professional is at least somewhat bound by a code of ethics to serve clients and the bureaucratic professional is as well. The corporate employer of professionals is not. Worse still, individual clients would be forgiven for distrusting the hybrid or corporate organisational form, the very form that outsources their job, lowers their incomes, and puts corporate profits ahead of community welfare (see Khurana 2007).

Professions as trusted interpreters of information

Related to the concept of professionals as risk managers is the concept of professionals as trusted interpreters of information (Evetts 2006; Kuhlman 2006; Olgiati 2006). Here the professional in the twenty-first century (and would-be consumers) are bombarded with information from a variety of sources, all made widely available on the internet (Castells 1996; Nichols 2017). But this unmediated access to information does not put the consumer in a better position than they were prior to the internet. The information is provided by individuals, corporations, interest groups, political parties, think tanks, and myriad of other organisations. All have specific agendas. Customer and individual wellbeing is not one of them. In fact, the internet represents the type of globalised market and cultural free-for-all that neo-liberalism and post-modernism embraces (Castells 1997; Nichols 2017). The consumer is placed in the position of telling good information from bad, which information applies to their specific situation and which information will make their situation worse if acted upon.

As Evetts (2013) points out, professionals stand in task domains where disembodied information needs to be interpreted for the benefit of specific clients in their life worlds. The embodied professional becomes not only the voice for the information but the negotiator of the relevance for the client in active interaction with them. Far from being a passive recipient of professional expertise and interpretation, the client is in active dialogue with the professional and may co-interpret the information the professional provides, bring forward new and independent sources of information for consideration, and actively steer intervention in directions that are consistent with their personal circumstances and life commitments. Obviously, a fair amount of the dialogue here involves the interpretation and management of risks (such as whether a course of action is legal or which course of treatment should be followed for cancer). In this situation access to information and access to other professionals to help interpret that information is critical for the individual client. The individual liberal practitioner is not in a good position compared to bureaucratic and corporate organisational forms that link a variety of professional groups in omnibus professional service firms (see Greenwood, Hinings and Brown 1990; Suddaby, Cooper and Greenwood 2007). If the client has an omnibus point-of-contact that navigates the information system in the professional service firm, and the relationship between the client recommendations and the products or services marketed by this firm is clear, the promise of the aggregation of professional services into new organisational forms can benefit individual as well as corporate clients.

Professions as values and ideology

Tied to the concept of professionals as risk managers and interpreters is a larger issue for societies and cultures around the world. This issue is linked to the values and ideological role professionals are expected to play and the wider acceptance of that role by policymakers and publics (Evetts 2013). At a basic level a global economic system that has disinvested in high-quality jobs in favour of higher profits probably produces a public longing for some triumph of professional values and ideology tied to meaning and public service. This is what people strive for and wish for themselves.

But publics have aspirations as consumers too. The world of competing risks and information overload has consumers looking for those that will exercise fiduciary responsibility toward them in areas like health, wellbeing and finance. Mid-twenty-first-century individuals are not likely to believe that unfettered free markets will deliver the best outcomes for them. Further, especially in the United States, consumers may question the sources of disembodied expertise that seem to control everything from what they eat to what they can write-off on their taxes. Instead, the client in a free-wheeling globalised world needs a locally-embodied professional to deliver face-to-face expert advice in the clients' interest. The nature and training of these experts may change but the basic idea will be there.

The general value placed on professions as values and ideology transcends specific organisational forms and heads in the direction of the larger institutional environment. Corporate and bureaucratic organisational forms can provide clients with the right information in a complex risk society and ways to interpret that information to promote individual health and wellbeing. Liberal professions can do the same thing. The big issue is not organisational form so much as intentions, ideology, and discourse. The ideology and discourse of professional work may be wide-ranging window dressing, but most people view it as superior to short-term profit seeking and hoarding by non-professionals or elite professionals controlling professional work.

A broader and unaddressed question is where this leads professional groups that are more dependent on the state, either in a clientele or corporatist fashion. If the appearance of limited autonomy affects greatly what professionals can do and advise, the professions risk de-legitimation as the state becomes 'too small for the big decisions' and 'too big for the small decisions' of life (Giddens 1994). In these cases, the ability of professionals to assert autonomy and act as coherent interest groups means they may eventually serve as an intermediary between individuals seeking good sources of information and advice and impersonal states that appear distant and uncaring.

Professionals as promoters of endogenous institutional change

Finally, professional work helps to aggregate information in different task domains and provides 'voice' to larger institutional forces that may be ignored by clients and publics. Professionals can therefore bring best practices to different locations and promote endogenous institutional change (Suddaby and Viale 2011). This conception of professional work is easiest to see in business services where tying specific firms to larger institutional practices is crucial. These institutional practices may have a nomadic base spread through the activities of the profession itself. Or professionals may play a substantial role in interpreting coercive and mimetic institutional pressures ('The new parliament law says ...' or 'Similarly situated companies have generated new revenues by ...'). Researchers and critical observers could question how much of this institutional change is truly necessary or whether the promotion of change lines the pockets of professionals more than clients. But in the business case it is becoming harder to interpret what markets want and what the political and regulatory environment is like. Strategically placed entrepreneurial professionals can provide concrete 'voice' to these environmental influences and engage in active dialogue with clients regarding their responses.

To a great extent the role of professions as a source of institutional change complements the view of professions as trusted interpreters of information. We expect professionals (liberal, entrepreneurial, and corporate) to collect information, interpret it, and then come up with a plan of action that maximises client welfare. This includes affirmative recommendations ('buy 100 shares of British Leyland now ...') and negative recommendations ('you need to lose a few pounds or your blood pressure will get worse ...' or 'in light of the new wage and hours laws you need to revise your hiring practices ...'). We expect professions to enact change we can't enable ourselves. The fact that some of these changes are individual and others are cultural or corporate really doesn't change the expectation very much. However, there is one caveat to this – professionals must be increasingly mindful of who is at the table making demands for professionals to solve. Most professionals make ethical commitments to promote the general welfare and the fragmentation accompanying neo-liberal and post-modern cultural change will push this capacity to the limit.

The challenges of the 'war on expertise', post-modern scepticism, and neo-liberalism point to the continual need to revisit the status of professional work and the prerogatives and arrangements that come with it. These trends by themselves leave consumers and clients in a good position to make important decisions about their real lives. In the end, the future of entrepreneurial professions depends on their ability to transcend the local and the global, representing and embedding themselves with local clients who may distrust expert knowledge but also distrust turning their lives over to impersonal market forces. That is a delicate balancing act which future generations of professionals will have to address.

References

Antonio, R. (2000) 'After post-modernism: Reactionary tribalism', *American Journal of Sociology* 106: 40–87.

Antonio, R. and Bonanno, A. (1996) 'Post-Fordism in the United States: The poverty of market-centered democracy', *Current Perspectives in Social Theory* 16: 3–32.

Baudrillard, J. (1983) *Fatal Strategies*, Paris: Editions Grasset.
Bauman, Z. (1992) *Intimations of Postmodernity*, New York: Routledge.
Bauman, Z. (1993) *Post-modern Ethics*, Oxford: Blackwell.
Beck, U. (1992) *The Risk Society: Towards a New Modernity*, Thousand Oaks, CA: Sage.
Beck, U., Giddens, A. and Lash, S. (1994) *Reflexive Modernization: Politics, Tradition and Aesthetics in the Modern Social Order*, Stanford, CA: Stanford University Press.
Bell, D. (1976) *The Coming of Post-industrial Society*, New York: Basic Books.
Bottery, M. (1996) 'The challenge to professionals from new public management: Implications for the teaching profession', *Oxford Review of Education* 22: 179–97.
Bourgeault, I., Benoit, C. and Hirschkorn, K. (2009) 'Comparative perspectives on professional groups: Current issues and critical debates', *Current Sociology* 57(4): 475–85.
Castells, M. (1996) *The Information Age: Economy, Society and Culture: The Rise of Network Society*, Oxford: Blackwell.
Castells, M. (1997) *The Information Age: Economy, Society, and Culture: The Power of Identity*, Oxford: Blackwell.
Christiansen, T. and Laegreid, P. (1999) 'New Public Management: Design, resistance, or transformation? A study of how modern reforms are received in a civil service system', *Public Productivity and Management Review* 23: 169–93.
Cummings, S. L. (ed.) (2011) *The Paradox of Professionalism: Lawyers and the Possibility of Justice*, Cambridge: Cambridge University Press.
DiPrete, T., Eirich, G. and Pittinsky, M. (2010) 'Compensation benchmarking, leapfrogs and the surge in executive pay', *American Journal of Sociology* 115: 1671–1712.
Dunleavy, P., Margetts, H., Bastow, S. and Tinkler, J. (2005) 'New public management is dead – Long live digital-era governance', *Journal of Public Administration Research and Theory* 16: 467–94.
Eagleton, T. (1996) *The Illusions of Post-Modernism*, Oxford: Blackwell.
Esping-Anderson, G. (1989) *Three Worlds of Welfare Capitalism*, Oxford: Polity Press.
Evetts, J. (2006) 'Trust and professionalism: Challenges and occupational changes', *Current Sociology* 54(4): 515–41.
Evetts, J. (2013) 'Professionalism: Value and ideology', *Current Sociology* 61(5/6): 778–96.
Fourcade, M. (2006) 'The construction of a global profession: The transnationalization of economics', *American Journal of Sociology* 112: 145–94.
Frank, D. J. (1997) 'Science, nature, and the globalization of the environment, 1870–1990', *Social Forces* 76: 409–35.
Frank, D. J., Meyer, J. W. and Miyahara, D. (1995) 'The individualist polity and the prevalence of professionalized psychology: A cross-national study', *American Sociological Review* 60: 360–77.
Freidson, E. (2001) *Professionalism: The Third Logic*, Chicago, IL: University of Chicago Press.
Gamble, A. (2014) *Crisis Without End: The Unraveling of Western Prosperity*, London: Palgrave Macmillan.
Giddens, A. (1994) *Beyond Left and Right: The Future of Radical Politics*, Stanford, CA: Stanford University Press.
Greenwood, R., Hinings, C. R. and Brown, J. (1990) 'P2-form strategic management: Corporate practices in professional partnerships', *Academy of Management Journal* 33: 725–55.
Grusky, D., Western, B. and Wimer, C. (eds) (2011) *The Great Recession*, New York: Russell Sage.

Gutmann, A. (ed.) (1994) *Multiculturalism: Examining the Politics of Recognition*, Princeton, NJ: Princeton University Press.

Habermas, J. (1984) *The Theory of Communicative Action: Reason and the Rationalization of Society*, Boston, MA: Beacon Hill Press.

Hanlon, G. (1999) *Professionals, State and the Market: Professionalism Revisited*, London: Macmillan.

Ironside, M. and Roger, S. (2003) *Facing Up to Thatcherism*, Oxford: Oxford University Press.

Jameson, F. (1984) 'Postmodernism, or the cultural logic of late capitalism', *New Left Review* 146: 53–92.

Jencks, C. (1986) *Modern Movements in Architecture*, Harmondsworth: Penguin.

Kaboolian, L. (1998) 'The New Public Management: Challenging the boundaries of the management vs. administration debate', *Public Administration Review* 58: 189–93.

Khurana, R. (2007) *From Higher Aims to Hired Hands: The Social Transformation of American Business Schools and the Unfulfilled Promise of Management as a Profession*, Princeton, NJ: Princeton University Press.

Krause, E. A. (1995) *Death of the Guilds: Professions, States and the Advance of Capitalism, 1930s to the Present*, New Haven, CT: Yale University Press.

Krugman, P. (2009) *The Return of Depression Economics and the Crisis of 2008*, New York: W. W. Norton and Company.

Kuhlmann, E. (2006) 'Traces of doubt and sources of trust: Health professions in an uncertain society', *Gender and Society* 54: 607–20.

Kuhlmann, E., Allsop, J. and Saks, M. (2009) 'Professional governance and public control: A comparison of medicine in the United Kingdom and Germany', *Current Sociology* 57(4): 511–28.

Kumar, K. (1995) *From Post-Industrial to Post-Modern Society: New Theories of the Contemporary World*, Oxford: Blackwell.

Leicht, K. (2016) 'Market fundamentalism, cultural fragmentation, post-modern skepticism, and the future of professional work', *Journal of Professions and Organization* 3: 103–17.

Leicht, K. and Fennell, M. (2008) 'Institutionalism and the professions', in Greenwood, R., Oliver, C., Suddaby, R. and Sahlin-Andersson, R. (eds) *The Handbook of Organizational Institutionalism*, Thousand Oaks, CA: Sage.

Leicht, K. and Fitzgerald, S. (2014) *Middle Class Meltdown in America: Causes, Consequences, and Remedies*, New York: Routledge, 2nd edition.

Leicht, K. and Lyman, E. (2006) 'Markets, institutions, and the crisis of professional practice', *Research in the Sociology of Organizations*, 24: 17–44.

Leicht, K., Walter, T., Sainsaulieu, I. and Davies, S. (2009) 'New Public Management and new professionalism across nations and contexts', *Current Sociology* 57(4): 581–606.

Lynn, L. E. (1998) 'The new public management: How to transform a theme into a legacy', *Public Administration Review* 58: 231–37.

Lyotard, J. (1984) *The Postmodern Condition: A Report on Knowledge*, Minneapolis, MN: University of Minnesota Press.

Malhotra, N., Morris, T. and Hinings, C. R. (2006) 'Variation in organizational form among professional service organizations', *Research in the Sociology of Organizations* 24: 171–202.

Nichols, T. (2017) *The Death of Expertise: The Campaign Against Established Knowledge and Why It Matters*, Oxford: Oxford University Press.

Nicholson, L. (1996) 'To be or not to be: Charles Taylor and the politics of recognition', *Constellations* 3: 1–16.

Olgiati, V. (2006) 'Shifting heuristics in the sociological approach to professional trustworthiness: The sociology of science', *Current Sociology* 54(4): 533–47.

Paradis, T. (2009) 'The statistics of the Great Recession', *Huffington Post* 10 October. Available at: www.huffingtonpost.com/2009/10/10/the-statistics-of-the-gre_n_316548.html

Pippenger, N. (2017) 'Know-nothing nation', *The Chronicle of Higher Education*. Available at: www.chronicle.com/article/Know-Nothing-Nation/238873?cid=cp84

Reich, R. (2012) *Beyond Outrage: What's Gone Wrong with Our Economy and Democracy and How to Fix It*, New York: Vintage Books.

Reschenthaler, G. B. and Thompson, F. (1996) 'The information revolution and the New Public Management', *Journal of Public Administration and Theory* 6: 125–43.

Rifkin, J. (2004) *The European Dream*, New York: Penguin.

Rogers, D. T. (2017) 'When truth becomes a commodity', *Chronicle of Higher Education*. Available at: www.chronicle.com/article/When-Truth-Becomes-a-Commodity/238866?cid=cp84

Sanbonmatsu, J. (2003) *The Post-Modern Prince: Critical Theory, Left Strategy and the Making of a New Political Subject*, New York: Monthly Review Press.

Savoie, D. (1995) 'What's wrong with the New Public Management?' *Canadian Public Administration* 38: 112–21.

Scott, W. R., Ruef, M., Mendel, P. J. and Caronna, C. A. (2000) *Institutional Change and Healthcare Organizations*, Chicago, IL: University of Chicago Press.

Stein, J. (1995) *Monetarist, Keynesian, and New Classical Economics*, Cambridge: Cambridge University Press.

Stiglitz, J. (2013) *The Price of Inequality: How Today's Divided Society Endangers Our Future*, New York: W. W. Norton.

Suddaby, R., Cooper, D. J. and Greenwood, R. (2007) 'Transnational regulation of professional services: Governance dynamics of field-level organizational change', *Accounting, Organizations and Society* 32: 333–62.

Suddaby, R. and Viale, T. (2011) 'Professionals and field-level change: Institutional work and the professional project', *Current Sociology* 59(4): 423–42.

Webb, J. (1999) 'Work and the New Public Service Class?', *Sociology* 33: 747–66.

Zizek, S. (1997) 'Multiculturalism, or, the cultural logic of multinational capitalism', *New Left Review* 225: 28–51.

3 Professions and professional service firms in a global context
Reframing narratives

John Flood

Introduction

It is often argued that the superior cognitive powers of *homo sapiens* enabled them to overcome the limitations of the Neanderthals through better abilities to make tools and diversify their agricultural processes. As a result, they had better nutrition and were stronger and so dominated others. Yuval Harari (2015) in his magisterial history, *Sapiens*, argues another case which is to do with humans' abilities to communicate and learn from such communication, or more simply the ability to gossip. It might sound trite, but from one's communicative abilities come myths, stories and fictions. And it is this which makes professions so successful – their capacity to create myths and legends to ensure their place within society (Boje 2008; Czarniawska 2004). All that has changed today is there is now intense competition among creators and interpreters of myths. The narratives told are often contradictory, even among professionals who ought to agree. Knowledge and expertise – often ignored in the studies of professions – are crucial to understanding the situation of professions and professionalisation today, which is more precarious now than before. This shift in the precariousness of professions might be put down to the following:

- The democratisation of knowledge through such intermediaries as the internet.
- Increasing difficulty of distinguishing between scientific and non-scientific knowledge.
- The loss of self-regulation of professions, including loss of trust within and between professionals and clients.
- The increased role of external regulation and audit, which are part of governmentality.
- The growing role of states intervening in delivery and training of professional services and professions.
- The move towards bureaucratic organisations as the mode of professional delivery with a consequent adoption of new audit methods such as New Public Management.
- Increasing permeability of professional boundaries – who controls whom?

- The rise of marketisation and financialisation of professions.
- Professionals' loss of autonomy and subsequent 'gain' in discretion.
- The disruptive (rather than sustaining) power of technology to hollow out professional skill sets.
- Better understanding of how the mind works, via cognitive science, especially in relation to hive minds versus individual limitations.

This list is by no means exhaustive and some may question its content, but it forms a starting point for exploring professional groups and professional service firms in modern societies in a global context, through the reframed narratives that both we and they use for interpretation. These narratives are the subject of this chapter, which in the process provides a selective overview of the contemporary issues regarding the professions set out above – creating a helpful backdrop to a number of subsequent chapters in this volume.

Narrative, legends and myths

The strength of narrative has several consequences. One of these is that it enables organisations and institutions to create lifeworlds that become self-sustaining and powerful (Habermas 1987). Within enterprise cultures narrative becomes a dominant force in creating domination. Consider, for example, how Apple has created a self-contained technological microcosm that is hermetically sealed from open source software (Isaacson 2011). Consumers allow themselves to be captured by the compelling narratives that Apple spins around ideals of 'the good life'. Tesla, more recently, has created a new lifeworld centred on energy capture and storage that enables self-sufficiency of a kind through batteries and continuously updated electric cars (Vance 2015). By contrast, Samsung was ensnared in crisis management when its phones started spontaneously combusting and it rapidly lost its grip over the ensuing stories (Moynihan 2017). Stories, while enabling us to communicate, are ways of creating and losing trust.

Stories also teach us about difference. Professions are replete with many stories from the charismatic to the bureaucratic and formal. The implicit appeal to Weber is deliberate in that he warned us about the relentless grip of the iron cage of bureaucracy, which he saw as the culmination of various historical, social and economic processes (Weber 1968). Many students of the professions are Weberians or neo-Weberians in some manner (for example, Parkin 1979; Saks 2010). But the emphasis here is on market closure and the retention and promotion of monopoly and status rather than knowledge and expertise. But it is a powerful story that has grown in substance in the twentieth and twenty-first centuries.

Narratives have many roles to play and the argument is that professions have to recreate their stories and myths or risk losing their established positions in society. Stories create the capability to retain their legitimacy and power. These are the stories told to the world about how essential professions are to civilised society. They justify their use of power and self-regulation, their status, and of course their earnings (Liljegren and Saks 2016). They are about trust and usefulness, the value of their knowledge and expertise. There is a double aspect to storytelling for professions. They must consider the internal dynamics of the institution: how will it reproduce itself and with whom? The production of producers is not a mechanical process. Different professions are in competition with each other to get the best graduates from business and law schools. If professions lack legitimacy, they will diminish in attraction to graduates. So, the two sets of narratives must mesh and mutually reinforce each other. But this is beset with difficulties because the trajectories of the narratives can run at different speeds causing a kind of arhythmical disjunction. This was evident in the Great Recession in 2008 where professional service firms laid off many associates while preserving the positions of the partners and senior members. Disjunctions such as these affect the building of trust and respect. Without them the *raison d'être* of professions disappears. Narrative is therefore the connective tissue that enables various scenarios in professions to play out and hopefully thrive. Managing divergent and convergent streams of narratives is complex and difficult and never-ending (Brock 2006; Adams 2012).

Professions and professionalism

Let us return to the history of the study of professions and professionalism (Brock and Saks 2015; Saks 2016). Early theorists of the professions such as Carr-Saunders and Wilson (1964), Greenwood (1957) and Parsons (1939, 1954) essentially adopted a functionalist approach that outlined the traits that denominated a profession. Often these included extensive training and education, a code of ethics, and a representative association. The trait approach carries within it the ideology of long-developed expertise justifying monopoly over the course of the professional's career. Moreover, professions were seen as a stabilising and civilising part of society – they were essentially practising for the public good. Critics pointed out that any exclusionary force of this theory was quite weak as any occupational group could adopt the traits and hence call themselves professionals. For example, there is an Association of Professional (Golf) Tour Caddies (APTC at http://theaptc.com/), which states "The APTC is a channel to educate the public about our profession and the role we play in professional golf". Indeed, we can recollect that the original trinity of professions was law, the church, and medicine, none of which in their early phases possessed the traits outlined above.

Interactionists like Hughes (1958) and Becker (1962) focused on the actual work and the actors involved. Small groups were key sites of study – Goffman (1952) showed, for example, how professional con artists cooled out their marks when they were completing their stings. This approach is micro-oriented: examining the small and subtle exchanges that take place rather than looking at larger social structures based on power. Later theorists have been more Marxist (Larson 1977) or Weberian (Abel 1989) in their outlooks, focusing on monopoly rents and market closure. Social ecologists, such as Abbott (1988, 2005, 2016), have examined how professions are in constant conflict, aggressively attacking others' jurisdictions and attempting to capture their work. We only have to look at the near constant battles between accountants and lawyers over who possesses the mandate to do tax work to illustrate this. And in the case of accountants, that attack has spread to the core areas of legal work as well. The nineteenth-century struggles between mainstream allopathy and homeopathy in the United States to determine who should be the primary diagnostician are also well documented (Starr 1982). The allopaths were able to mobilise stronger political resources, combined with the might of the hospital to gain dominance, a position strongly defended today. The arrest and imprisonment of midwives in Hungary is another example of professional domination as the state sides with doctors to outlaw midwifery for home births (Hill 2012). The medicalisation of births, to be carried out in hospital, is the only professional activity sanctioned by the state.

The taxonomic approach to professions has not completely disappeared, as we know from the work of Eliot Freidson (2001) who argued that professions constituted a third logic between the market and bureaucracy where market refers to consumer control and bureaucracy refers to control by managers. Professionalism is therefore an organised occupation that has the power to determine who will perform certain tasks. Law in most countries appears to fit this model. Lawyers are granted monopolistic powers by the state, which places them *primus inter pares* among those who work in the legal industry. The last part of the twentieth century has seen this market closure eroded and authority given to a growing paralegal body of workers as the division of legal labour has intensified (Cannon 2014). Freidson (2001) also adopted the Weberian method of establishing ideal types in order to model professionalism in the world. When applied to the real world of medicine he demonstrates how the profession of medicine has altered through the twentieth century into the twenty-first century. The rise of insurance, hospitals and the incursion of the state into medical practice have attenuated the power of the medical practitioner, although doctors remain an esteemed and well-remunerated profession. However, a number of researchers on the professions caution us about the prevalence of universalistic models of professionalism arguing for distinctions between Anglo-American and European models – in addition to differentiation in specific societies (Brock and Saks 2015; Liu 2013; Sciulli 2005).

Professions and knowledge

We must note here that of the various characteristics of professions examined, little attention is given to the content of the knowledge base of professions. As Conley and O'Barr (1990), Flood (2013) and Sandefur (2015) ask, what is it that professionals do? Is there, for instance, any theoretical justification or scientific explanation for a canonical set of topics that define the content of legal education and the practice of law? In my sceptical way I do not see any (LETR 2013). Thomas Brante (2010) takes a Foucauldian line and provides the example of the American Psychological Association's *Diagnostic and Statistical Manual of*

Mental Disorders (DSM), which is in its fifth edition from its birth in 1952. DSM provides a bewildering number of conditions that it describes by the various symptoms ascribed to them. It is atheoretical and descriptive in that it fails to offer any causes for the conditions. So, while on the face of it, it appears objective and scientific, and is openly biomedical and biological, it contains many cultural biases based around the medicalisation of psychiatry. It ignores non-Western ideas on illness. And with the medicalisation of psychiatric disorders it has given free rein to the pharmaceutical industry. Since DSM-I the number of diagnoses has risen by over 300 per cent from 106 to 365. Following Foucault (1979) we see how the thought style or paradigm has created institutions in medicine of significant power and authority in which the professions are complicit in its exercise of governmentality.

Certainly, if we look at professions today they are remarkably different to the nineteenth century and earlier. The degree to which most are regulated, have their training monitored and measured, and their qualifications and credentials calibrated and equated for cross-border movement is profound and palpable. For example, Australia is working on interstate equivalence of legal qualifications (Rogers, Kingsford Smith and Chellew 2017). Moreover, the history of the Establishment Directive on qualifications and practice in the European Union shows how apparently incommensurable and incompatible systems can be brought into harmony with the right political will (and pressures from the big law firms) (CCBE 2001). It does not mean local bar associations have not fought to protect their turf through the European Court of Justice. Their fears concerned forms of regulatory and educational arbitrage emerging, but another way of seeing the changes is the curbing of monopoly power.

In the list earlier, reference was made to the democratisation of knowledge. This speaks to the shift from a class-based occupational category to one founded on apparent meritocracy and talent, despite family and social background. We could probably say education, grades, and credentials became important around the nineteenth century in modern societies. The academy was fighting to become the gatekeeper of professionalism and so professionalise itself in the process. Medicine became increasingly scientific and law degrees were established. Craft was still probably the most common route into the professions. Articles and apprenticeships gave the feeling of learning to master subjects, becoming skilled like a carpenter or cabinetmaker. Yet they also allowed social contacts to flourish as the key entry point to the professions. For instance, the Ivy League universities in the United States still give favours to 'legacy students', the children of graduates and donors (Nisen 2013). Jared Kushner, President Trump's son-in-law, could also be considered as an exemplar. However, the big welfare state reforms of the twentieth century have enabled children from all classes to access higher education and move into the professions (see, among others, Jencks and Riesman 1977).

Not only did this expansion of knowledge and entrants stimulate interest in the professions, and indeed expand the number of professions – not least in software and Information Technology – the narratives of the professions subtly shifted as well. The shift coincides with the move to regulatory control and globalisation. A new set of myths was emerging caught between a hankering for the past 'golden age' and the brashness of the new regime. Boje (2008) characterises sense-making narratives as legend, myth, and folk tale. Each attempt to reconstruct the present by creating a new past acts as a controlling vision for the present. The most common form of the legends is the founding story of an institution. The way the law firm of Cravath Swaine and Moore in New York presents itself as *primus inter pares* by virtue of its in-house training and partner selection processes is a classic legend that is still retold in the modern day. Stories of how Joe Flom remade Skadden by turning it into a mergers and acquisitions powerhouse (Caplan 1994) or how Marty Lipton created the poison pill (Starbucks 1993) give their heroes mythic status. But the activities of individuals also have elements of folk wisdom in them.

Organised professionals

To capture this paradigm shift we now examine the transformation of professional education and professional organisations. To justify their market positions, professions had to claim to be founded on scientific principles. This even applied to law to some extent, but for medicine and accounting the claim was easier to make. Medicine had the body to analyse and treat. It based itself on chemistry and biology with a smattering of mechanics. The scientific method was the *grundnorm* for medicine making it unassailable to attack unless you could disprove its science. Science gave legitimacy to a craft that used to be a sideline for barbers. This was why it was important to solidify and implant that legitimacy in the minds of the populace and the state. Medicine created its own symbolic order that became almost priest like (van Quaquebeke, Zenker and Eckloff 2009; Lipworth *et al.* 2013). The English medical profession displays an interesting take on this. As one ascends the medical hierarchy and attains the senior status of 'consultant', the prefix 'Doctor' is dropped in favour of a return to the honorific 'Mr' or 'Mrs'. Is there any scientific justification for this change? There is none whatsoever. It is purely a signifier of status and esteem granted by the profession to its own without consideration for patients' understanding. It apparently matters little that it confuses patients who might worry who is treating them and reintroduces notions of class, status, and difference. The fact they have been referred to such a doctor provides a type of safety net for their fears. The narrative here is almost masonic in its ideological fervour. It also shows the power and authority of longstanding institutions such as the Royal College of Physicians and the Royal College of Surgeons. However, the rise of a commercialised public accountability often placed professionals in antagonistic or loosely co-ordinated assemblages with the managerial class (Hanlon 1998) and nudged them towards a more enterprising form of professionalism (Misztal 2002). Dent (2003) shows this in action in a hospital threatened with closure where the professionals became enmeshed in the project of saving the hospital and so came to accept they had a managerial responsibility as well as a professional one.

Accounting has made claims of a scientific value. Luca Pacioli codified double-entry bookkeeping in the late-fifteenth century (Yamey 2007), but it was not until the nineteenth century that the profession of accounting emerged. Accountants were among the lower strata of professional type occupations until the caste of lawyers decided in their Brahmin-like way to disown dealing with bankruptcy. The nineteenth century was in Britain and elsewhere a boom time for railway construction. To build a line, a consortium had to win a dispensation from Parliament. Huge amounts of money were spent on making representations to parliamentary committees. It was the time when the City law firm came into its own. Senior partners often sat on the boards of the companies they advised, including railways. Barristers and Queen's Counsel did the advocacy before the committees. Norton Rose, now a global law firm, operated leverage rates of one partner to up to 100 managing clerks during the height of the boom (St George 1995). Legal fees were enormous. Of course, those that lost the parliamentary battles often went bankrupt. But such work was beneath the dignity of the City lawyer. It was funereal: a matter of dealing with corpses. This did not deter the accountants who saw a ready income stream in bankruptcy work. On the back of this, accountants professionalised and achieved respectability, although not to the same level as lawyers (Matthews 2006). Accountants also exploited the state's need to understand business operations and tax liabilities and so became indispensable through their audit work, which gave them unparalleled insight into business operations. Yet if we compare the growth of accounting and law firms, accountants have successfully capitalised on their early achievements. The world's largest law firm, Dentons-Dacheng, has some 7,700 lawyers, but the world's largest accounting firm, PwC, has over 223,000 professionals on its staff. It is interesting to reflect that when the first significant big law merger occurred in 1989 resulting in Clifford Chance (Flood 1996), one of its aims was to merge with an accounting firm on equal terms – perhaps indicating hubris?

One of the biggest changes for professionals and one where the professional narrative becomes confusing is in the role of large organisations. This harks back to Weber's iron cage. Julia Evetts (2013) has pointed out how the vast majority of professionals are now employed within organisations and these organisations are imposing controls from above rather than the professional ethos emerging from the professionals themselves (see Moorhead 2014). In one respect this is the story of deskilling and deprofessionalisation, but managers are keen to promote the rhetoric of professionalism as a major value. It is different from earlier conceptions of professionalism which celebrated vocation and autonomy. Indeed, even the managers in these organisations consider themselves professionals, as professionals see themselves as managers (Kirkpatrick, Ackroyd and Walker 2005). The discourse of enterprise becomes the dominant narrative. We know what this entails: performance reviews, hierarchy, customer service and audit. How many academics groan as they fill out another performance review detailing their publications for the year, grants, and teaching reviews? Hospitals, architecture practices, engineering companies all contain similar programmes that monitor the outputs of professionals and other employees (Power 1999).

And, of course, the enterprise discourse encourages competition between employees for various rewards, which is completely antithetical to the values of collegiate professionalism (Cheetham and Chivers 2005). The promotion of individualisation by managers, being founded on accountability, is in constant tension as professionals try to make sense of their roles in organisations.

These tensions have intensified as the roles of professionals within organisations have changed along with globalisation and the effects of the Great Recession. The classic model of the professional law firm is the tournament for partnership (Galanter and Palay 1991; Malhotra, Morris and Smets 2012) where associates compete for the prize of partnership. The model is an extension of the Cravath system (Swaine 1946, 1948) which was, and still is largely, predicated on the 'up or out' approach. If at the end of the probationary period an associate is not considered suitable for promotion, an exit strategy is planned that often enables the associate to join a client's legal department. For the Cravath firm the strategy has created a strong alumni network that has helped build the firm and establish it as a central point in the legal universe of firms. A key element of this has been the creation and maintenance of trust among the actors.

Since the end of the twentieth century there has been a shift in the composition of professional service firms. The classic shape of a law firm under the tournament model was that of a pyramid with the associates at the base in great numbers and the partners clustered at the top. Because of the rewards available to partners, the contest among associates was considered worth joining. Periods of eight to twelve years' probation around different departments gave sufficient opportunity for partners to evaluate the associates' promise. Associates could be tested on work, client responsiveness and billings but the crucial test was the ability to 'make rain' or bring in business. To an extent, the latter was speculative and junior partners would be given time to prove their capacity for business creation.

Competition among professional service firms has deepened as client relationships changed along with firm composition. Traditionally, firms would cultivate clients with the aim of providing a wide portfolio of services to the client. With pressures on cost cutting in corporate legal departments, client relationships have altered from being long term and wide to short term and transactional. Moreover, clients are more selective, through the use of procurement specialists, about which external counsel personnel will be used on legal matters. Firms have had to respond to these challenges by altering the customary rainmaker relationships and instituting instead 'client relationship managers' who act as the interface between the client and the firm. Some in-house counsel, too, are refusing to pay for the use of first year associates for the reason that they are essentially trainees rather than true fee earners (Sullivan 2017). The result is that law firms' staffing policies have to adapt to client demands rather than firm preferences. For partners retrenchment was necessary to preserve their status and incomes, thus those of associates had to change. The prospect of partnership became remote – the tournament no longer appeared fair.

To enable the restructuring of the tournament, a new narrative had to be constructed that re-characterised the meaning of contingency in the associate contest. Associates were no longer to be part of a win-lose contest, but there would be a pre-tournament contest that would provide the opportunity to participate in the tournament. As a result, a new shape came into being, superseding the pyramid – the diamond. The diamond introduced a new raft of positions and levels. The simple division in the pyramid of associates and partners transformed into a shrunk partner category at the top matched by a diminished supply of associates entering at the bottom, whereas the expanded middle absorbed new roles. Although some associates played the traditional tournament, most were destined to remain in subordinate roles along the lines of professional support staff, outsourced labour, permanent senior associates, and salaried partners (Pinnington and Morris 2003). Partnership shifted from a permanent status with high rewards to one where the position introduced significant uncertainty and contingency. Partners would be given between two and three years to prove their business cases otherwise their partnerships were terminated. Indeed, instead of cutting down workloads on promotion, partners were loaded up more heavily than when they were associates. They still had to match their associate billable hours on top of which they would have to hone their business development skills. The pressures to stay competitive with the firm were considerable and could result in wayward and erratic behaviours (Regan 2006).

The new narrative was not hard to create. Law has always been and still is a fiercely competitive business, generally awarding the star individual the lion's share of the rewards. Traditionally, law firms were collegiate putting the organisation first before the individual. Old-line City of London law firms claimed lockstep remuneration (cohort based pay) and promoted the co-operation of skills and clients (Galanter and Roberts 2008). Lateral hires into partnerships were rare since newcomers might not fully understand and adapt to the firm culture. The Cravath model was predicated on similar grounds. Some New York law firms also used lockstep. However, upstart firms like Finley Kumble (Eisler 2004) and Skadden Arps (Caplan 1994) accentuated the ideal of the individual rainmaker who commanded awe, respect and fear. The fear was in the rainmaker moving to another firm and taking clients away. These fears intensified the move of law firms from lockstep towards meritocratic reward ('eat what you kill') (Regan 2006). The majority of law firms now adhere to meritocratic remuneration. The increased pressures to ramp up fees have reduced the incentives to train associates as potential partners (Wilkins and Gulati 1998). Whereas under the traditional tournament model, partners extended their human capital by using and training associates; the opportunity cost of training exceeds its returns.

With the growth in size of professional service firms customary modes of self-regulation built around shared values, schooling and class proved inadequate for the task. More robust processes of governance and governmentality were introduced, such as New Public Management (Dunleavy *et al.* 2005). This was in part a response to collapsing trust in professions leading to legislation like the Legal Services Act 2007 (Flood 2013). For Saks (2014) these processes cast professions from a zoo into the realm of the circus where, for public safety, state control of performance is necessary and mandatory. Massey and Pyper (2005) trace the roots of collapsing trust back to the attacks on elitist professionals by Ivan Illich (1977) in his classic book *Disabling Professions*. Professions needed to be made more customer focused and to see customers, not clients, as active participants in the relationship. This was apparent in the targets set for seeing patients in the National Health Service in Britain within certain time frames and for their operations to be carried out in set periods. Websites reviewing hospitals and doctors were actively encouraged. Medical and financial needs were given equal weight: if surgery had to be postponed to ensure the books were balanced, or to ensure a smaller deficit, then that would override medical concerns. The government created internal markets within the National Health Service to make hospitals and doctors' practices compete for resources and patients. The results were intensive game playing to circumvent the rules or subvert them.

Perhaps one of the most extreme examples of this mindset is the 1986 Challenger disaster when an O-ring failed at launch and the Challenger blew up killing all on board. Despite warnings about the reliability of the O-ring, managers at NASA and the manufacturer considered the ring to be within normal ranges of flight risk. John Glenn aptly summed it up when he said:

> I guess the question I'm asked the most often is: 'When you were sitting in that capsule listening to the count-down, how did you feel?' Well, the answer to that one is easy. I felt exactly how you would feel if you were getting ready to launch and knew you were sitting on top of two million parts – all built by the lowest bidder on a government contract.
> (See www.marketwatch.com/story/that-famed-john-glenn-quote-about-a-rockets-2-million-lowest-bidder-parts-2016–12–11)

So, organisational control and New Public Management are about governmentality and governance where organisational accountability and professional values and ethics may largely coincide, but when they differ the organisation's rules will trump those of the professionals. And the principles of New Public Management have migrated into the private sector, especially as the private sector takes over more of the public sector's roles, including public–private partnerships.

To make all this work for the good of the public and community, there has to be trust. Without it professionals are unable to make the claims they do. Luhmann (2017) characterised trust as a means of coping with risks. We trust by internally examining the external risks to our wellbeing. Among family members and close friends, it is not difficult to assume trust, but in a neo-liberal market economy it is a different matter. In the classic move from *Gemeinschaft* to *Gesellschaft* with increasing urbanisation our range of unfamiliar situations has increased exponentially, inducing all kinds of fears and anxieties. Professional values and codes are meant to reassure us that whatever is to be done to us or on our behalf is done from the purest of motives, for our good, not the professional's own benefit. It is a hard distinction to maintain in the modern era.

One could argue that organisational professionalism is ideally suited to engender trust in service delivery. We are no longer in thrall to the caste and class system of yore, and paternalism is no longer acceptable to most people. People want transparency and accountability. The newspaper consumer complaints pages show us what it is like when businesses fail to live up to consumer expectations and we have to turn to another profession, the media, to get recompense. For law this came to a head with the manoeuvres of a disgruntled client who created a website called 'Solicitors from Hell' (http://johnflood.blogspot.com.au/2011/07/is-solicitors-from-hell-criminal.html). 'Solicitors from Hell' allowed clients to put up their stories of bad treatment by lawyers, which created uproar among lawyers who cried foul in the strongest terms. The courts found the website defamatory and it was closed down. But the legal profession was rather naïve and failed to understand mirroring – so 'Solicitors from Hell' still exists on mirror sites, only in other jurisdictions. Law is not the only sufferer from lack of trust. Accounting firms seem to be regularly in the news for misconstruing a company's account – over reporting profits, not predicting the imminent collapse of a business and so forth. The most spectacular example was that of Arthur Andersen which imploded when a rogue partner in Texas shredded documents connected to Enron (McClean and Elkind 2004). Governments are now wary about prosecuting big accounting firms as they have diminished in number from eight to the present Big Four. It was uncertain for KPMG a few years back in the United States when the Department of Justice considered indicting the firm for marketing abusive tax shelters. It held back because the idea of the Big Three was a step too far.

Globalisation and professions

The increased urgency of globalising and locating offices where clients were situated also made the traditional model of organising professional service firms much harder to sustain. Ideals of partnership varied from place to place and the difficulty of creating 'one firm' arrangements remains alive and pressing. Muzio and Faulconbridge (2013) show us that in Italy status and financial rewards are very much tied to the *ancien regime* of small, elite practice rather than modern bureaucratic law firms. The tendency, however, towards super-global professional service firms has shown gaps in the way globalisation operates. Globalisation also intensifies matters. How does one trust the *behemoth* of 7,700 lawyers at Dentons-Dacheng spread across the world? At one time, Baker & McKenzie, a large global law firm, was disparagingly referred to as 'Baker & McDonalds' because of the perceived inconsistency of its global offices (Flood 1995). This may have been bad mouthing on the part of competitors, but the firm created an office of global quality and education whose head spent nine months of the year travelling from office to office. For corporations, global reach is often a necessity: it helps overcome agency-principal problems. No one ever gives full credence to legal directories. To use Baker & McKenzie further, it operated as an Illinois partnership for many years of its existence (Baumann 1999). Given the vast majority of the firm's lawyers were overseas and foreign, the artificiality of the Illinois partnership became apparent. To overcome the limitations of the original system Baker & McKenzie converted to a Swiss *verein*. In so doing, it provided an international framework that sat over different local rules. The firm could internationalise fee sharing and work, while honouring local ethical and bar association rules.

The push to globalisation came from finance and business, which needed to use Western hegemony to ensure its products were sold all over the world. It was further reinforced by the twin cities of New York and London that provided the world's capital for expansion (Sassen 2001). Globalisation was also seen as a mechanism to exploit the fixity of labour as against the mobility of capital, often to the detriment of labour. In law and accounting moves to outsource as much work as possible were driven by the need to reduce costs, driven by corporate clients, and sustain profits. India became the hotspot for business and legal outsourcing and offshoring (Kuruvilla, Noronha and D'Cruz 2016). The new priesthood of unbundling and decomposing work pushed the rationalities of specialisation and offloading work to its cheapest possible human resource. Back office work, document analysis and discovery were shipped to India or the Philippines or South Africa. Outsourcing became the apologia for professional service firms who decreased their associate training to a minimum. The narrative of competition, external forces, and need to remain viable and entrepreneurial were the dominant aspects of the discourse. Accordingly, the firms themselves could not be blamed as it was all beyond their control. There were, and are, consequences: as business and professional service firms became more remote from their consumers, questions arose around quality, speed and reliability.

In addition, globalisation and diversification brought increasing complexity to professional–client relationships. Dyads were earlier referred to as being the ideal type of professional relationship, but we know that this has little resonance in the modern complex world of international business and commerce. Virtually every professional–client relationship is at least triadic in nature. It might be a bank or an insurance company or a private health provider, but consumers are dealing with third parties who do not always make themselves known. They hide behind the curtains: 'No you can't have this treatment', 'We insist on settling this case'. When a lawyer is advising on arranging finance for a client's business, who then is prominent in their mind? Is it the client or the bank for which they will work again? This can be illustrated by the example of the sale of Canary Wharf (Flood 2016), a beacon of neo-liberalist, Thatcherite property development, in East London. When it was being auctioned in the early 2000s after a bankruptcy, a dispute arose between a potential buyer and a bank. The buyer's law firm was Freshfields, a big London firm. The buyer wanted to sue the bank, but Freshfields refused to act claiming that it was conflicted by being a member of the bank's legal panel. In fact, the panel had around 120 London law firms as members. Not a single law firm in London would act against the bank. In the end a barrister was found who would accept instructions direct from the buyer. This is why trust is a problem: 'My lawyer says no because he has a financial arrangement with your opponent'. This finally brings us to whether there is a future for professionalism.

The future of professionalism

In this regard, a key question in light of the foregoing is whether trust can be reinvigorated? Can professions construct a narrative that will appeal both to its members and its users? It would seem so. We need professions and professionals, or people who behave professionally. We need intermediaries who help us tackle a complex world, which in most cases is now beyond our comprehension. According to IBM, 90 per cent of the data in the world today was produced in the last two years (Dragland 2013). From Gutenberg to big data means the idea of the polymath professional is more or less lost to us.

We can characterise professionalism as externalised knowledge and expertise, but our problem is that knowledge is often opaque, and we need transparency. There ought to be no difficulty in professionals disclosing how they arrive at their conclusions. Cognitive science is now showing that most of us estimate our knowledge of phenomena as greater than it actually is (Sloman and Fernbach 2017). Try to explain how a toilet works? My explanation of its operation would be fairly superficial. Evolution has spurred the mind to do the least to improve the fitness of its host, but because we are a social species we have dispersed knowledge throughout the community. This applies to humanity as a whole but we can see how it works in relation to professionals. The division of labour and specialisation are so finely grained that the hive mind has developed so we become intuitively adept at co-operating – and given the complexity of professional services firms the hive mind is essential.

But what I have outlined here could probably apply to any occupation including car mechanics and golf caddies, but boundaries are important. We have little difficulty in distinguishing between genuine scientific medicine and quack remedies (Gieryn 1999). We comprehend the latter has little or no scientific basis. Boundary work will always cause difficulties, as it should. But, nevertheless, we search for abstracted knowledge, a scientific basis; 'know-why' instead of 'know-how', as Brante (2010) puts it. We recognise boundaries are fluid and open to reconfiguring, but perhaps we should not oversell to ourselves the significance of boundaries and perimeters (Rodda 2014). The distinction between the professions of law and accounting is diminishing such that one can imagine a future blending of law, accounting and management consultancy. Take, for example, Wiggin, a media law firm in the United Kingdom. Under rules denoting alternative business structures, Wiggin has now become a firm that does film production, game development, as well as legal work (see www.wiggin.co.uk).

Let me try to draw this together. The erosion of trust is palpable and exists between professionals and clients and between professionals themselves and between professionals and managers in organisations. Various propositions can be put forward and I will leave the trust issue between professionals and clients until last. The nexus of control between managers and professional employees is unlikely to change. Neo-liberalism is firmly entrenched and shows no signs of changing. Professionals can make two responses to the New Public Management and organisations: one is to subvert them which is not difficult to do, circumventing rules and playing games with the interpretation of which academics and lawyers are expert (Cornford 1908). Such a strategy is ultimately self-defeating for the organisation, the professional and the client – a zero sum game. Instead, we must begin to recognise that professionals are stakeholders in organisations and have the capacity to provide creative solutions to problems that emerge. In a sense, organisations and managers have to recreate collegiality since command and control is likely to lead to subversion instead.

This ties into the relations between professions. There will always be competition between them as they compete and challenge each other over work jurisdictions and clients. This leads to demarcation disputes, something that was visible among various trades in the 1950s and 1960s. Who was responsible for inserting a screw into wood – a carpenter or a metal worker? It has been argued that formal organisational structures reflect the myths of their institutional environments instead of the demands of their work activities. William Ouchi (1980) suggests clans are way of coping with complex organisations. Clans are antithetical to hierarchies and instead interpose network structures that create opportunities for productive and shared interactions between groups of professionals (Hanlon 2004). They similarly create a space for types of autonomy to re-emerge as professionals recognise their shared features. This is not an argument for a resistance force, but a different way for professionals to co-exist and co-operate in complex organisations and so engender trust. The norms of reciprocity and interdependence enable exchange and understanding of values. There are questions of whether in globalised professional service firms such values can be inculcated. Social distance alongside physical and cultural distance becomes a barrier to common values. Add to this shortened career trajectories and the adoption of portfolio careers, and the plight of professional service firms becomes one of efficient management and audit.

Turning to the professional–client relationship, it is clear that it is difficult. Even in institutions such as hospitals where close contact with the patient's body is normal, the nature of the relationship is altering, after the scandals involving health professionals in Britain of Shipman and the Mid-Staffordshire NHS Hospital Trust (see respectively O'Neill 2000; Francis 2013). As with paralegals and legal process outsourcers taking on more lawyers' work, there has in the medical world been a devolution of work activity from doctors to other subordinate groups – nurses, in particular, who are now a profession in their own right, and paramedics. Doctors do triage and the specialised work that requires specific medical licensing. They are becoming more remote from the patient rather than the body. For example, in Cleveland Ohio, a major health care company has established a remote intensive care unit (www.advancedicucare.com/insights/southern-ohio/). Using the full range of technologies available a centre can monitor up to 150 intensive care patients scattered around the region. Using big data, they can begin to predict the onset of problems and aim to prevent them. When signals show changes in vital signs local medical carers can be notified to take on-the-ground action. This is emblematic of the hospital as the air traffic controller rather than the doctor as pilot – and also brings us to the conclusion of the chapter.

Conclusion: the power of technology

As the above narrative indicates, part of the solution to the future of professions lies in the increased use of technology, which might seem counter-intuitive. The old ideas of professional domination no longer hold. Virtually everyone has access to the internet and can check WebMD or Divorce Online, even if they get it wrong. But herein lies the answer – empowerment of the consumer. An empowered consumer no longer feels dominated, but more of a partner in the relationship. The development of health apps on iPhones and the like places responsibility on the individual to be cognisant of their own state of health, not to predict trouble but to behave in a manner that prevents medical interventions. Moreover, no one judges you. Take for example, donotpay.co.uk, an app developed by a tech student at Stanford University. Essentially the details of the parking ticket are inputted and the app asks questions until it has sufficient information. The donotpay app uses IBM's Watson as its artificial intelligence resource. When done, the app suggests it writes a letter appealing your ticket and it directs it to the correct local authority office. All this is free. So far donotpay has had a 70 per cent success rate in appeals. Local governments detest it as it lowers revenues. We can also download such legal documents as wills, leases, and contracts for free. We can do our divorce online and our tax – and Britain is now introducing online courts (Bowcott 2017).

In parallel, big law firms are increasingly using technology to deliver services relating to making term sheets, checking MIFID compliance and more. This means professionals are dealing more with processes, systems and structures – all artificial constructs. In law this is almost a return to the era of fictions. Lawyers are becoming designers and engineers. Perhaps in states where monopoly controls are strict – not least in the United States and Australian states like Queensland – the potential to develop new structures will be limited. LegalZoom had to fight a number of unauthorised practice battles with state bars before it could relax and do business (Ambrogi 2014). Some things are better done by technology. For example, in the United States there are 78,000 agencies issuing business licences at federal, state, county, city, municipal and board levels, none of which communicate with each other. It is a nightmare for any business from Amazon to a pizza parlour. LegalZoom have automated the process. One tells them what the business is, and they procure all the licences you need and do the renewals as well (www.legalzoom.com/business/business-operations/business-licenses-overview.html). Human time is too valuable to waste on such boring activities (Goodman 2016).

The power of technology here, which is not replacing all professionals, is that it can transfer to the consumer the ability to negotiate a set of risks in a safe manner. For example, virtual reality would allow patients and clients to experience many procedures and processes in ways that 2D cannot do. Virtual reality could become a forum for court hearings themselves as well as a way of presenting evidence to jurors. For professionals, technology enables them to escape much of the humdrum work they do. Take e-discovery where the trick is to devise the right algorithm to find the correct documents rather than having a poor associate spend sleepless nights going through thousands of documents manually – or virtual deal rooms where the parties and their professional advisers can communicate and interact. Technology reshapes trust and places consumers in a partnership or network with professionals.

For those entering – or considering entering – professions, they potentially have more freedom to express themselves. They will not necessarily be enslaved into long probationary periods as professional career trajectories are fundamentally different to those of the nineteenth and twentieth centuries. Entering a tournament for partnership is illusory since it no longer signifies durability and security. Partners no longer have the time or resources to ensure their human capital is expended in the best form. Partnership is not a marriage for life, rather than a unanimous vote of all partners, a combination of two senior partners is sufficient to remove a partner these days. As new types of institutions and entities evolve, professionalism has the opportunity to recreate and reinvent itself in a meaningful and significant way. To invoke Yuval Harari (2017) again in his new book, *Homo Deus: A Brief History of Tomorrow*, we are no longer bound by the evolutionary forces of old. With the powers we have gained we can actually invent futures, we can redesign humans and of course institutions. We need to learn to be creative and the stories and narratives that professionalism tells must adapt to the new age.

References

Abbott, A. (1988) *The System of Professions: An Essay on the Division of Expert Labor*, Chicago, IL: University of Chicago Press.

Abbott, A. (2005) 'Linked ecologies: States and universities as environments for professions', *Sociological Theory* 23(3): 245–74.

Abbott, A. (2016) 'Boundaries of social work or social work of boundaries?', in Liljegren, A. and Saks, M. (eds) *Professions and Metaphors: Understanding Professions in Society*, Abingdon: Routledge.

Abel, R. (1989) *American Lawyers*, Berkeley, CA: University of California Press.

Adams, K. F. (2012) 'The discursive construction of professional-ism: An episteme of the 21st century', *Ephemera* 12(3): 327–43.

Ambrogi, R. (2014) 'Latest legal victory has LegalZoom poised for growth', *ABA Journal* Available at: www.abajournal.com/magazine/article/latest_legal_victory_has_legalzoom_poised_for_growth

Baumann, J. (1999) *Pioneering a Global Vision: The Story of Baker & McKenzie*, Chicago, IL: Harcourt.

Becker, H. (1962) 'The nature of a profession', in National Society for the Study of Education (ed.) *Education for the Professions*, Chicago, IL: University of Chicago Press.

Boje, D. (2008) *Storytelling Organizations*, Thousand Oaks, CA: Sage.

Bowcott, O. (2017) 'Government's £1bn plan for online courts "challenges open justice"', *Guardian* 15 March.

Brante, T. (2010) 'Professional fields and truth regimes: In search of alternative approaches', *Comparative Sociology* 9(6): 843–86.

Brock, D. (2006), 'The changing professional organization: A review of competing archetypes', *International Journal of Management Reviews* 8(3): 157–74.

Brock, D. and Saks, M. (2015) 'Professions and organizations: A European perspective', *European Management Journal* 34(1): 1–6.

Cannon, T. A. (2014) *Ethics and Professional Responsibility for Paralegals*, New York: Wolters Kluwart, 7th edition.

Caplan, L., (1994) *Skadden: Power, Money, and the Rise of a Legal Empire*, New York: Farrar, Strauss and Giroux.

Carr-Saunders, A. and Wilson, P. (1964) *The Professions*, London: Frank Cass.

CCBE (2001) *Guidelines on the Implementation of the Establishment Directive (98/5/EC of 16th February 1998)*, issued by the CCBE for Bars and Law Societies in the European Union. Available at: www.ccbe.eu/fileadmin/speciality_distribution/public/documents/ FREE_MOVEMENT_OF_LAWYERS/FML_Position_papers/EN_FML_20011101_ Guidelines_on_the_Implementation_of_the_Establishment_Directive__985EC_of_16th_ February_1998__issued_by_the_CCBE_for_Bars_and_Law_Societies_in_the_European_Union.pdf

Cheetham, G. and Chivers, G. (2005) *Professionals, Competence and Informal Learning*, Cheltenham: Edward Elgar.

Conley, J. and O'Barr, W. (1990) *Rules versus Relationships: The Ethnography of Legal Discourse*, Chicago, IL: University of Chicago Press.

Cornford, F. M. (1908) *Microcosmographia Academica: A Guide for the Young Academic Politician*. Available at: www.maths.ed.ac.uk/~aar/baked/micro.pdf

Czarniawska, B. (2004) *Narratives in Social Science Research*, Thousand Oaks, CA: Sage.

Dent, M. (2003) 'Managing doctors and saving a hospital: Irony, rhetoric and actor networks', *Organization* 10(1): 107–27.

Dragland, A. (2013) 'Big Data, for better or worse: 90% of world's data generated over last two years', *Science News* 22 May. Available at: www.sciencedaily.com/releases/2013/05/130522085217.htm

Dunleavy, P., Margetts, H., Bastow, S. and Tinkler, J. (2005) 'New Public Management is dead – Long live digital-era governance', *Journal of Public Administration Research and Theory* 16: 467–94.

Eisler, K. I. (2004) *Shark Tank: Greed, Politics, and the Collapse of Finley Kumble, One of America's Biggest Law Firms*, New York: Beard Books.

Evetts, J. (2013) 'Professionalism: Value and ideology', *Current Sociology* 61(5/6): 778–96.

Flood, J. (1995) 'The cultures of globalization: Professional restructuring for the international market', in Dezalay, Y. and Sugarman, D. (eds) *Professional Competition and Professional Power: Lawyers, Accountants and the Social Construction of Markets*, London: Routledge.

Flood, J. (1996) 'Megalawyering in the global order: The cultural, social and economic transformation of global legal practice', *International Journal of the Legal Profession* 3(2/3): 169–214

Flood, J. (2013) *What Do Lawyers Do? An Ethnography of a Corporate Law Firm*, New Orleans, LA: Quid Pro Books.

Flood, J. (2016) 'Corporate lawyer-client relationships: Bankers, lawyers, clients and enduring relationships', *Legal Ethics* 19(1): 76–96.

Foucault, M. (1979) *The Birth of the Clinic*, London: Routledge.

Francis, R. (2013) *Report of the Mid-Staffordshire NHS Foundation Trust Public Inquiry*, London: The Stationery Office.

Freidson, E. (2001) *Professionalism: The Third Logic*, Cambridge: Polity Press.
Galanter, M. and Palay, T. (1991) *Tournament of Lawyers: The Transformation of the Big Law Firm*, Chicago, IL: University of Chicago Press.
Galanter, M. and Roberts, S. (2008) 'From kinship to Magic Circle: The London commercial law firm in the twentieth century', *International Journal of the Legal Profession* 15(3): 143–78.
Gieryn, T. (1999) *Cultural Boundaries of Science: Credibility on the Line*, Chicago, IL: University of Chicago Press.
Goffman, E. (1952) 'On cooling the mark out: Some aspects of adaptation to failure', *Psychiatry: Journal of Interpersonal Relations* 15(4): 451–63.
Goodman, J. (2016) *Robots in Law: How Artificial Intelligence is Transforming Legal Services*, London: ARK Group.
Greenwood, E. (1957) 'The attributes of a profession', *Social Work* 2(3): 45–55.
Habermas, J. (1987) *Life-World and System: A Critique of Functionalist Reason*, Boston, MA: Beacon Press.
Hanlon, G. (1998) 'Professionalism as enterprise: Service sector politics and the redefinition of professionalism', *Sociology* 32(1): 43–63.
Hanlon, G. (2004) 'Institutional forms and organizational structures: Homology, trust and reputational capital in professional service firms', *Organization* 11(2): 187–210.
Harari, Y. (2015) *Sapiens: A Brief History of Mankind*, New York: Harper Collins.
Harari, Y. (2017) *Homo Deus: A Brief History of Tomorrow*, New York: Harper Collins.
Hill, O. (2012) 'Hungarian home births champion to move from house arrest to jail', *Guardian* 27 April.
Hughes, E. (1958) *Men and Their Work*, Glencoe, IL: Free Press.
Illich, I. (1977) *Disabling Professions*, London: Marion Boyars.
Isaacson, W. (2011) *Steve Jobs*, New York: Simon & Schuster.
Jencks, C. and Riesman, D. (1977) *The Academic Revolution*, Chicago, IL: University of Chicago Press.
Kirkpatrick, I., Ackroyd, S. and Walker, R. (2005) *The New Managerialism and Public Service Professions: Change in Health, Social Services and Housing*, Houndmills: Palgrave Macmillan.
Kuruvilla, S., Noronha, E. and D'Cruz, P. (2016) 'Globalization of commodification: Legal process outsourcing and Indian lawyers', *Journal of Contemporary Asia* 46(4): 614–40.
Larson, M. S. (1977) *The Rise of Professionalism: A Sociological Analysis*, Berkeley, CA: University of California Press.
LETR (2013) *Setting Standards: The Future of Legal Services Education and Training Regulation in England and Wales*. Available at: www.letr.org.uk/wp-content/uploads/LETR-Report.pdf.
Liljegren, A. and Saks, M. (2016) 'Introducing professions and metaphors', in Liljegren, A. and Saks, M. (eds) *Professions and Metaphors: Understanding Professions in Society*, Abingdon: Routledge.
Lipworth, W., Little, M., Markham, P., Gordon, J. and Kerridge, I. (2013) 'Doctors on status and respect: A qualitative study', *Journal of Bioethical Inquiry* 10(2): 205–17.
Liu, S. (2013) 'The legal profession as a social process: A theory on lawyers and globalization', *Law and Social Inquiry* 38(3): 670–93.
Luhmann, N. (2017) *Trust and Power*, Cambridge: Polity Press.
McClean, B. and Elkind, P. (2004) *The Smartest Guys in the Room: The Amazing Rise and Scandalous Fall of Enron*, New York: Penguin.

Malhotra, N., Morris, T. and Smets, M. (2012) 'New career models in UK professional service firms: From up-or-out to up-and-going-nowhere?'. Available at: https://research.aston.ac.uk/portal/files/1441783/Malhotra_Morris_Smets_forthcoming_New_career_models_in_UK_professional_service_firms.pdf

Massey, A. and Pyper, R. (2005) *The Public Management and Modernisation in Britain*, London: Palgrave Macmillan.

Matthews, D. (2006) *A History of Auditing: The Changing Audit Process in Britain from the Nineteenth Century to the Present Day*, London: Routledge.

Misztal, B. (2002) 'Trusting the professional: A managerial discourse for uncertain times', in Dent, M. and Whitehead, S. (eds) *Managing Professional Identities: Knowledge, Performativity and the 'New' Professional*, London: Routledge.

Moorhead, R. (2014) 'Precarious professionalism: Some empirical and behavioural perspectives on lawyers', *Current Legal Problems* 67(1): 447–81.

Moynihan, T. (2017) 'Samsung finally reveals why the Note 7 kept exploding', *Wired* 22 January 2017. Available at: www.wired.com/2017/01/why-the-samsung-galaxy-note-7-kept-exploding/

Muzio, D. and Faulconbridge, J. (2013) 'The global professional service firm: "One firm" models versus (Italian) distant institutionalized practices', *Organization Studies* 34(7): 897–925.

Nisen, M. (2013) 'Legacy kids' still get a staggering college admissions advantage and it needs to end', *Business Insider*. Available at: www.businessinsider.com.au/legacy-kids-have-an-admissions-advantage-2013-6#CGAFOgGFpDmErTgX.99

O'Neill, B. (2000) 'Doctor as murderer: Death certification needs tightening up, but it still might not have stopped Shipman', *British Medical Journal* 320(7231): 329–30.

Ouchi, W. (1980) 'Markets, bureaucracies, and clans', *Administrative Science Quarterly* 25(1): 129–41.

Parkin, F. (1979) *Marxism and Class Theory: A Bourgeois Critique*, London: Tavistock.

Parsons, T. (1939) 'The professions and social structure', *Social Forces* 17: 457–67

Parsons, T. (1954) 'A sociologist looks at the legal profession', in Parsons, T. *Essays in Sociological Theory*, Glencoe, IL: The Free Press.

Pinnington, A. and Morris, T. (2003) 'Archetype change in professional organizations: Survey evidence from large law firms', *British Journal of Management* 14: 85–99.

Power, M. (1999) *The Audit Society: Rituals of Verification*, Oxford: Oxford University Press.

Regan, M. (2006) *Eat What You Kill: The Fall of a Wall Street Lawyer*, Ann Arbor, MI: University of Michigan Press.

Rodda, M. (2014) 'The diagrammatic spectator', *Ephemera* 14(2): 221–44.

Rogers, J., Kingsford Smith, D. and Chellew, J. (2017) 'The large professional service firm: A new force in the regulative bargain', *University of New South Wales Law Journal* 40(1): 218–61.

St George, A. (1995) *A History of Norton Rose*, London: Granta Books.

Saks, M. (2010) 'Analyzing the professions: The case for the neo-Weberian approach', *Comparative Sociology* 9(6): 887–915.

Saks, M. (2014) 'The regulation of the English health professions: Zoos, circuses or safari parks?', *Journal of Professions and Organization* 1(1): 84–98.

Saks, M. (2016) 'A review of theories of professions, organizations and society: The case for neo-Weberianism, neo-institutionalism and eclecticism', *Journal of Professions and Organization* 3(2) 1–18.

Sandefur, R. (2015) 'Elements of professional expertise: Understanding relational and substantive expertise through lawyers' impact', *American Sociological Review* 80(5): 909–33.

Sassen, S. (2001) *The Global City: New York, London, Tokyo*, Princeton, NJ: Princeton University Press.

Sciulli, D. (2005) 'Continental sociology of professions today: Conceptual contributions', *Current Sociology* 53(6): 915–42.

Sloman, S. and Fernbach, P. (2017) *The Knowledge Illusion: Why We Never Think Alone*, New York: Penguin Random House.

Starbucks, W. (1993) 'Keeping a butterfly and an elephant in a house of cards: The elements of exceptional success', *Journal of Management Studies* 30(6): 885–921.

Starr, P. (1982) *The Social Transformation of American Medicine*, New York: Basic Books.

Sullivan, C. (2017) 'Is Deutsche Bank's refusal to pay junior lawyers misguided?', *Bloomberg Law: Big Law Business*. Available at: https://bol.bna.com/is-deutsche-banks-refusal-to-pay-junior-lawyers-misguided/

Swaine, P. (1946) *The Cravath Firm and Its Predecessors*, Volume 1, New York: Ad Press.

Swaine, P. (1948) *The Cravath Firm and Its Predecessors*, Volume 2, New York: Ad Press.

van Quaquebeke, N., Zenker, S. and Eckloff, T. (2009) 'Find out how much it means to me! The importance of interpersonal respect in work values compared to perceived organizational practices', *Journal of Business Ethics* 89(3): 423–31.

Vance, A. (2015) *Elon Musk: Tesla, SpaceX, and the Quest for a Fantastic Future*, New York: Harper Collins.

Weber, M. (1968) *Economy and Society*, Berkeley, CA: University of California Press.

Wilkins, D. and Gulati, M. (1998) 'Reconceiving the tournament of lawyers: Tracking, seeding, and information control in the internal labor markets of elite law firms', *Virginia Law Review* 84: 1581–1681.

Yamey, B. S. (2007) 'The historical significance of double-entry bookkeeping: Some non-Sombartian claims', *Accounting, Business and Financial History* 15(1): 77–88. Available at: http://dx.doi.org/10.1080/09585200500033089

4 Professional strategies and enterprise in transnational projects

Jacob Hasselbalch and Leonard Seabrooke

Introduction

This chapter explores how transnational professionals develop new markets for their services and products through knowledge and framing strategies. We respond to the call for a 'transnational sociology of the professions' (Faulconbridge and Muzio 2012) that is interested in identifying how professionals forge and maintain markets. Much of this activity comes through professional enterprises that operate in 'thin' transnational environments and are decoupled from 'thick' domestic environments (Seabrooke 2014). Transnational projects operate in a unique 'social space' in that they blend interactions between the national, local, international and transnational (Morgan 2001). As activity is stretched across these levels, it offers room for professionals to push forward and establish markets for their expertise and skills. Professionals create and drive enterprises to make the most of these opportunities, using knowledge and framing strategies to assert their control over professional markets and generate demand for their services within them. Here we outline how professionals use enterprises and their network to pursue knowledge and framing strategies to push forward their transnational projects. Knowledge strategies include knowing how to *leverage* institutional and organisational fields (Boussebaa, Sturdy and Morgan 2014; Greenwood, Suddaby and Hinings 2002), engaging in '*epistemic arbitrage*' (Seabrooke 2014) and establishing oneself as an *arbiter* of appropriate professional knowledge. Framing strategies include *disrupting* current professional and institutional orders (Vollmer 2013), *contesting* what is appropriate professional knowledge for transnational issues, and *normalising* who is best suited to controlling professional jurisdictions within transnational professional projects (Fligstein and McAdam 2012). Both knowledge and framing strategies are examples of 'institutional work' done by professionals as they pursue their transnational projects (Lawrence, Suddaby and Leca 2011).

While most attention on how professionals pursue transnational projects has focused on global professional service firms (see Faulconbridge and Muzio 2017), we focus on professionals who develop transnational projects to mediate between markets and regulators. Tensions between market activity and regulation force professionals to develop strategies to defend and further their enterprises. To do so they must develop strategies to exercise jurisdictional control over which professionals are permitted to work on what tasks in transnational space (Seabrooke and Henriksen 2017). This chapter first outlines issues concerning transnational projects, namely transnationality, professional decoupling, and the establishment of organisational fields, and then delves into the knowledge and framing strategies noted above.

Transnational professionals

Transnationality

To say that something is transnational is to differentiate it from both the domestic and the international. Whereas domestic domains or affairs are circumscribed by the borders of nation-states, international matters are defined as taking place *between* nation-states, as in operating through channels that depend on the existence of nation-states in the first place. A high-level summit of heads of state to discuss trade matters is an international affair, for example. The boundaries of states still matter in terms of constituting the identities of the involved parties and binding them to a history of past obligations (Dezalay and Garth 2016).

Transnationality, on the other hand, cares not for boundaries or for nation-states. When something is transnational, it *transcends* borders and nation-states, which is to say that these qualities have no bearing whatsoever on transnational phenomena. This is a strong version of the distinction between transnationality and internationality that makes more analytical sense than practical – in reality, the two are much more closely intertwined, and we will not find it easy to distinguish clearly between international and transnational entities. For example, global warming is a transnational phenomenon, but emerging responses to the problem contain both international and transnational elements. The world of transnational enterprise, similarly, will find it hard to completely disavow the existence of national boundaries and the different sets of rules and institutions that go along with them.

Nonetheless, there are good reasons to take transnationality more seriously in the study of professions in the global economy. While the domestic and the international still matter, they are not necessarily the most important sites or channels of interaction working upon the professions any longer – although this certainly varies from one professional group to another. Transnationality first and foremost implies a 'rescaling' of the professional world: mobility, connections, clients, work, and regulation have become freed from the confines of the nation-state. This has led Faulconbridge and Muzio (2012: 149) to argue for a need to:

> replace in neo-Weberian sociologies of the professions the traditional focus on the nation-state with broader governance regimes; of inserting a new actor, the firm and GPSFs [global professional service firms] in particular within existing frameworks; and of understanding users, universities and practitioners as multi-scalar actors.

The rescaling and multi-scalar qualities of transnationality imply that dialogues between international, transnational, national, and local actors are increasingly pertinent to the system of professions. Many professionals will find that transnational enterprise itself has become the primary site of professional regulation and control (Cooper and Robson 2006; Henriksen and Seabrooke 2016), more so than any domestic or international institutions. Moreover, transnational enterprises are strategically oriented towards global rather than domestic markets for their services, meaning that global standards of professional conduct and expertise need to be defined and defended (Faulconbridge and Muzio 2007). One tendency that exemplifies this is the emergence of transnational professional associations and their growing importance in re-regulating professional service markets and institutionalising new jurisdictions (Evetts 1995). Such emerging transnational regimes, coupled with the global outlook of transnational enterprise, are likely to further erode nationally specific knowledge bases and qualification trajectories (Tsingou 2017).

While the discussion so far would suggest that transnationality matters mostly because it changes the conditions of professional life, this would underestimate the capacity of professionals to exploit transnationality themselves in pursuit of particular goals. Professionals are not passive targets of transnational pressures, but are integral drivers of transnationalisation. This is connected to comparisons between the 'thick' domestic environment with the 'thin' transnational one: domestic settings are densely populated by jurisdictions and institutions that provide clear divisions of work between professional groups. Capacities to act transnationally have preceded the emergence of strongly defined institutions and jurisdictions in the transnational space, meaning that professionals have a greater scope for laying claim to work tasks and areas of expertise.

Transnational social space is 'thin' because it is more likely to be characterised by 'structural holes' (Burt 1992; Seabrooke 2014). For Burt (1992), structural holes are missing relationships in a network that would otherwise permit the flow of information. The 'thinness' of transnational social space (in other words, the sparsely populated institutional landscape) translates to structural holes in network terms. What we see in transnational space is that actors and institutions in one issue area frequently share little or no flows of information or people with adjacent issue areas (see, for example, Seabrooke and Tsingou 2015). This creates opportunities for those who can jump between issue areas and cross the structural holes in a network, which we expand on in the third section of this chapter.

There is a wealth of research on how professionals create markets for their services by building transnational governance regimes that favour their particular form of expertise (for example, Dezalay and Garth 1996, 2002; Djelic and Quack 2010; Fourcade 2006; Seabrooke and Tsingou 2014; Suddaby, Cooper and Greenwood 2007). In particular, this happens by professionals organising transnationally (Henriksen and Seabrooke 2016) in order to project global authority over some domain and then seeking to redraw the institutional frameworks and rules that govern that domain on domestic, international and transnational levels.

It is precisely the 'thin' nature of transnational environments that lets them do this. In order to implement the new rules, many studies also highlight the role of the interrelationships that are forged between actors on different planes of the rescaled global order. For example, professionals in the transnational domain can productively engage with either international organisations on the one hand, such as the European Union or World Trade Organisation (see, for example, Dezalay and Garth 1996), or local actors on the other, such as Latin American law firms, universities or think tanks (see, for instance, Dezalay and Garth 2002). In these ways, transnationality both shapes and is shaped by professionals: the transnational space is full of opportunities for professionals who know how to seize them, but the pressures of globalisation and transnational enterprise are also changing what it means to be a professional.

Decoupling

One way to make sense of this mutual interaction between professionals and transnationality is through the concept of 'decoupling'. Meyer and Rowan (1977) introduced the concept to institutional theory as a way to make sense of the global spread of certain formal organisational structures. They explain the similarity in organisational structure observed worldwide by arguing that organisations "dramatically reflect the myths of their institutional environments instead of the demands of their work activities" (Meyer and Rowan 1977: 341). Even in very different settings, organisations look the same in order to maintain ceremonial conformity with the prevailing institutions, thereby deriving measures of support and legitimacy that make them seem credible and serious. However, because efficiency criteria vary from one setting to another, organisations are forced to endure gaps between their formal structures and actual work activities. In other words, the form and content of organisations are *decoupled* from one another.

We can understand the changing context of professionalism through the metaphor of decoupling. In one sense, and as mentioned earlier, professional work activities in the transnational domain are increasingly decoupled from the formal structures (especially national structures) of the professions. This applies to all aspects of professional life, such as accreditations, associations, jurisdictions, knowledge bases, and so on. Many transnational professionals have no obvious need to become formal members of national associations (a contrary view can be found in the legal profession, see Dezalay and Garth 2016). National associations have traditionally supplied the legitimacy supporting professional activities, but transnational professionals obtain their legitimacy from being networked into peer groups that recognise their expertise (Seabrooke and Tsingou 2014). Some have taken this argument even further, demonstrating that national or other traditional forms of professional accreditation or membership can be seen as a direct impediment to gaining prestige within transnational networks of professionals (Sending 2015). This can lead to 'wormhole effects' (Johnson 2006) where professionals avoid domestic actors in order to engage in transnational interactions with their peers.

All of this suggests that professionals can use decoupling strategically to pursue different goals. A critical take on this suggests that professional rhetoric and practices can be decoupled and deployed as a performative discourse and disciplinary mechanism to exert managerial control over workers in professional and non-professional contexts alike (Dent and Whitehead 2002). There are also some who see the last 'vestige of formal imperialism' (Seabrooke 2014) apparent in the current dominance of Anglo-Saxon transnational professionals (Annisette 2000). These notions of decoupling are also especially prevalent in studies that demonstrate the interlinkages between neo-liberalism and various professionalisation projects of lawyers, accountants and economists (for example, Fourcade 2006; Chwieroth 2010; Mennicken 2010). Indeed, Faulconbridge and Muzio (2012) argue that the imperatives of neo-liberal capitalism are inextricably tied to the transnational professional projects of the most powerful actors involved in the institutionalisation of new professional practices and privileges.

Organisational fields

Under conditions of intense decoupling and a rescaling of the professional world, we require new ways of viewing and conceptualising the system of professions that extend traditional neo-Weberian theories that placed nation-state institutions centrally (Abbott 1988; Burrage and Torstendahl 1990; Freidson 2001; Larson 1977). As we demonstrate in later sections, many are taking up this call. In addition to the call by Faulconbridge and Muzio (2012) for a transnational sociology of the professions, Muzio, Brock and Suddaby (2013) have also indicated the value added from a more institutionalist sociology of the professions. One concept that has been borrowed from institutional theory to help make sense of transnational professional life is the idea of an 'organisational field' (DiMaggio 1991; Scott 1995; Wooten and Hoffman 2008).

Organisational fields imply "the existence of a community of organizations that partakes of a common meaning system and whose participants interact more frequently and fatefully with one another than those actors outside the field" (Scott 1995: 56). This means that organisational fields are relationally defined around issues rather than given by some set of formal criteria or boundaries. The field is the 'centre of common channels of dialogue and discussion' in which issues (such as environmentalism in the chemical industry) get treated by organisations that often have disparate purposes, attitudes and beliefs (Hoffman 1999). Organisational fields are marked by contestation as 'arenas of power relations' (Brint and Karabel 1991) or 'fields of struggles' (Bourdieu and Wacquant 1992).

The advantage of viewing transnational professional life through the lens of organisational fields is that it allows you to view transnationalisation as a process of changing organisational systems, structures, and procedures. This makes it possible to conceptualise transnational social space as a community of organisations that are embedded in networks with each other, guided by both common and distinct institutional elements. These elements make up the issues that are negotiated and transformed by the actions of professionals through 'institutional work' (Lawrence, Suddaby and Leca 2011). Some of this institutional work is highly mediated by political interests, especially in focal intergovernmental organisations (for a case on the International Monetary Fund (IMF) see Kentikelenis and Seabrooke 2017). But the bureaucracy and structures of nation-states, prevalent in neo-Weberian theories of professionalism, need not always feature in organisational fields. Organisational fields thereby make it possible to answer questions about how professionals can provoke larger-scale structural changes in the thinly networked and institutionalised transnational domain, which has otherwise been a puzzle for institutional theory (Suddaby and Viale 2011). It also permits us to think through how some transnational projects can become the dominant means of professional practice, such as the role of large multinational firms that operate in 'mature' organisational fields, including the Big Four accountancy firms (Suddaby and Greenwood 2006).

The following sections put some of these ideas into practice by reflecting on innovative empirical research that has been undertaken in this domain, focusing on the strategies of professionals to develop new markets for their products and services through knowledge strategies and framing strategies.

Knowledge strategies

For professionals to succeed in their transnational projects they need to develop strategies to obtain and control knowledge. Knowledge combines information about what is going on, as well as know-how in how that information can be used for professional purposes. Especially important is how knowledge permits jurisdictional control over who and what organisations work on particular issues (Seabrooke and Henriksen 2017). The thinness of transnational social space means that knowledge strategies can be particularly effective for professionals who seek to avoid being entrenched in battling national professional associations, as well as for those who use transnational enterprises to change how professional work is being conducted – and who benefits most from such changes.

Leveraging

A common strategy in transnational professional projects is to control knowledge as a means of leveraging interests and creating and maintaining power asymmetries. Yves Dezalay and Bryan Garth (1996, 2002, 2010) have demonstrated how lawyers and economists have constructed transnational professional projects that leverage American geopolitical and economic interests to reshape legal and economic professional practices, especially in Latin America, and East and Southeast Asia. Leverage comes from control over what knowledge is deemed appropriate for professional practices – such as legal and economic reforms – that originate in the relationship between the state and professions in the 'core' country (in this case the United States) that then inform battles over professional knowledge in the periphery. Those exercising leverage are professional elites, such as the 'Chicago School' of economists (Dezalay and Garth 2002), whose students are overrepresented in international organisations (Chwieroth 2010; Kentikelenis and Seabrooke 2017; Nelson 2017) and who have formed a transnational network that affirms the interests of the core. Professionals can use leveraging of elite status to control knowledge and further transnational projects. Such status can come from the state-professions relationship within 'thick' domestic spaces which is then used as a form of power in thin transnational space.

The work of Mehdi Boussebaa (2009, 2017) demonstrates how global professional service firms engage in leveraging to control how knowledge flows from the core to the periphery, and vice versa, as well as to leverage power asymmetries to exploit professional expertise in peripheral countries as a form of 'cheap labour'. Global professional service firms have followed a deliberate strategy to make themselves transnational enterprises by creating corporate forms that rely on playing off national legal jurisdictions while building a common cross-national culture (Spence et al. 2015). With colleagues Boussebaa has convincingly shown how global professional service firms create knowledge hierarchies that are neo-colonial or neo-imperial in character (Boussebaa, Morgan and Sturdy 2012; Boussebaa, Sturdy and Morgan 2014). As such, firms are typically headquartered in core economies in which they have the greatest control over client management and 'talent' search. The 'Englishization' of global professional work affirms these power asymmetries (Boussebaa and Brown 2017; Boussebaa, Sinha and Gabriel 2014). This permits core professionals to leverage their status to control what knowledge is received by clients and also what professionals create from this knowledge at prices that favour 'transnational professionals' located in the core economies. For example, a London-based professional in charge of a global professional service firm's client management may outsource the professional tasks to employees in Warsaw, paying the Polish professionals a third of what is then billed to the end-user client (Boussebaa 2017). Furthermore, professionals in the core leverage their status to deflect or ignore knowledge coming from professionals in the periphery to the core within the global professional service firm structure, affirming that professionals in London and New York know best and should earn higher compensation based on their revenue-making (see also Paik and Choi 2005). In short, professionals using leveraging can turn status and position – nearly of all of which is beyond their own making – into power and money.

Epistemic arbitrage

Those who are percieved as knowing may well have strategies in addition to leveraging (Lazega 1992). One of them is to position themselves between different pools of professional knowledge and use 'epistemic arbitrage' to signal that they are well qualified to control transnational professional projects (Seabrooke 2014). The concept of epistemic arbitrage is particularly appropriate for transnational activities, where canny professionals can exploit the thin social space. By acting as brokers between established professional groups, those engaging in epistemic arbitrage can influence what knowledge is viewed as most relevant and who is perceived as knowing well. The sociology of professions has long held the view that knowledge 'lives through its agents' (Freidson 1986), and should be seen as a resource rather than simply information. Seeing knowledge as a resource about how professional practices are enacted or transmitted also differs from the focus in much literature on transnational actors that stresses the importance of 'ideas', or the traditional view of professions as steeped in a particular form of abstracted knowledge provided by specialised training and associational credentials (Abbott 1988). Professionals engaging in epistemic arbitrage use knowledge as a strategic resource in attempts to be viewed by others as 'knowing well' (Lazega 1992). They can do so by finding 'structural holes', gaps in networks that would otherwise permit information transfer between actors (Burt 1992). These gaps often exist between professional bodies of knowledge, permitting brokers to use epistemic arbitrage to position themselves as knowing well. These brokers can also use hierarchies of professional knowledge in asserting their positions. Those who can call upon concepts and applications from economists, for example, are able to position themselves as authoritative among other actors trained in other professions (Fourcade, Ollion and Algan 2015). Actors who can successfully work between different pools of professional knowledge are more likely to be seen as those carrying 'good ideas'. But not all actors are successful with this strategy. Arbitrage can also fail, especially on issues where professional jurisdictions at the domestic level are particularly defensive (Mudge and Vauchez 2012) and/or where issues lack political salience – as on, for example, fertility issues (see Seabrooke and Tsingou 2016).

Epistemic arbitrage has been identified as a knowledge strategy used by professionals in a range of cases, including those related to enterprise. Thistlethwaite and Paterson (2016) have documented how professionals pushed forward new environmental and social standards in the area of green accounting by using epistemic arbitrage between professional associations, non-governmental organisations, and the Big Four accountancy firms. By using knowledge about environmental standards and technical accounting information, these professionals established standards boards in London and Washington that changed green accounting. On a less upbeat note, Eskelinen and Ylönen (2017) trace how professionals engaged in epistemic arbitrage on international taxation and, separately, trade law developed strategies to defend Panama. Experts were able to counter 'anti-tax haven' measures directed at Panama by Argentina and Colombia by appealing to international trade law, while also promoting legal tax avoidance activities. Finally, Holzscheiter (2017) has demonstrated how the strong development of 'global health boundary organisations' comprised of multiple stakeholders and organisations has enabled professionals to engage in epistemic arbitrage. In doing so, the organisational efforts to create a more coherent transnational health regime are diminished by professionals who play these organisations off against each other and encourage fragmentation. Furthermore, those well positioned in global health networks are increasingly recognised not only as those who know well, but also as those who are the best judges of what professional practice should be.

Epistemic arbiters

A third knowledge strategy is to actively sit in judgement on what is appropriate professional knowledge and who should have jurisdiction over issues in transnational projects. Epistemic arbiters can acquire this position through extreme forms of leveraging, such as from high status acquired by elite institutional affiliation, personal and family wealth (Tsingou 2015), or by engaging in epistemic arbitrage so successfully that the professional changes from being a broker in issue networks to a gatekeeper overseeing them (Seabrooke 2014). The key knowledge strategy used by epistemic arbiters include control over knowledge production by organisations in which they have power, including the selection of professionals to work on transnational issues. Epistemic arbiters also rely heavily on inducing deference in others through style of engagement and form of communication (Seabrooke 2011), as well as relying on knowledge from third parties to affirm their positions.

Epistemic arbiters are relatively easy to identify in transnational professional projects, both in public and private enteprises. For example, in post-financial crisis debates about necessary changes to the banking sector prominent professionals were active in policy commissions that put forward official and unofficial proposals. The presence of particular professionals on commissions that produced opposing recommendations during the same window of time was notable. These epistemic arbiters were not acting as brokers to push forward a reform agenda, but using their authority as knowing best to occupy positions in the policy space to prevent certain changes from occurring (Seabrooke and Tsingou 2014). This problem has recurred in recent debates on the transnational problem of 'shadow banking' (Ban, Seabrooke and Freitas 2016).

Epistemic arbiters also control who is hired to produce knowledge. Within the IMF, for example, the establishment of a 'Committee of Eminent Persons' in 2007 to reconsider the IMF's 'business model' was indicative of important changes in knowledge management in the organisation by epistemic arbiters. The use of external consultants to support existing professional skills in the IMF shifted to an emphasis on high-end private sector consultants hired for their expertise, experience, and market knowledge (Seabrooke and Nilsson 2015). Similarly, executive search firms place themselves as positioned to find those who know best and have promoted a form of 'corporate professionalisation' in how knowledge is treated (Muzio *et al.* 2011). The role of consultants in acting as gatekeepers over what kinds of professional knowledge is produced is ever increasing, with governments and international organisations relying on them more as the best arbiters of what is world best practice (Sturdy and Wright 2011; Sturdy, Wright and Wylie 2015).

Framing strategies

In contrast to knowledge strategies, which are manoeuvres to control the supply and demand of expertise on transnational issues, framing strategies are strategic communications meant to affect the network of relations between involved actors in different ways. Typically, framing strategies aim at building coalitions by eliciting support from other participants or instigating collective action by enrolling new stakeholders and making them care about an issue. Framing has been accused of being a 'scattered conceptualisation' and lacking a general statement of framing theory, but in part this is due to the successful incursion of the term into a very broad spectrum of social science disciplines (Entman 1993). What all studies on framing have in common is that they emphasise the power of a communicating text or discourse over human consciousness. Entman (1993: 52) offers the following definition:

> Framing essentially involves selection and salience. To frame is to *select some aspects of a perceived reality and make them more salient in a communicating text, in such a way as to promote a particular problem definition, causal interpretation, moral evaluation, and/or treatment recommendation* for the item described.
>
> (Emphasis in original)

The book *Frame Analysis* by Goffman (1974) laid the foundations for much of the work that has been done to popularise framing in the social sciences. For Goffman, to frame something is to produce the social context of a situation – to tell participants what they are looking at and why it matters. Successive and multiple instances of framing add up to produce social order and established understandings of phenomena. Frames therefore diagnose, evaluate, and prescribe (Benford and Snow 2000).

On the issues that unite different groups of professionals and organisations in the organisational fields that make up the transnational domain, having the power to diagnose, evaluate and prescribe is equivalent to having the power to redraw transnational governance regimes and institutional frameworks in your own favour (or in pursuit of preconceived ends such as neo-liberalism). Instances of framing and counter-framing supply the momentum that drives the evolution of transnational professional projects and governance regimes. In the following sections, we will look closer at how framing strategies were employed in an enterprise context on the transnational policy issues of hydraulic fracturing (fracking) and electronic cigarettes (e-cigarettes). Our analysis draws on original research on how these issues were negotiated by transnational professionals in recent years working to influence how the European Union would approach the disruptions (Hasselbalch 2016, 2017). The application of framing to these controversial technologies should be immediately clear; fracking can be presented as ecological disaster or energy boom and e-cigarettes as a public health threat or opportunity. It depends on which elements that make up

Disruptions

Framing strategies are often oriented around disruptions. Disruptions are events that cause a breakdown in the prevailing understanding of an issue, leading to an opportunity for involved actors to reframe the situation and reorganise the institutional landscape (Vollmer 2013). The flow of social action during such episodes have also been conceptualised as beginning with shocks and field ruptures, leading to episodes of contention, and ending with a new settlement (Fligstein and McAdam 2012).

E-cigarettes and fracking are both good examples of disruptions that rupture an organisational field. E-cigarettes are disruptive in the sense that they turn prevailing assumptions about tobacco control on their head. Current best estimates say they are 95 per cent less harmful than conventional cigarettes (McNeill *et al.* 2015), and there is good evidence to support the fact that they actually help people quit smoking (Brown *et al.* 2014). At the same time, they have grown in under a decade into a multi-billion-dollar market, with some analysts projecting a compound annual growth rate in excess of 20 per cent until 2020 (Research and Markets 2016). It is not far-fetched to imagine them completely replacing conventional cigarettes in the future. This has created a conundrum for those professionals engaged on tobacco control – in other words, the public health professionals and medical doctors that organise in transnational associations and networks to influence regimes of tobacco control (such as the European Respiratory Society or the European Public Health Alliance). The conundrum asks: should e-cigarettes be embraced in their current form as a different kind of cigarette that can reduce the harm of smoking, or should they be rejected and turned into a pharmaceutical product used solely for the purposes of quitting smoking? There is no immediate answer to the question as the disruption of e-cigarettes challenges the expectations that used to govern professional conduct in tobacco control.

When it comes to fracking, it is not so much an issue that divides professional groups internally (as in the e-cigarette example) as it brings different professional groups into direct confrontation with each other. The disruption of fracking has led some to argue that we are entering a new era of fossil fuel abundance, which should be embraced to the extent that we can substitute coal for natural gas (Helm 2012). Fracking has completely changed the energy picture worldwide: ten years ago, analysts agreed that the United States would remain a natural gas importer for the foreseeable future, and facilities to import liquefied natural gas were under construction (Zuckerman 2013). Now the United States is on track to become a net gas exporter by 2018 (United States Energy Information Administration 2016), and the liquefied natural gas facilities are being retrofitted for export. On the other hand, academics and environmentalists have drawn attention to the risks to groundwater, air quality and climate from extensive fracking activities (Food and Water Europe *et al*. 2012; Howarth, Santoro and Ingraffea 2011). The 2010 documentary film *Gasland* (Fox 2010) also sparked a wave of protest and instigated a transnational social movement against fracking. For the professionals working in transnational enterprises such as global oil and gas companies or in transnational environmental organisations, fracking brings up numerous difficult questions about how to prioritise trade-offs between energy security, jobs, economic growth, environmental quality and global warming.

Contests

One of the most basic insights about the process of framing is that it is prone to manipulation and exploitation (Goffman 1974). Disruptions, in being so provocative to the settled expectations, assumptions and institutions governing an issue area, open discursive spaces in which professionals have room to manoeuvre by using framing strategically in order to align the disruption with their preferred set of rules and institutions.

Framing contests unfold over time through a series of moves and countermoves by participants working in the disrupted organisational field. We can observe frames in many different ways. Interviews can reveal the background assumptions and perceptions from which frames are constructed, but we should also take an interest in the communicative texts or discourses that are propagated throughout the organisational field. These could be press releases, political programmes, studies, fact sheets, stakeholder consultations, pamphlets, social media posts, legislative documents, meeting minutes, newspaper articles and so on. The fracking and e-cigarette controversies initiated dense interactions and communications between the professionals in the organisational field centred around the European policymakers engaged on drawing up policy on the issues.

In the e-cigarette debate, the core institution structuring the organisational field of tobacco control was the notion of abstinence and the tobacco endgame (Hasselbalch 2016). According to these ideas, centrally enshrined in tobacco control through the World Health Organisation's Framework Convention on Tobacco Control, the object of tobacco control is to eliminate nicotine dependency completely from the population. Tobacco controllers driven by these ideas cannot envision a future role for e-cigarettes outside of a completely medicalised version that serves as a pharmaceutical quitting tool. The problem, according to the norm of abstinence, is not the harm from smoking, but nicotine dependency in itself and the fact that an industry is profiting from it. To contest the norm of abstinence, e-cigarette users, companies, liberal politicians and public health campaigners on the fringes of tobacco control banded together around an alternative frame that communicated e-cigarettes as harm reduction devices. Their argument was founded on the assumption that nicotine dependency is not a problem as such, according to the well-known saying in public health that 'people smoke for the nicotine, but they die from the tar' (Russell 1976). While the contending norm of harm reduction has found mainstream approval among public health professionals when it comes to needle-exchange programmes, it is a much more controversial idea in tobacco control, and something that has met much resistance from medical doctors specialised in respiratory matters, who see little reason to inhale anything that is not air. But the harm reduction frame was able to build a broad coalition that enrolled many different kinds of professionals and stakeholders, lending e-cigarettes a greater semblance of public support in the eyes of policymakers.

In fracking, much of the contestation revolved around the idea of natural gas as a 'bridge fuel' (Cotton 2015; Howarth 2014). According to this idea, also endorsed by Helm (2012) and mentioned earlier, natural gas should be embraced in the short to medium term in order to bridge our current energy system with a more sustainable future – one built on renewables. The logic of the argument is that natural gas only emits 50 per cent of the carbon dioxide of coal, but it is not feasible to completely abandon coal overnight. Therefore, we should substitute coal for gas until we can phase it out at a later stage. Most environmental organisations contest this idea, saying that we are way past the point where such convenient solutions can be considered. According to this norm of rapid decarbonisation, the climate challenge demands that we move swiftly and completely to a low carbon energy system and economy, and gas as a bridge fuel would only lock us in to a new cycle of carbon dependency that we cannot afford.

During this episode of contestation, which pitted transnational professional activists against lobbyists in the oil and gas industry, both sides made strategic use of framing strategies to build coalitions to further their cause. Whereas framing in the e-cigarette case successfully challenged the core institutions of the organisational field, this was impossible in fracking owing to the contrast in the strongly held beliefs of the different sides. Rather than seek some form of compromise position, professionals turned their attention towards using framing to enrol new stakeholders into the negotiation. Activists exploited the popularity of the *Gasland* documentary by staging screenings and inviting the director to the European Parliament (The Greens/European Free Alliance 2013). They concentrated on communicating through social media and emphasizing the risks to groundwater and air quality that made fracking especially salient in the eyes of the general public. On the other hand, industry lobbyists focused their efforts on higher-level business associations and national politicians of different European Member States in order to frame fracking as a competitiveness bargain and energy security opportunity that could substitute for Russian imports and increase independence. These divergent strategies demonstrate the flexibility of framing when transnational professionals try to build or consolidate their network positions.

Normalisation

The ultimate goal of framing strategies is to normalise or settle the disruption around a stable set of institutions, bringing the period of contestation to an end and establishing a new state of social affairs (Fligstein and McAdam 2012;

Vollmer 2013). Professionals will seek to ensure that the new state of affairs favours their particular set of skills and services, which is why disruptions and framing strategies are opportunities for professionals to advance in transnational social space.

Following the contestation from the harm reduction coalition in the e-cigarettes debate, the European Commission was forced to soften their position on e-cigarettes in the Tobacco Products Directive (Hasselbalch 2016). Not only did this provide market benefits for the professionals and organisations in the e-cigarette category, it also created a demand for harm reduction expertise among public-health professionals, moving them closer into the centre of the organisational field and challenging the position of medical doctors. Re-framing e-cigarettes through the lens of harm reduction was instrumental in providing a counterpoint to the mainstream position that medicalisation was inevitable, and the re-framing also ensured a broad base of support to pressure policymakers. In the fracking debate, re-framing fracking as energy security shifted attention away from the technical details of its environmental and climate impact in which negotiations had become mired (Hasselbalch 2017). This allowed key Member States and transnational business associations to pressure the European institutions into refraining from overregulating the practice with a binding Directive, settling instead on non-binding voluntary recommendations (European Commission 2014). For public affairs professionals in the transnational oil and gas enterprises, this was an example of the strategic use of framing to ensure the commercial viability of a product while giving them access to higher-level political debates on questions of energy security and foreign policy. Framing can in this matter also support strategic moves to enter new networks.

The examples here demonstrate how framing is a useful vehicle for exploring the scope for transnational professionals to act strategically in issues of transnational policy in order to further their position and claim resources for themselves and their organisations. In all its manifestations as outlined in this section framing is therefore a useful analytical tool in the arsenal of those who concern themselves with understanding the actions of professionals and transnational enterprises in the global economy. This brings us to our overarching conclusion regarding professional strategies in transnational projects.

Conclusion

As we have seen, one aspect that differentiates framing strategies from knowledge strategies is that knowledge strategies work well when epistemic closure is realistic, while framing strategies work well when it is unrealistic. By epistemic closure we mean the capacity of professionals to successfully occupy network positions in which they are recognised as 'knowing well' (Eyal, 2013; Lazega 1992; Seabrooke 2014). In especially controversial issue areas such as fracking and e-cigarettes, where the scientific basis is uncertain, and the issues are fast-moving and always evolving, such epistemic closure will be difficult for professionals to attain. These debates are driven to a greater degree by clashes in opposed normative assumptions or relations of trust and mistrust (Hasselbalch 2017). Our aim in this chapter has been to outline how professionals use knowledge and framing strategies in transnational projects with a focus on enterprise, and to give examples of how we can identify when they are employed, when they succeed, and when they fail. We have described knowledge strategies such as leveraging, epistemic arbitrage and epistemic arbiters, as well as framing strategies including disruptions, contests and normalisation. These strategies are regular activity in organisational fields and help us to understand when decoupling takes place. We suggest that the prevalence of these strategies is also more likely in transnational projects because transnationality offers a thin social space that can empower the professionals so involved in enterprise and other contexts – and can work to their own benefit, as well as that of the organisations with whom they operate.

References

Abbott, A. (1988) *The System of Professions: An Essay on the Division of Expert Labor*, Chicago, IL: University of Chicago Press.

Annisette, M. (2000) 'Imperialism and the professions: The education and certification of accountants in Trinidad and Tobago', *Accounting, Organizations and Society* 25: 631–59.

Ban, C., Seabrooke, L. and Freitas, S. (2016) 'Grey matter in shadow banking: International organizations and expert strategies in global financial governance', *Review of International Political Economy* 23(6): 1000–33.

Benford, R. D. and Snow, D. A. (2000) 'Framing processes and social movements: An overview and assessment', *Annual Review of Sociology* 26: 611–39.

Bourdieu, P. and Wacquant, L. J. D. (1992) *An Invitation to Reflexive Sociology*, Cambridge and Oxford: Polity Press and Blackwell Publishers.

Boussebaa, M. (2009) 'Struggling to organize across national borders: The case of global resource management in professional service firms', *Human Relations* 62(6): 829–50.

Boussebaa, M. (2017) 'Global professional service firms, transnational organizing and core/periphery networks', in Seabrooke, L. and Henriksen, L. F. (eds) *Professional Networks in Transnational Governance*, Cambridge: Cambridge University Press.

Boussebaa, M. and Brown, A. D. (2017) 'Englishization, identity regulation and imperialism', *Organization Studies* 38(1): 7–29.

Boussebaa, M., Morgan, G. and Sturdy, A. (2012) 'Constructing global firms? National, transnational and neocolonial effects in international management consultancies', *Organization Studies* 33(4): 465–86.

Boussebaa, M., Sinha S. and Gabriel, Y. (2014) 'Englishization in offshore call centres: A postcolonial perspective', *Journal of International Business Studies* 45(9): 1152–69.

Boussebaa, M., Sturdy, A. and Morgan, G. (2014) 'Learning from the world? Horizontal knowledge flows and geopolitics in international consulting firms', *International Journal of Human Resource Management* 25(9): 1227–42.

Brint, S. and Karabel, J. (1991) 'Institutional origins and transformations: The case of American Community Colleges', in Powell, W. W. and Dimaggio, P. J. (eds) *The New Institutionalism in Organizational Analysis*, Chicago, IL: University of Chicago Press.

Brown, J., Beard, E., Kotz, D., Michie, S. and West, R. (2014) 'Real-world effectiveness of e-cigarettes when used to aid smoking cessation: A cross-sectional population study', *Addiction* 109(9): 1531–40.

Burrage, M. and Torstendahl, R. (eds) (1990) *Professions in Theory and History: Rethinking the Study of Professions*, London: Sage Publications.

Burt, R. S. (1992) *Structural Holes*, Cambridge, MA: Harvard University Press.

Chwieroth, J. M. (2010) *Capital Ideas: The IMF and the Rise of Financial Liberalization*, Princeton, NJ: Princeton University Press.

Cooper, D. J. and Robson, K. (2006) 'Accounting, professions and regulation: Locating the sites of professionalization', *Accounting, Organizations and Society* 31: 415–44.

Cotton, M. (2015) 'Stakeholder perspectives on shale gas fracking: A Q-method study of environmental discourses', *Environment and Planning A: Economy and Space* 47(9): 1944–62.

Dent, M. and Whitehead, S. (eds) (2002) *Managing Professional Identities: Knowledge, Performativity and the 'New' Professional*, London: Routledge.

Dezalay, Y. and Garth, B. G. (1996) *Dealing in Virtue: International Commercial Arbitration and the Construction of a Transnational Legal Order*, Chicago, IL: University of Chicago Press.

Dezalay, Y. and Garth, B. G. (2002) *The Internationalization of Palace Wars: Lawyers, Economists, and the Contest to Transform Latin American States*, Chicago, IL: University of Chicago Press.

Dezalay, Y. and Garth, B. G. (2010) *Asian Legal Rivals: Lawyers in the Shadow of Empire*, Chicago, IL: University of Chicago Press.

Dezalay, Y. and Garth, B. G. (2016) '"Lords of the dance" as double agents: Elite actors in and around the legal field', *Journal of Professions and Organization* 3(2):188–206.

Dimaggio, P. J. (1991) 'Constructing an organizational field as a professional project: US Art Museums, 1920–1940', in Powell, W. W. and Dimaggio, P. J. (eds) *The New Institutionalism in Organizational Analysis*, Chicago, IL: University of Chicago Press.

Djelic, M. and Quack, S. (2010) *Transnational Communities: Shaping Global Economic Governance*, Cambridge: Cambridge University Press.

Entman, R. M. (1993) 'Framing: Toward clarification of a fractured paradigm', *Journal of Communication* 43(4): 51–58.

Eskelinen, T. and Ylönen, M. (2017) 'Panama and the WTO: New constitutionalism of trade policy and global tax governance', *Review of International Political Economy* 24(4): 629–56.

European Commission (2014) 'Commission Recommendation of 22 January 2014 on minimum principles for the exploration and production of hydrocarbons (such as shale gas) using high-volume hydraulic fracturing', *Official Journal of the European Union*. Available at: http://eur-lex.europa.eu/legal-content/EN/TXT/PDF/?uri=CELEX:32014 H0070&from=EN

Evetts, J. (1995) 'International professional associations: The new context for professional projects', *Work, Employment and Society* 9(4): 763–72.

Eyal, G. (2013) 'For a sociology of expertise: The social origins of the autism epidemic', *American Journal of Sociology* 118(4): 863–907.

Faulconbridge, J. R. and Muzio, D. (2007) 'Reinserting the professional into the study of professional service firms', *Global Networks: A Journal of Transnational Affairs* 7(3): 249–70.

Faulconbridge, J. R. and Muzio, D. (2012) 'Professions in a globalizing world: Towards a transnational sociology of the professions', *International Sociology* 27(1): 136–52.

Faulconbridge, J. R. and Muzio, D. (2017) 'Global professional service firms and institutionalization', in Seabrooke, L. and Henriksen, L. F. (eds) *Professional Networks in Transnational Governance*, Cambridge: Cambridge University Press.

Fligstein, N. and McAdam, D. (2012) *A Theory of Fields*, New York: Oxford University Press.

Food and Water Europe, Friends of the Earth Europe, Greenpeace and Health and Environment Alliance (2012) Position statement on shale gas, shale oil, coal bed methane and 'fracking'. Available at: www.foeeurope.org/sites/default/files/press_releases/foee_shale_gas_joint_position_240412_3.pdf

Fourcade, M. (2006) 'The Construction of a global profession: The transnationalization of economics', *American Journal of Sociology* 112(1): 145–94.

Fourcade, M., Ollion, E. and Algan, Y. (2015) 'The superiority of economists', *Journal of Economic Perspectives* 29(1): 89–114.

Fox, J. (2010) *Gasland*, USA: HBO Documentary Films.

Freidson, E. (1986) *Professional Powers*, Chicago, IL: University of Chicago Press.

Freidson, E. (2001) *Professionalism: The Third Logic*, Chicago, IL: University of Chicago Press.

Greenwood, R., Suddaby, R. and Hinings, C. R. (2002) 'Theorizing change: The role of professional associations in the transformation of institutionalized fields', *Academy of Management Journal* 45(1): 58–80.

Goffman, E. (1974) *Frame Analysis: An Essay on the Organization of Experience*, Cambridge, MA: Harvard University Press.

Hasselbalch, J. (2016) 'Professional disruption in health regulation: Electronic cigarettes in the European Union', *Journal of Professions and Organization* 3(1): 62–85.

Hasselbalch, J. (2017) *The Contentious Politics of Disruptive Innovation: Vaping and Fracking in the European Union*, University of Warwick. Available at: http://wrap.warwick.ac.uk/93146/

Helm, D. (2012) *The Carbon Crunch: How We're Getting Climate Change Wrong – and How to Fix It*, New Haven, CT: Yale University Press.

Henriksen, L. F. and Seabrooke, L. (2016) 'Transnational organizing: Issue professionals in environmental sustainability networks', *Organization* 23(5): 722–41.

Hoffman, A. J. (1999) 'Institutional evolution and change: Environmentalism and the U.S. chemical industry', *Academy of Management Journal* 42(4): 351–71.

Holzscheiter, A. (2017) 'Coping with institutional fragmentation? Competition and convergence between boundary organizations in the global response to polio', *Review of Policy Research* 34(6): 767–89.

Howarth, R. W. (2014) 'A bridge to nowhere: Methane emissions and the greenhouse gas footprint of natural gas', *Energy Science and Engineering* 2(2): 47–60.

Howarth, R. W., Santoro, R. and Ingraffea, A. (2011) 'Methane and the greenhouse-gas footprint of natural gas from shale formations', *Climatic Change* 106(4): 679–90.

Johnson, J. (2006) 'Two-track diffusion and central bank embeddedness: The politics of Euro adoption in Hungary and the Czech Republic', *Review of International Political Economy* 13(3): 361–86.

Kentikelenis, A. and Seabrooke, L. (2017) 'The politics of world polity: Script-writing in international organizations', *American Sociological Review* 82(5):1065–92.

Larson, M. S. (1977) *The Rise of Professionalism: A Sociological Analysis*, Berkeley, CA: University of California Press.

Lawrence, T. B., Suddaby, R. and Leca, B. (eds) (2011) *Institutional Work: Actors and Agency in Institutional Studies of Organizations*, Cambridge: Cambridge University Press.

Lazega, E. (1992) *Micropolitics of Knowledge*, New York: Aldine de Gruyter.

McNeill, A., Brose, L. S., Calder, R., Hitchman, S. C., Hajek, P. and McRobbie, H. (2015) *E-cigarettes: An Evidence Update*, London: Public Health England. Available at: www.gov.uk/government/uploads/system/uploads/attachment_data/file/457102/Ecigarettes_an_evidence_update_A_report_commissioned_by_Public_Health_England_FINAL.pdf

Mennicken, A. (2010) 'From inspection to auditing: Audit and markets as linked ecologies', *Accounting, Organizations and Society* 35(3): 334–59.

Meyer, J. W. and Rowan, B. (1977) 'Institutionalized organizations: Formal structure as myth and ceremony', *American Journal of Sociology* 83(2): 340–63.

Morgan, G. (2001) 'Transnational communities and business systems', *Global Networks* 1(2): 113–30.

Mudge, S. L. and Vauchez, A. (2012) 'Building Europe on a weak field: Law, economics, and scholarly avatars in transnational politics', *American Journal of Sociology* 118(2): 449–92.

Muzio, D., Brock, D. M. and Suddaby, R. (2013) 'Professions and institutional change: Towards an institutionalist sociology of the professions', *Journal of Management Studies* 50(5): 699–721.

Muzio, D., Hodgson, D., Faulconbridge, J., Beaverstock, J. and Hall, S. (2011) 'Towards corporate professionalization: The case of project management, management consultancy and executive search', *Current Sociology* 59(4): 443–64.

Nelson, S. C. (2017) *The Currency of Confidence: How Economic Beliefs Shape the IMF's Relationship with Its Borrowers*, Ithaca, NY: Cornell University Press.

Paik, Y. and Choi, D. Y. (2005) 'The shortcomings of a standardized global knowledge management system: The case study of Accenture', *Academy of Management Executive* 19(2): 81–8.

Research and Markets (2016) *Global E-cigarette Market 2016–2020*. Available at: www.researchandmarkets.com/research/q2w6rq/global

Russell, M. A. (1976) 'Low-tar medium-nicotine cigarettes: A new approach to safer smoking', *British Medical Journal* 1(6023): 1430–3.

Scott, W. R. (1995) *Institutions and Organizations*, London: Sage.

Seabrooke, L. (2011) 'Economists and diplomacy: Professions and the practice of economic policy', *International Journal* 66: 629–42.

Seabrooke, L. (2014) 'Epistemic arbitrage: Transnational professional knowledge in action', *Journal of Professions and Organization* 1(1): 49–64.

Seabrooke, L. and Henriksen, L. F. (eds) (2017) *Professional Networks in Transnational Governance*, Cambridge: Cambridge University Press.

Seabrooke, L. and Nilsson, E.R. (2015) 'Professional skills in international financial surveillance: Assessing change in IMF policy teams', *Governance* 28(2): 237–54.

Seabrooke, L. and Tsingou, E. (2014) 'Distinctions, affiliations, and professional knowledge in financial reform expert groups', *Journal of European Public Policy* 21(3): 389–407.

Seabrooke, L. and Tsingou, E. (2015) 'Professional emergence on transnational issues: Linked ecologies on demographic change', *Journal of Professions and Organization* 2(1): 1–18.

Seabrooke, L. and Tsingou, E. (2016) 'Bodies of knowledge in reproduction: Epistemic boundaries in the political economy of fertility', *New Political Economy* 21(1): 69–89.

Sending, O. J. (2015) *The Politics of Expertise. Competing for Authority in Global Governance*, Ann Arbor, MI: University of Michigan Press.

Spence, C., Dambrin, C., Carter, C., Husillos, J. and Archel, P. (2015) 'Global ends, local means: Cross-national homogeneity in professional service firms', *Human Relations* 68(5): 765–88.

Sturdy, A. and Wright, C. (2011) 'The active client: The boundary-spanning roles of internal consultants as gatekeepers, brokers and partners of their external counterparts', *Management Learning* 42(5): 485–503.

Sturdy, A., Wright, C. and Wylie, N. (2015) *Management as Consultancy: Neo-Bureaucracy and the Consultant Manager*, Cambridge: Cambridge University Press.

Suddaby, R., Cooper, D. J. and Greenwood, R. (2007) 'Transnational regulation of professional services: Governance dynamics of field level organizational change', *Accounting, Organizations and Society* 32: 333–62.

Suddaby, R. and Greenwood, R. (2006) 'Institutional entrepreneurship in mature fields: The Big Five accounting firms', *Academy of Management Journal* 49(1): 27–48.

Suddaby, R. and Viale, T. (2011) 'Professionals and field-level change: Institutional work and the professional project', *Current Sociology* 59(4): 423–42.

The Greens/European Free Alliance (2013) *Unfracked*. Available at: www.greens-efa.eu/unfracked-10219.html

Thistlethwaite, J. and Paterson, M. (2016) 'Private governance and accounting for sustainability networks', *Environment and Planning C: Government and Policy* 34(7): 1197–221.

Tsingou, E. (2015) 'Club governance and the making of global financial rules', *Review of International Political Economy* 22(2): 225–56.

Tsingou, E. (2017) 'New governors on the block: The rise of anti-money laundering professionals', *Crime, Law and Social Change*. Available at: https://doi.org/10.1007/s10611-017-9751-x

United States Energy Information Administration (2016) *Annual Energy Outlook 2016*, Washington, DC: USEIA. Available at: www.eia.gov/forecasts/aeo/pdf/0383(2016).pdf

Vollmer, H. (2013) *The Sociology of Disruption, Disaster and Social Change: Punctuated Cooperation*, Cambridge: Cambridge University Press.

Wooten, M. and Hoffman, A. J. (2008) 'Organizational fields: Past, present and future', in Greenwood, R., Oliver, C., Suddaby, R. and Sahlin, K. (eds) *The SAGE Handbook of Organizational Institutionalism*, London: Sage.

Zuckerman, G. (2013) *The Frackers: The Outrageous Inside Story of the New Billionaire Wildcatters*, New York: Penguin.

Part II
Changes in professionalism in an enterprise context

5 Professionalism as enterprise

Service class politics and the redefinition of professionalism (with Postscript: Extinguishing professionalism?)

Gerard Hanlon

Introduction

The changing nature of the class structure has largely been held responsible for the decline of Labour politics and the emergence of the New Right over the past decade. The thrust of this thesis is that the traditional working class, which was the bulwark of the labour movement both industrially and politically, has declined and been replaced by the service class in most of the advanced economies (see Lash and Urry 1987; Fox Piven 1991). Such a transition has altered the nature of politics because the service class is inherently conservative (Goldthorpe 1982). This thesis is given great force when one examines the decline of labour politics in Britain. The percentage of the electorate supporting the Labour party in Britain fell from 36.4 per cent in 1945 to 23.2 per cent in 1987 (Crewe 1991). Such a marked decline led Crewe to comment:

> Given the outcome of the 1992 election Crewe was evidently right. Crewe lists four reasons for the decline of the Labour Party and, by implication, left-wing politics. These are (1) social mobility and the expansion of the service class; (2) internal migration; (3) mass unemployment; and (4) falling trade-union membership.

As with other writers, Crewe sees the growth of the service class as detrimental to radical politics. This chapter seeks to raise some questions about such an assumption. It will do so by examining the reasons given for the conservatism of the service class and to highlight some of the inadequacies of these assumptions.

The service class as a conservative force

The position of the service class as a unified homogeneous group which is inherently conservative is most closely identified with Goldthorpe (see Goldthorpe 1980, 1982, 1995; Erikson and Goldthorpe 1992). The conservative nature of the service class arises out of their experience of employment.

The service class is to be distinguished from other classes by four features (Goldthorpe 1982):

- Service-class workers are trusted.
- These workers have a code of service.
- They have relative security of employment.
- They have prospects of material and status advancement.

The service relationship and/or delegation of authority enjoyed by these workers means that their employers are not in a position to monitor them in the same way as they monitor other workers and therefore have to rely more on trust. A decade later Erikson and Goldthorpe (1992) reiterated that service-class workers maintained these relative benefits and continued to enjoy security of employment and well-defined career paths. It is this employment relationship that unites the service class and weakens any potential divisions within it such as, for example, the public sector versus the private sector. These divisions, although they exist, are of limited and indeed declining strength. Thus, central to the thesis appears to be the belief that service-class workers have benign relations with their employers. If it is the case that these employees enjoy a trust relationship with their employers, it is essential to ask why they are trusted, who exactly is trusted, and how do some come to be trusted and others not? In much of his work Goldthorpe appears to assume that people are trusted because they have the necessary technical and/or bureaucratic expertise (see Goldthorpe 1980, 1982). However, this chapter will suggest that such an assumption downplays some areas of potential conflict.

The rest of this chapter will question the 'conservative' thesis on a number of fronts. First, it will highlight possible structural divisions within the service class; second, it will attack the notion that the service class enjoys a trust relationship with employers; and third, it will argue that elements of the service class may well prove to be radical in the future. It will highlight all of this by analysing the changing nature of professionalism.

At this point, three issues need to be addressed. First, this chapter will only provide some tentative evidence concerning the fragmenting of the service class because fragmentation is in process and thus emphatic proof is impossible at this very early stage. Having stated this, there are indications that the hypothesis holds water. Second, it is necessary to provide some description of professional employment. Following the impressive lead of Abbott (1988), a definition of what makes up a profession will not be proffered. Abbott suggests that a better way of thinking about professional work is as something that is defined and redefined through continuous struggle between different occupational groups. Hence the values and attributes of professionals are fluid and subject to change and struggle. In short, professionalism is a shifting rather than a concrete phenomenon. In the light of this shifting nature I will not define what professionalism is but rather state that when I discuss professionals I am talking about groups such as doctors, academics, teachers, accountants, lawyers, engineers and civil servants, that is those groups commonly thought of as professional by the lay public, academics, the professionals themselves (Randle 1996 uses a similar formulation).

Third, some description of what is meant by trust is required. I use it in a twofold sense. It entails trust in a person's technical competence to do the job but it also entails trusting them and/or their professional colleagues to monitor and control their work and to ensure that the practices they perform are administered in a way that is agreed to be correct. This requires granting these occupational groups a wide range of autonomy and the freedom to manage and discipline themselves and their organisations or to have a meaningful collaboration in the managing of these organisations. Such managerial structures are based upon shared goals among all the important stakeholders (for example, the client – paying and non-paying – employees, the state and regulatory bodies).

Service-class divisions

The idea that there are divisions within the service class is not new. Many writers have highlighted possible divisions within this group (see Bourdieu 1984; Butler and Savage 1995; Carchedi 1975; Dunleavey 1980; Hanlon 1994; Perkin 1989; Savage et al. 1992; Wright 1985). Generally, these divisions are based either on economic sector, such as the public and private sectors, or upon the nature of the assets used to achieve and maintain a service-class position. This section will examine both approaches.

The public sector–private sector divide is commonly associated with Dunleavey (1980) and Perkin (1989). The argument is relatively straight-forward – the public and private sectors derive their economic and ideological basis from different sources, namely the state and the market, and therefore have different material interests (Hanlon 1994 also endorses such an argument). The public sector service class will seek an expansion of state resources and finance which will lead to higher taxes, whereas the private sector service class will aim to limit the expansion of the state and the public sector in order to lessen taxes. Perkin (1989) suggests that the rise of Thatcherism in Great Britain was really the emergence of an open feud between public and private sector professionals locked in a struggle to impose their vision of society. He suggests that at present the private sector is in the ascendancy, but it still has not won the war. This ascendancy is reflected in the government's attempts to limit expenditure, the reaction against the power and privileges of professionals, the attack on corporatism, the re-emergence of a free market ideology. Perkin suggests that this is an important political shift as he argues that for most of this century public sector professionals imposed their view of society onto the British political landscape.

The public sector–private sector split argument is persuasive but unsubstantiated in Dunleavey's and in Perkin's work. In terms of political behaviour the evidence of such a divide has been weak and does not appear to be substantial enough to override the possibility that the two groups share more in common and will hence act as one political force (see Heath and Savage 1995). However, despite the limited nature of supporting evidence this is a theme we will return to.

The second group of theories which analyses the fragmentation of the service class relates to the assets required to guarantee membership, although within this group there are differences. Carchedi (1975) highlights the functions performed by the service class in terms of co-ordinating the labour process and controlling the labour process. He suggests that the degree to which these two functions are mixed affects one's class position, that is the more controlling functions one has, the greater the likelihood one will be a member of the bourgeoisie, whereas if one merely co-ordinates the labour process the greater the likelihood that one will be a member of the proletariat. Service-class members fulfil both roles hence they are in a contradictory position. However, the distribution of functions within this position is important. In the light of this, the structure of the service class itself may become an important political feature.

Others have adopted different interpretations of the assets required to gain service-class access. Wright (1985) argues that there are three types of asset which may allow one access to the service class. These are ownership of capital, control of organisational assets, and/or skill or credential assets. The degree to which a person has one or all of these assets dictates their class position. As with Carchedi, Wright attempts to place individuals and the roles they play within the class structure. Unfortunately, the end result of Wright's analysis is problematic. He finishes up with twelve class positions, seven of which he views as contradictory. Within this there are examples that offend common sense, for example a pilot has less autonomy than a cleaner (for a critique of Wright, see Marshall *et al.* 1988).

In many respects the work that has gone furthest in examining the use of different assets to establish service-class membership and indeed the heterogeneity of the service class has been written by Bourdieu (1984) or inspired by him (Savage *et al.* 1992). Bourdieu suggests that society is divided along two major fault lines which he calls economic and cultural capital. These lines divide people into different classes and split classes into fractions or segments. He argues that economic assets are the safest means of guaranteeing membership of a privileged class and are the easiest form of asset to pass on. However, cultural capital is also an important source of privilege and one that people seek to pass on to their children via the education system and educational credentials. Cultural capital is largely independent of economic capital and the degree to which one's cultural capital is legitimised by society (which is itself a matter of historic conflict) dictates the level of skill one is deemed to have and hence the level of reward one receives. Thus, cultural battles dictate who is considered highly skilled and who is not. Therefore, the battle to legitimise cultural capital influences the occupational structure and hence the social structure. Social structure is flexible and subject to change by the practices of individuals and groups within society. One of the contested terrains within this flexible structure is what is considered cultural capital and what is not, that is what are considered important skills or sets of practices and what are not. It will be argued that one of the key sources of division within the service class is one such struggle. This struggle is being played out in the context of what defines professionalism.

Savage and colleagues (1992) have critically applied Bourdieu's work to Britain. They have argued that Bourdieu's twofold system should be expanded to form a threefold series of fault lines. They add organisational assets to Bourdieu's distinction of economic assets (Savage *et al.* call these 'property assets') and cultural assets. The key distinction between cultural and organisational assets is based on independence. Savage and colleagues (1992) suggest that cultural assets, through the education and credentialing systems, allow people independence from the organisation they work for, thereby providing them with other means of maintaining or improving their class position. The key group to use cultural assets successfully is the professions. Professionals have successfully argued that their cultural capital is important and have translated these skills into a means of earning a successful reward. Another key advantage of having recognised cultural capital is that the individual worker can decide how their skill is transferred to a specific context; this gives them independence from any one organisation. In contrast to this, organisational assets are organisation specific and less likely to be legitimised at a wider level or through the credentialing system. These assets are usually managerial or administration based. Thus organisational/managerial skills are context dependent and allow the worker little autonomy from the employing organisation.

The way in which privilege is derived is of crucial significance to both Bourdieu and Savage and colleagues. The assets exploited to maintain a service-class position are different and theoretically may be in conflict. As a result of this the service class is fragmented along two or three axes. This chapter examines the struggle within the professions and beyond to define and redefine what the cultural capital of professionalism should be and hence to legitimise certain skills while downgrading others.

Trust and the service class

The crucial element of the Goldthorpe thesis is that service-class employees enjoy a different relationship with their employers to other workers. In short, the service class is trusted and in return it responds with a code of service. This relationship blossoms out to ensure that service-class employees enjoy careers and long-term security. Trust is the main uniting factor among the service class. However, to accept this one needs to be sure what this trust entails. Trust is not a reified concept; it changes and reforms itself in the light of ongoing struggles. Hence it is vital that we examine these struggles, examine how they impact upon the political behaviour of the service class, and crucially examine whether or not these struggles split the service class into discrete blocs.

In order to do this, we need to examine the nature of the employment relationship in specific contexts. One, admittedly limited, way of doing this is to examine the contest to define and redefine professionalism. This is important because professionals are an important part of the service class and they are possibly the primary group of workers to exploit cultural assets. It is with this issue that the rest of the paper will concern itself.

Professionalism is an area of struggle between important economic actors within Britain and the Anglo-American world (Perkin 1989, 1996; Hanlon 1994; Hanlon 1999). This struggle revolves around whose definition of professionalism emerges as hegemonic and therefore who has access to significant economic resources. In other words, this struggle centres on which form of cultural capital is seen as the most legitimate. The contest, however, does not appear to be purely between the public and private sectors (although this is an important area of cleavage) nor does it appear to be between one homogeneous group of professionals against another homogeneous group (although again these cleavages are important), rather it appears to cut across the public and private sector and to fragment previously relatively homogeneous professions. This split is centred around whether or not the old version of professionalism based on the notion of social service of Marshall (1939) predominates or whether it is replaced by a new commercialised version of professionalism. In order to develop this argument further we need to examine these contending definitions of professionalism.

The social service ethos of professionalism was outlined by Marshall (1939). It is centred around providing a service on the basis of need rather than ability to pay (this became a crucial element in nearly every major definition of what professionalism meant over the next thirty years – see Goode 1957; Hughes 1963; Parsons 1954; Wilensky 1964). He suggests that such a definition of professionalism was itself new. The newness of this definition was the fact that it was different to the previously dominant notion of professionalism which he suggested was an individualistic professionalism. This individualistic professionalism entailed adherence to the idea of servicing those people who could pay, and on being a 'gentleman'. The new social service ideology emerged at a time when the professions were being forced to provide, and wanted to provide, services to the whole of society rather than one element of it. Such a transition was not painless nor were the professionals concerned naively altruistic. They were willing to provide a service to people on the basis of need, provided they were adequately reimbursed by the state. For example, the British Medical Association (BMA) fought tooth and nail with the government to ensure that they were well paid and that doctors had control of the emerging National Health Service (NHS). When these assurances were not forthcoming the BMA advocated that doctors should boycott the NHS until their demands were met. The doctors demanded twice the estimated annual cost of a patient from the state as the price for their involvement in the Health Service after the passing of the 1911 National Health Insurance Act. In the end they received up to 75 per cent of the fees they claimed, but still doctors continued to make demands throughout the 1920s. These struggles were resolved by a compromise which largely favoured the professionals (see Carr-Saunders and Wilson 1933). Likewise, the Law Society resisted the emergence of legal aid schemes until such time as they were given control over the state legal aid budget (Goreily 1994). Similar, more or less successful, tales could be recounted for teachers, social workers and other professional groups (Perkin 1989). The ability of these professions to control the resources of the state and provide services on the basis of need also benefited these professionals in other ways. Perkin (1989) suggests that such provision by certain professionals, especially those in the public sector, increased their standing among the general public. If this is true, it would have increased the legitimacy of their cultural capital, thereby empowering them still further.

The question must be asked: why did this redefinition of professionalism come about in the 1930s and thereafter? The emergence of such a definition of professionalism during the 1930s and 1940s is not a coincidence. It was during this period that the social consensus which is generally called Fordism began to emerge. One of the chief developments of this consensus was the creation and expansion of the welfare state wherein one was guaranteed certain rights on the basis of citizenship (Jessop 1994). Many of these rights were delivered by professionals, those in healthcare, education, social welfare, and health and safety at work, to name but a few. As a result of this consensus the state professional sector expanded rapidly so that its definition of professionalism, that is social service professionalism, came to dominate. This definition also reinforced the prevailing economic and political climate (Hanlon 1996a). If the economic boom of the Fordist era had not taken place and hence allowed for a mode of societal regulation based on full employment, provision of a welfare state and a limited redistribution of wealth (Lipietz 1987), such a definition might well not have emerged.

In the 1970s and 1980s this definition of professionalism came under attack and over the past decade or more there has been a struggle for the soul of professionalism as elements within established professions, previously less important professions, and newly emerging professions seek to define and redefine what professionalism means. This contest reflects wider socio-economic forces and represents a structural fragmentation of the service class based on different forms of economic sustenance.

The competing definition of professionalism which gained increasing acceptance over the 1980s has been called 'commercialised professionalism' (see Hanlon 1994, 1996a). This version of professionalism stresses the need to have managerial and entrepreneurial skills. To date it has emerged most strongly in areas of the private sector such as accountancy (Grey 1994; Hanlon 1994, 1996a), law (Hanlon 1999; Hanlon and Shapland 1997) and engineering (Causer and Jones 1990, 1996; Whittington, McNulty and Whipp 1994). This professionalism normally stresses three factors:

1 Technical ability – this will allow one to practice in the profession, but it will not guarantee advancement nor success.
2 Managerial skill — this is the ability to manage other employees, the ability to balance budgets and the capacity to manage and satisfy clients.

3   The ability to bring in business and/or act in an entrepreneurial way. The extent to which one has all three skills determines how successful one will be in the profession.

The need for these three skills has a number of implications. First, the ability to bring in new business is directly related to your ability to create a profit and hence it weakens the capacity to provide a service on the basis of need. In short, personal professional success is related to profitability, not to serving clients in need. Second, ability to generate a profit and the managerial skills of keeping the paying client happy give the client a powerful voice in the creation of the professional service and hence allow, indeed ensure, that the service is tailored to the needs of the large and/or powerful client rather than the needs of all clients or the profession (Hanlon 1996a, 1996b). This is different from the past wherein professionals supposedly provided solutions to a largely ignorant client base (Cain 1983; Hughes 1963). This ignorant client base may be fundamentally changing in the light of the suggestion by Giddens (1991) suggestion that one of the basic characteristics of high modernity is that individuals no longer simply 'trust' expert systems. High modernity's emphasis on reflexivity encourages people to question and learn from their interaction with society thereby altering knowledge. Such an environment means they use (and believe in) expert systems but also question expert solutions thereby undermining the passivity inherent in the 'ignorant client' thesis. In this sort of society there are fewer and fewer ignorant clients. Third, the technical function has been downgraded in the sense that in the past success was theoretically based on one's technical ability rather than other factors such as managerial or entrepreneurial skills (Perkin 1989). These three features differentiate this version of professionalism from its social service counterpart.

Both professional ideologies are engaged in a struggle to define professionalism and to make their definition, and by implication their cultural capital, legitimate in the eyes of the market, the state and the general public. This contest is one of the key fissures within the service class and it has implications for the economic regeneration of competing groups within this class. It is in the light of this ongoing struggle that we should examine Goldthorpe's idea about the service class enjoying a trusting relationship with their employers. Why is this redefining taking place? It is taking place because as different powerful actors have moved away from the shared goals and consensus of most of the post-war era, they have also indicated a lack of trust in those professionals that adhere to the social service ethos of professionalism. This has emerged as a result of the decline in profitability of capital in the late 1960s and 1970s (Lipietz 1987; Sassen 1991), the fiscal crisis of the state which also emerged at this point, and the shift on behalf of the state from a Fordist preoccupation with the welfare state to a post-Fordist preoccupation with international competitiveness (Hanlon 1994; Harvey 1989; Jessop 1994). Social service professionals are viewed as unresponsive to the needs of the client (Hanlon 1996a) and profligate in the use of and increasing demands for resources (Perkin 1989). In the private sector this has manifested itself through the desire of corporations to force their professional advisers to compete, to rein in their fees, and to demand that the service is tailored to the client's organisational needs.

In the public sector it manifested itself in the attempt by the state to control costs in the NHS, legal aid, education and the civil service. Such attempts to control costs have resulted in the restructuring of all of the above (see Burrage 1992; Carter and Fairbrother 1995; Ferlie 1992; Fitzgerald, Ashburner and Ferlie 1995; Jessop 1994; Sinclair, Ironside and Seifert 1996; Whittington, McNulty and Whipp 1994). The key thrust of these reforms has been to make the professionals accountable and to enforce financial and managerial discipline upon them. That is to commercialise them by introducing quasi-markets. The reason for this is that a social service professional ethos is perceived as a luxury which the state can no longer afford as it shifts its priorities from a Keynesian welfare state to one where the state's primary function is to ensure international competitiveness rather than welfare based on citizenship (see Jessop 1994).

Thus, the issue of who is trusted and who is not trusted and how some come to be trusted and others do not is of vital importance. As society shifts from a Fordist regime of accumulation to a post-Fordist or flexible regime of accumulation the issue of trust comes clearly into focus. Under Fordism, society was regulated on the basis of the welfare state and this legitimised a professionalism which was founded on serving people on the basis of need and citizenship. As we move from Fordism to Flexible Accumulation such a form of professionalism is under attack because powerful actors – the state and large-scale capital – no longer deem it appropriate, that is they no longer trust the ethos to deliver what is required, increasing profitability and international competitiveness. Such a process has created opportunities for some service-class members while threatening others. These opportunities and threats are not simply sectorally based; they cut across the public sector divide.

Fissures in the service class?

Although the public sector–private sector divide is important the picture is more complex than this. As suggested, the state has a vital role to play in this restructuring, but it is important to note that this role reaches beyond the public sector. For example, legal aid is public money that had traditionally been managed by the Law Society and given to private law firms. In the 1980s this changed as the state sought to increase its control of these funds and to limit the resources used by legal aid (Goreily 1994). The state – via the Legal Aid Franchise Board – has recently sought to gain further control of the budget by establishing a franchise system wherein it will demand that certain criteria are met by private firms allowing them to bid for public money. Another element within this process of change is that legal aid fees should not match market-based fees, thereby making the work less profitable and somewhat second rate (Rice 1995). Thus, although legal aid is public money it does not solely affect public sector professionals. Likewise, the state has sought to weaken the power of lawyers by extending competition in other areas; for example, people are increasingly being encouraged to use non-legal counsellors for divorce (Dingwall 1995), and legal changes opened the conveyancing market to other professionals via the creation of licensed conveyancers in the 1980s (Sherr 1994).

On the positive side, from the lawyer's point of view, the property boom of the 1980s was assisted by the sale of public housing (Pierson 1994), which led to increased conveyancing for lawyers, and the privatisation programme, which brought huge incomes to the largest law firms (Lee 1992). Despite these pluses the overall impact for the profession has been negative with only the largest firms supporting government policy (Lee 1992), while small firms, which make up the bulk of the profession, appear to want to return to some form of Fordist past where social service professionalism is paramount (Sommerlad 1995). The state, therefore, has had a major influence upon this (largely private sector based) profession, much of which seems to have been unwelcome.

Likewise, the state has also influenced other areas, giving rise to a mixed set of winners and losers. Whittington, McNulty and Whipp (1994) have suggested that not all groups in the NHS or the scientific research centres (some of which have been privatised) have opposed the reforms that have been imposed upon them. In the past these organisations had structures where the medical and scientific professionals were largely in control. The recent changes have created new professional groups or allowed previously excluded professionals into these organisations, thereby providing them with new opportunities. Likewise, not all of the medical or scientific professionals are against the changes, indeed some actually welcomed and saw opportunities in them. Thus, the role of the state is important, but it is complex and multifaceted.

As with the state, large-scale capital is restructuring, and this has also been a mixed bag for professionals. This restructuring has entailed a shift in attitude towards expert labour. This shift has been centred around increasing vigilance and policing in the area of purchasing professional services externally and a downgrading or externalisation of many professional (and indeed other) services which were previously provided in-house (Atkinson 1984; Hanlon 1994; Harrison and Bluestone 1988; Sassen 1991). The increased globalisation of business, corporate restructuring and an increasingly sophisticated and differentiated market have created global empires that are paradoxically increasingly tightly controlled from a handful of spatial locations (Sassen 1991). Some of the key benefactors in this process are the professional advisers such as accountants via management consultancy, lawyers via international take-overs, mergers and indeed privatisation (Flood 1995), marketing people who attempt to manipulate the market place and bankers through the internationalisation of finance. Hanlon (1996a) has outlined how these transformations have altered the economic base of the largest accountancy firms so that today they are less dependent on auditing and more involved in management consulting, tax advice, information technology services and corporate restructuring, that is in attempting to control this new flexible economy. Similar patterns appear to be emerging in the largest law firms (Hanlon and Shapland 1997; Hanlon 1999). However, other professional groups seem to have lost out. Engineers and scientists in privatised research centres and doctors in the NHS are being forced to concede power to financial professionals (Whittington, McNulty and Whipp 1994), in pharmaceuticals there is evidence that scientists are coming under increasing managerial pressures as management attempt to gain greater control over their labour process (Randle 1996), in the privatised water industry engineers are coming under increasing supervision from management (Ogden 1996), and in many organisations the whole concept of having a particular professional role may be under attack (Watson 1995). Added to this, is the fact that even among the beneficiaries there are casualties. For example, the accountancy profession has been polarised into two completely separate hemispheres of large and small firms which operate in completely different markets in a way that did not occur in the past; in effect this means that many are being denied access to much lucrative work.

What is it that the beneficiaries, across both the public and the private sectors, have which enables them to benefit? I would suggest that they subscribe to the new commercialised professionalism. That is, they prioritise profit, meet budgets, and manage clients and staff in a way that the social service professional does not. In short, they are driven by a commercial rather than a technical logic. If one does not live up to this commercialised logic, then one will not enjoy the benefits Goldthorpe suggests are common to the service class. Those professions (or probably more accurately elements of those professions) that have endorsed this redefinition are starting to restructure. For example, the largest law and accountancy firms (which endorse this form of professionalism above all others) have attacked ideas such as guaranteed career paths for their staff, staff who do not live up to the new commercialised standards are ostracised within the firms and/or quickly pushed out, employed professionals often perform unpaid work or skimp on the technical quality of the job rather than go over budget, firms are developing increasingly sophisticated appraisal schemes to ensure workers meet the new standards, employment is no longer secure – in fact these organisations have begun to get rid of non-performing partners because they are deemed unsuitable (see Hanlon 1994, 1996a, 1996b). In other areas as well, similar processes have taken place. Halford and Savage (1995) have highlighted how careers in local authorities have been altered so that promotion is dependent upon 'personal' factors and skills rather than seniority or previous job title and that for senior personnel short-term contracts have been introduced forcing them consistently to meet performance targets or face non-renewal of contract. Carter and Fairbrother (1995) have also highlighted the changing nature of management and control within the civil service so that supervisory grades behave in a much more managerial way than in the past. In the NHS this commercial behaviour is also beginning to emerge. Fitzgerald, Ashburner and Ferlie (1995) suggest that clinicians within trusts earn the respect of other members of the board of directors if they prove to be competent managers and that health professionals in different hospitals are reluctant to share information if the hospitals are in competition. Thus, this redefinition is forcing change as professionals seek to prove their trustworthiness. However, herein lies a contradiction, senior professionals who should feel that their trustworthiness is beyond dispute, given their seniority, now have to prove their trustworthiness on a regular basis and on an increasingly changed set of criteria. If the social service professionalism which dominated when these people joined the professions still dominated it is a moot point whether or not this would be the case.

However, at an individual level adherence to this commercialised logic does not guarantee success. Access to certain structures is also important. For example, a commercialised professional in accountancy or law will only gain access to the most prestigious and lucrative clients by working in a handful of firms (Hanlon 1994, 1999). Only by being in one of these firms can an accountant or lawyer access the exceptionally privileged lives which top professionals in these major international professional service firms live. By adhering to a commercialised professionalism in, say, law or accountancy, one's agency is enhanced as it opens up access to powerful organisations such as a Big Six accounting firm in a way that a social service professionalism will not (Hanlon 1996a). However, other structures continue to be dominated by a social service professional and will hence limit the agency of a commercialised professionalism within these structures or sharpen the conflict between individuals and groups in their quest for organisational resources.

In short, individual agency is bound by a number of elements, for instance, organisational structures, compatibility of an individual's version of professionalism with the dominant organisational culture, with colleagues, with clients, and other powerful actors. If all of these factors are favourable then one can have considerable agency and influence upon one's career and the organisation one works for (see Hanlon 1996b, for examples of this in law and accounting). However, it is equally possible that these factors are unfavourable, thereby weakening one's agency and forcing one to accept this or to generate alternative courses of action, such as leaving the organisation for a more compatible one or changing one's version of professionalism. If replicated enough such individual actions can have a significant impact at a group and organisational level. Thus, the actions of individuals have an influence upon wider structures and can reinforce or weaken these structures and the version of professionalism that dominates an organisation. However, such a process is heavily influenced by and bounded by structural factors (see Bourdieu 1977 for a greater analysis of these processes at a societal level).

A radical service class?

If the divisions mapped out are accurate then there appears to be a definite cleavage among professionals in the service class. This cleavage is not simply one of the public and private sectors, although obviously this is important. Instead, it appears to be one of winners and losers in the changes of the past twenty years or so. In reality the struggle between these versions of professionalism is not over, although it is difficult to mobilise around these issues given that they have fragmented certain occupational groups as the interests of different sections of each group become conflictual. Both camps are still seeking to impose their vision on society and hence to legitimise their cultural capital. Political action will have a key role to play in the ensuing battle as the state, through its reforms, has been made ever more powerful while also seeking to impose the new commercialised professionalism (Burrage 1992). Thus, advocates for those groups who have lost out or who are unsure about whether they will win or lose have been called into action. Professional bodies such as the Law Society, the Bar Council, the BMA, the National Union of Teachers, have all opposed the majority of the reforms (Burrage 1992; Lee 1992; Sherr 1994) and elements of the redefinition, like the NHS and education reforms, became issues in the 1992 and 1997 general elections. Likewise, the commercialised professionals have come under attack in the recent past, for example, large accountancy firms have been subject to long and sustained attacks over scandals such as the BCCI (Bank of Commerce and Credit International) and Maxwell affair (Sikka, Willmott and Lowe 1989). Thus, the debate rages on and will become significant in terms of the political future of Britain. There appears to be very limited evidence – and its limitations must be stressed – that the different segments in this struggle are beginning to side with different political parties and possibly to have different political agendas.

Heath and Savage (1995) have demonstrated the changing nature of the service-class vote within Britain over the past twenty years. This evidence is, I would suggest, a limited indicator of fragmentation (although Heath and Savage would probably disagree with my interpretation of their work). The overall level of identification with the Conservative Party has remained roughly consistent over the 1972–1989 period at about 60 per cent (Evans, Heath and Lalljee 1996 suggest that voting behaviour is a good indicator of wider political belief). However, it did drop slightly from 61.4 per cent to 58.4 per cent. But such aggregate figures appear to mask another trend. This second trend reflects the polarisation of the service-class vote between those groups that strongly identify with the Conservatives and those that quite strongly identify with left and/or centre groups. Thus, in the 1980s higher education lecturers, junior civil servants, scientists, social workers, doctors and dentists were all less enthusiastic supporters of the Conservatives than their class colleagues. Indeed, the evidence for the 1972–1989 period shows that doctors and dentists had shifted their allegiance from the Conservatives quite substantially. In 1972, 80 per cent of these professionals voted Conservative whereas by 1989 the figure was 50 per cent. Over the same period the shift in terms of social workers was from 37.5 per cent to 11.5 per cent, and for scientists 58.6 per cent to 38.9 per cent, and teachers and judges may also be moving away from the Conservatives. It is plausible that the 1989 figures are unrepresentative as the reforms outlined earlier have had time to have an impact, thereby further undermining the social service version of professionalism and alienating those professional groups that adhere to it. For example, in 1987 51 per cent of doctors voted Conservative (a figure very similar to the 1989 above) whereas only 28 per cent intended to before the 1992 election.

In contrast to this, 37 per cent intended to vote Labour whereas only 20 per cent had in 1987 (see Burrage 1992). However, other groups are increasing their already strong support for the Conservatives. Thus, the bourgeoisie have increased their support, the security forces have also moved to the right, likewise accountants, lawyers, senior civil servants and engineers appear to be Conservative supporters whose support is increasing.

What do these figures tell us about the service class? Heath and Savage (1995: 291) suggest that, because the shifts within the service class cancel each other out and the class has remained stable in its political support, we are not witnessing a fragmentation of the service class. I dispute this conclusion. I think we are witnessing a very unclear and messy fragmentation. This fragmentation arises out of socio-economic restructuring and the desire by different groups of professionals to legitimise their cultural capital. The basic struggle is over who legitimises the working practices and behaviour of professionals. Is it the professionals themselves, as it largely was in the past (Perkin 1989), or is it to be powerful actors such as the state and/or capital in negotiation with these weakened professional groups? This struggle is getting played out in terms of whether or not professionals should be primarily concerned with technical competence, servicing on the basis of need and citizenship, or whether they should possess managerial, budgetary, indeed entrepreneurial skills that are used to define the service according to the needs of the client (although in reality this becomes the powerful, informed and resourceful client). This struggle is ongoing in areas such as education, the NHS, the auditing world, law and the civil service with winners and losers in different economic sectors and indeed within the same professions. It is not solely a public sector–private sector divide (there are, for example, increasing levels of support for right-wing policies among the security forces) although this is an important area of division. In many respects the struggle is between those who support a previous regime of accumulation which benefited social service professionals and allowed them to control large areas of social life and those who have the opportunity and capacity to exploit an emerging one. The political arena may well be a crucial one to the resolution of this struggle given the leading role the state has played in the battle so far. Given the state's role these service sector fractions may well develop different political agendas and hence lead one segment to adopt a radical posture. Paradoxically, social service professionals as the forces of conservation may well vote for the left in an attempt to conserve the version of professionalism which empowers them. However, the likelihood of their being able to simply reproduce such a situation becomes doubtful given the increasing reflexivity of individuals in high modernity. The constant questioning which this implies may give rise to opportunities for professionals and experts, but it also constantly challenges their knowledge (Giddens 1991). As such, it undermines one of the pillars of social service professionalism – namely the idea that the ignorant client trusts the professional to provide solutions to their problems. In the light of this, it seems more likely that a victorious social service professionalism would have had to alter in order to maintain or increase its popular support among clients.

Discussion and methodological issues

This chapter argues that the service class is not homogeneous and, indeed, that it is in the process of fragmenting. The line of cleavage examined is based on the ongoing struggle by different service-class members to have society recognise their cultural capital as more legitimate than other forms of capital in those areas of work commonly thought of as professional. Such legitimacy would allow the successful candidates complete or partial control of vast areas of social life, such as education, health and access to justice. I have argued that this conflict is probably most explicit in the struggle between those service-class members who adhere, on the one hand, to a social service professional ethos and, on the other hand, their colleagues who support a newer commercialised version of professionalism. The guerrilla warfare between these two groups has split professions which were previously relatively homogeneous, and it has blurred the public sector–private sector split which Perkin and others have suggested is the main form of cleavage among the service class as both camps have adherents on either side of this divide. I would suggest that we are witnessing a slow and messy fragmentation which reflects broader changes in the socio-economic structure of Britain as it undergoes a long period of socio-economic restructuring.

As outlined, restructuring is taking place and the fragmentation of the service class is possibly one element in this process. It is not complete by any means and indeed I would argue that it still has a long way to go. This presents researchers with two methodological difficulties. First, before we can understand broader intra-class shifts we need to understand single professional occupations which are themselves undergoing a period of transformation and fragmentation upon a social service-commercialist axis and to understand why this is happening, when it took place or is taking place and the spatial, gender, ethnic and class impacts of such a fragmentation within the occupation itself. Only when we have a set of data on a wide range of such occupations can we begin to systematically theorise and understand broader changes. Hence, we need more analysis of occupational change at this end of the labour market. Second, intra-class fragmentation will obviously be a slow process – long-term party voters will not change their long-term allegiances overnight and added to this is the fact that the process of occupational change will be a slow one and it will only be one issue upon which people base their social and political identity (although it will be a centrally important one). On top of this is the fact that the process of reform and change will accelerate and recede at different points in time thereby heightening or lessening the struggle for cultural capital legitimation. Thus, there will not be a sudden change in the political or class allegiances of service-class members, change will work itself through in a much slower fashion. However, there is evidence which indicates that change will work itself through. These two factors mean that the evidence to support the hypothesis presented is necessarily weak and will remain so for some time. Critics may argue that these occupational changes are superficial and are merely ephemeral but given the evidence referenced in this chapter such a proposition seems unlikely. A more likely scenario is that the changing nature of work for many professional occupations will continue even if change is slow and that the ongoing guerrilla campaigns by the two camps will continue and spill over into the political arena in a variety of ways. At this point suffice to say the jury is still out and probably will be for some time.

Conclusion

Does the nature of trust between the service class and its employers lead the service class towards conservatism? I have argued that the answer is no. This is not to say that the service class will necessarily emerge as a radical force. I have tried to highlight one source of cleavage within the service class and to link this to the class's future political behaviour. The issue of trust is a fluid concept which undergoes redefining at different times. These times may relate to specific individual groups or occupations or they may be more broadly based and impact upon a wider spectrum. Changing regimes of accumulation as outlined by Lipietz (1987), Harvey (1989) and Sassen (1991) obviously affect large numbers of occupational groups. We are experiencing one of these shifts – hence the issue of trust, who is trusted, and why they are trusted is up for grabs. I have argued that one of the terrains where this is being played out is the area of professionalism and its definition. This struggle reflects different bids by different groups to legitimise their cultural capital and thus ensure their place at the table. However, there is not room for everyone so if Petra gets to the table Paula is excluded and this sharpens the conflict. Ironically, some of the groups that will possibly be excluded, or at least given less elbow room at the table, are long-established members who in the past were conservative because they wanted to maintain the *status quo*. But now the *status quo* may be moving against them and in order to shift the balance back they may well switch their political allegiance in a bid to increase their influence on the nature of the social settlement entailed in the next regime of accumulation. To be sure this radicalism may be short lived, but it is a source of cleavage and it may be radical in its consequences, because if the state has been politicised and radical in its impact over the past two decades surely it can be so again? I believe the force of this argument is significant and seriously questions the homogeneity and conservatism of the service-class argument.

Acknowledgements

Grateful thanks are due to Sage for permission to reproduce in Chapter 5:

Hanlon, G. (1998) 'Professionalism as enterprise: Service class politics and the redefinition of professionalism', *Sociology* 32: 43–63.

The Postscript to this chapter is an original contribution from the author concerned.

References

Abbott, A. (1988) *The System of Professions*, Chicago, IL: University of Chicago Press.
Atkinson, J. (1984) 'Management strategies for flexible organisations', *Personnel Management* 16 (August): 28–31.
Bourdieu, P. (1977) *Outline of a Theory of Practice*, London: Routledge and Kegan Paul.
Bourdieu, P. (1984) *Distinction: A Social Critique of the Judgement of Taste*, London: Routledge and Kegan Paul.
Burrage, M. (1992) 'Mrs Thatcher against deep structures: Ideology, impact, and ironies of her eleven year confrontation with the professions', Working Paper 92–11, Institute of Governmental Studies, University of California at Berkeley.
Butler, T. and Savage, M. (eds) (1995) *Social Change and the Middle Classes*, London: UCL Press.
Cain, M. (1983) 'The general practice lawyer and the client – Towards a radical conception', in Dingwall, R. and Lewis, P. (eds) *The Sociology of the Professions*, London: Macmillan.
Carchedi, G. (1975) 'On the economic Identification of the new middle class', *Economy and Society* 4: 1–86.
Carr-Saunders, A. M. and Wilson, P.A. (1933) *The Professions*, London: Frank Cass.
Carter, B. and Fairbrother, P. (1995) 'The remaking of the state middle class', in Butler, T. and Savage, M. (eds) *Social Change and the Middle Classes*, London: UCL Press.
Causer, G. and Jones, C. (1990) 'Technical workers, work organisation and career structures in the electronics industry'. Paper presented at Organisation and Control of the Labour Process Conference, Aston University, March.
Causer, G. and Jones, C. (1996) 'Management and the control of technical labour', *Work, Employment and Society* 10: 105–23.
Crewe, I. (1991) 'Labour force changes, working class decline, and the Labour vote: Social and electoral trends in post-war Britain', in Fox Piven, F. (ed.) *Labour Parties in Postindustrial Societies*, Oxford: Polity Press.
Dingwall, R. (1995) 'Divorce mediation – Market failure and regulatory capture'. Paper presented at Conference on Liberating Professions – Shifting Boundaries?, University of Sheffield, July.
Dunleavey, P. (1980) 'The political implications of sectoral cleavages and the growth of state employment: Part 2 Cleavage structures and political alignment', *Political Studies* 28: 527–49.
Erikson, R. and Goldthorpe, J. (1992) *The Constant Flux: A Study of Class Mobility in Industrial Societies*, Oxford: Clarendon Press.
Evans, G., Heath, A. and Lalljee, M. (1996) 'Measuring left-right and libertarian-authoritarian values in the British electorate', *British Journal of Sociology* 47: 93–112.
Ferlie, E. (1992) 'The creation and evolution of quasi markets in the public sector', *Strategic Management Journal* 13: 79–97.
Fitzgerald, L., Ashburner, L. and Ferlie, E. (1995) 'Professions, markets, and managers: Empirical evidence from the NHS'. Paper presented at Professions in Late Modernity seminar, Centre for Corporate Strategy and Change, University of Warwick, March.
Flood, J. (1995) 'Cultures of professional restructuring for the international market', in Dezalay, Y. and Sugarman, D. (eds) *Professional Competition and Professional Power – Lawyers, Accountants and the Social Construction of Markets*, London: Routledge.
Fox Piven, F. (ed.) (1991) *Labour Parties in Postindustrial Societies*, Cambridge: Polity Press.

Giddens, A. (1991) *Modernity and Self-Identity*, Cambridge: Polity Press.
Goldthorpe, J. (1980) *Social Mobility and Class Structure in Modern Britain*, Oxford: Clarendon Press.
Goldthorpe, J. (1982) 'On the service class, its formation and future', in Giddens, A. and Mackenzie, G. (eds) *Social Class and the Division of Labour*, Cambridge: Cambridge University Press.
Goldthorpe, J. (1995) 'The service class revisited', in Butler, T. and Savage, M. (eds) *Social Change and the Middle Classes*, London: UCL Press.
Goode, W. J. (1957) 'Community within a community – The professions', *American Sociological Review* 22: 194–200.
Goreily, T. (1994) 'Rushcliffe fifty years on – The changing role of civil aid within the welfare state', *Journal of Law and Society* 21: 545–66.
Grey, C. (1994) 'Career as a project of the self and labour process discipline', *Sociology* 28: 479–97.
Halford, S. and Savage, M. (1995) 'The bureaucratic career: Demise or adaptation?', in Butler, T. and Savage, M. (eds) *Social Change and the Middle Classes*, London: UCL Press.
Hanlon, G. (1994) *The Commercialization of Accountancy — Flexible Accumulation and the Transformation of the Service Class*, London: Macmillan.
Hanlon, G. (1996a) 'Casino capitalism and the rise of the commercialised service class — An examination of the accountant', *Critical Perspectives on Accounting* 7: 339–63.
Hanlon, G. (1996b) 'Law and the market — Relationships as law's core'. Paper presented at Economists' Club Seminar, Institute for the Study of the Legal Profession, University of Sheffield, January.
Hanlon, G. (1999) *Lawyers, the State and the Market – Professionalism Revisited*, Basingstoke: Macmillan.
Hanlon, G. and Shapland, J. (1997) 'Professional disintegration? – The case of law', in Broadbent, J., Dietrich, M. and Roberts. J. (eds) *The Transformation of the Professions – Theory and Practice*, London: Routledge.
Harrison, B. and Bluestone, B. (1988) *The Great U-Turn – Corporate Restructuring and the Polarising of America*, New York: Basic Books.
Harvey, D. (1989) *The Condition of Postmodernity*, Oxford: Basil Blackwell.
Heath, A. and Savage, M. (1995) 'Political alignments within the middle classes, 1972–89', in Butler, T. and M. Savage, M. (eds) *Social Change and the Middle Classes*, London: UCL Press.
Hughes, E. C. (1963) 'Professions', *Daedalus* 92: 655–68.
Jessop, B. (1994) 'The transition to post-Fordism and the Schumpeterian workfare state', in Roger, B. and Brian, B. (eds) *Towards a Post Fordist Welfare State?*, London: Routledge.
Lash, S. and Urry, J. (1987) *The End of Organised Society*, Cambridge: Polity Press.
Lee, R. G. (1992) 'From profession to business – The rise and rise of the City law firm', *Law and Society* 19: 31–48.
Lipietz, A. (1987) *Mirages and Miracles: The Crisis of Global Fordism*, London: Verso.
Marshall, T. H. (1939) 'The recent history of professionalism', *Canadian Journal of Economics and Political Science* 5: 325–40.
Marshall, G., Newby, H., Rose, D. and Vogler, C. (1988) *Social Class in Modern Britain*, London: Hutchinson Education.
Ogden, S. (1996) 'The role of accounting in organisational change'. Paper presented at Critical Perspectives on Accounting symposium, City University, New York, April.

Parsons, T. (1954) *Essays in Sociological Theory*, New York: Free Press of Glencoe.
Perkin, H. (1989) *The Rise of a Professional Society*, London: Routledge.
Perkin, H. (1996) *The Third Revolution – Professional Elites in the Modern World*, London: Routledge.
Pierson, C. (1994) 'Continuity and discontinuity in the emergence of the "post-Fordist" welfare state', in Burrows, R. and Loader, B. (eds) *Towards a Post-Fordist Welfare State?*, London: Routledge.
Randle, K. (1996) 'The white coated worker: Professional autonomy in a period of change', *Work, Employment and Society* 10: 737–54.
Rice, R. (1995) 'Government outlines scheme to cap aid', *Financial Times* 18 May: 11.
Sassen, S. (1991) *The Global City – New York, London, Tokyo*, Princeton, NJ: Princeton University Press.
Savage, M., Barlow, J., Dickens, P. and Fielding, T. (1992) *Property, Bureaucracy and Culture*, London: Routledge.
Sherr, A. (1994) 'Come of age', *International Journal of the Legal Profession* 1: 3–12.
Sikka, P., Willmott, H. and Lowe, T. (1989) 'Guardians of knowledge and public interest', *Accounting, Auditing and Accountability Journal* 2: 47–71.
Sinclair, L., Ironside, M. and Seifert, R. (1996) 'Classroom struggle? Market oriented reforms and their impact on the teacher labour process', *Work, Employment and Society* 10: 641–62.
Sommerlad, H. (1995) 'Managerialism and the profession: A new professional paradigm', *International Journal of the Legal Profession* 2: 159–86.
Watson, T. J. (1995) 'Speaking professionally – Soft postmodernist thoughts on some late modernist questions about work, occupations, and markets?'. Paper presented at Professions in Late Modernity seminar, Centre for Corporate Strategy and Change, University of Warwick, March.
Whittington, R., McNulty, T. and Whipp, R. (1994) 'Market-driven change in professional services: Problems and processes', *Journal of Management Studies* 31: 829–45.
Wilensky, H. (1964) 'The professionalisation of everyone', *American Journal of Sociology* 70: 137–58.
Wright, E. O. (1985) *Classes*, London: Verso.

Postscript
Extinguishing professionalism?
Gerard Hanlon

It is roughly twenty years since the paper 'Professionalism as enterprise: Service class politics and the redefinition of professionalism' was published in *Sociology* (Hanlon 1998) and, unsurprisingly, much has altered. Although picked up in the broader sociology of professions literature, on re-reading the paper it feels very British. It was an attempt to examine the manner in which professional ideology chops and changes with wider social re-composition. It challenged the idea that professionals were simply trusted as members of the service class to argue that this 'trust' was always contingent on wider class struggles. Furthermore, it argued the issue of trust and social recomposition meant the service class might fracture along the lines of commercialised or social service professionalism. These two versions of professionalism were not simply a matter of private verses public sector professionals – although this was a major line of cleavage. Social service professionalism stressed the importance of need rather than ability to pay and it was closely tied to an expanding welfare state which enabled it to become the dominant form of professional ideology in the post-war Fordist period. On the other hand, commercialised professionalism is tied to the post-Fordist economy, the retrenchment of the welfare state, and the desire to replace state solutions with market ones. In comparison to social service professionalism, it stressed different skills, that is technical ability, managerial skill, and an entrepreneurial capacity to grow the business. My contention was that this model of professionalism was replacing the earlier social service model as the dominant, but not sole, professional form. This seems to me to be even more true today than when I wrote this chapter, for example, with tuition fees, British academics no longer provide an education on the basis of need alone, new members of the university know they need to develop research grants and grow the business if they wish to succeed, and those manager-academics in senior positions are the highest paid academics within the system and increasingly distant from their professional colleagues – quite where social service is fostered here is hard to see.

However, the world has also changed. At the time of writing, Western labour parties had been in retreat and yet, a year after I had written the reprinted previous part of this chapter, the Labour Party in the United Kingdom won power with the largest majority in United Kingdom politics – an achievement it is often accused of squandering. We have since had a financial crisis which was used to further entrench neo-liberal-post-Fordist policies that only strengthen commercialised professionalism (Mirowski 2013); globalisation has transformed life (Steger 2017); societies are becoming increasingly managed across huge swathes of social life within and beyond organisations (Chertkovskaya and Loacker 2016); and in its origin, management as a practice is closely aligned to neo-liberalism (Hanlon 2016) so that it undermines non-profit oriented forces. In light of these issues, albeit that social service professionalism is entrenched in elements of the economy, it is also severely under threat and very much in retreat – at least until such time as the economy restructures society once more. None of this bodes well for professionalism in any meaningful sense of a non-profit-driven occupational outlook.

The United Kingdom class structure has altered since 1998. In the previous part of the chapter, I made use of the work of Savage and colleagues (1992) on class structure – especially their emphasis on property, organisational and cultural assets, to argue that which cultural assets and skills were seen as legitimate was a crucial question of struggle for professionals in the service class. Savage and other colleagues (2013) have continued to examine the class structure in suggesting that Britain now has seven classes – an elite, clearly separated from the rest of society and relatively closed; a precariat making up 15 per cent of the population; a new affluent working class of both white and blue collar employees; a technical middle class with technical, but not cultural, skills; the older established middle class (aka Goldthorpe's service class at 25 per cent of the population); an increasingly small traditional working class; and an emergent class of service workers with high cultural capital and education but modest pay, renting and young. Importantly, they also argue that neither occupation nor educational credentials neatly fit to class any longer. Fragmentation has happened.

This fragmentation reflects significant changes in global manufacturing which, if replicated in services, will radically alter professional life in the United Kingdom. Organisations have innovated in remarkable ways and this has had important impacts on how economies develop. Central here is what is often called the 'global value chain revolution' (Baldwin 2016; Nolan 2012) or, more traditionally, the new international division of labour (Fröbel, Heinrichs and Krevet 1978). This is basically a firm driven division of the production process across the globe which has deindustrialised the North and industrialised the South as firms look to slash expensive wages in Europe and the United States – while other countries, such as China, see their path to economic development located within global value chains (GVC) dominated by (Western) multinational firms. One consequence of this is the shipping of some knowledge from the North to the South; a second is the (partial) transfer of comparative advantage from the state to the firm; and a third is the recomposition of the global class structure which in the West as its occupational structure fragments, makes property ownership increasingly central to economic status (Baldwin 2016; Head 2014).

Thus far, this has been good for elements of many professions because some professionals have been at the heart of this capital-centric social transformation – for instance, accountants, lawyers, academics, Information Technology (IT) consultants, and even human rights professionals as they engage in a 'quest for perfection' (Head 2014; Scheper 2015; Sklair 2001). Within this change, the firm's knowledge base, IT corporate business systems, brand, intellectual property rights and so on matter more than its production capacity – indeed, many multinational corporations have very limited production capacity, for example famously Apple, but also Asia's largest textile firm Uniqlo survives on knowledge embedded in law, accountancy, marketing, IT and engineering (Baldwin 2016). Here it is the extremes of the 'smile curve' – the prefabrication and post-fabrication of the production process such as research and development, legal contracts, accounting frameworks and marketing, from which value is extracted. By weakening production and strengthening such services, these changes are (partly) responsible for the recent restructuring of the United Kingdom class system because they diminished unionised manufacturing employment and facilitated the growth of expert, professional and managerial control functions.

What has this, now old, story to do with professions? I think potentially quite a lot given my earlier argument that wider class forces shape professionalism. Although I disagree with the analysis of Baldwin (2016) that the GVC is the only road to economic development – see Nolan (2012) for an economic critique of this, Head (2014) for an ethical critique, and Quan (2014) for its latent Western chauvinism – I believe he is correct to say that what differentiates this globalisation from earlier versions is the ease with which ideas and knowledge systems can be moved. Knowledge movement exploded in the 1980s and 1990s and, while initially concentrated in low skilled manufacturing, it is spreading its tentacles to more skilled areas. For example, having deskilled labour and embedded knowledge in management systems and technology (Hanlon 2015), organisations could break down production into simpler and simpler stages within the Northern economies. As the cost of moving goods – and later ideas and knowledge systems – plummeted, the transportation of these now deskilled jobs to the South became easier.

Unlike the 1970s and 1980s, today firms like the aircraft company Bombardier are also relocating innovative skilled and professional production stages to Mexico because Mexican engineers earn $60 a day as opposed to $35 an hour in Canada (Baldwin 2016). If a company can enforce 'deep discipline' on a host state which ensures that the organisation's property rights, its freedom to move its assets, its physical resources and technology are protected, and it can leverage wage arbitrage between the expensive North and the cheaper South, as it has already done with deskilled work, why would it not do so with professional work? Surely this is especially possible, or probable, if this professional work is housed in branded bureaucracies such as Harvard University or KPMG? For instance, we can perform surgery remotely so into the (near) future, as the technology improves and cheapens, why is it not probable that the NHS purchases remote knee surgery from the United States' hospital provider Kaiser Permanente which has established a hospital for the provision of such remote services in Brazil? Have these two important organisations not got powerful brands which can be used to leverage wage advantages in the same way as Apple uses

Foxconn? Alternatively, are European or American universities with a presence in Asia not capable of leveraging global wage differentials between academics in order to sell education services? Could Harvard's Asian campus not sell university education to United Kingdom students remotely? In this example, Vietnam or China does not need to build up an internationally competitive university system, rather they need to specialise in one segment of the Harvard GVC. Given the proto-standardised mass production system of much European and United States undergraduate teaching, why is such not a possibility or a probability into the near future for students who attend a non-elite United Kingdom or American university? Could or will large reputable firms not do something similar in law or accountancy? So, if today we purchase our off-the-shelf will from the Co-op via telecommunications, tomorrow could we not receive tele-robotic dental check-ups from Tesco Lotus in Thailand?

In these examples, major professional service (or even non-professional) bureaucracies act as 'systems integrators' do in manufacturing (Nolan 2012). Systems integrators are the organising brains of a dispersed production system which produces in-house, off-shore or sub-contracted work. Accompanying this is the 'cascade effect' wherein the lead firm squeezes value from every point of the supply chain. Importantly in these systems it is the lead firm's reputation, not the country of production, which guarantees quality. Here, comparative advantage shifts from the country, for instance United Kingdom professional services, to the lead organisation such as KPMG, Lloyds, the NHS, Tesco, University of Oxford or the London School of Economics. Indeed, one could argue that nationally universities are already doing this. The University and College Union estimate that 49 per cent of all academic teaching staff in the United Kingdom are on insecure contracts – in some sense, they already are remote, outsourced, and off-shore. As students increasingly access standardised programmes via mass teaching platforms like Moodle, a question is raised of which they would prefer – an insecure or precarious academic in a mid-ranking UK university or a full-time secure, but cheaper, academic in a Harvard-branded Asian campus engaged with ever-improving tele-presence equipment or indeed a BPP University or Pearson Education Ltd overseas academic? Indeed, the intrusion of organisational behaviour is already partly there. For example, Sage Edge provides tutors with the following remote resources – Microsoft Word Testbank, Respondus Electronic Testbank, PowerPoint Slides, Chapter Objectives, Sample Course Syllabi, Discussion questions, Referencing links to other material, Video and Audio links to samples and cases, flashcards and web quizzes, and an array of journal articles which it has developed over the years. This is already remote education; what organisations have simply not done yet, is to create a GVC.

Is this the future of much professional work? The argument against this is that professional services are centrally influenced by co-presence and trust which allows the professional to decide the work routine and the desirable end point. However, today trust is no longer an insurmountable issue – most clients trust the organisation not the individual (if they trust experts at all (Beck 1992)). Furthermore, co-presence is rendered unnecessary by standardisation, for instance, conveyancing services in the United Kingdom or, indeed, mass university education and co-presence may be overcome via tele-presence and tele-robotics. For example, Brynjolfsson and McAfee (2016) highlight the way in which software replaced H&R Block Tax Preparers in the United States and how the fifteen people who designed the Instagram app helped to both increase the number of photos taken globally and undermine Kodak Eastman, which at one point employed 145,300 managerial, professional, skilled and semi-skilled employees. They also point out that IBM and a variety of partners are seeking to build a robot (Dr Watson) capable of diagnosing patients. It is claimed the computer will augment the physician's skill, but Brynjolfsson and McAfee (2016) hold out the possibility that one day it will 'be the world's best diagnostician'. They further claim the jobs most likely to be automated are cognitive and unskilled routine jobs. Many professional jobs entail large numbers of people engaged in just these cognitive activities. One could argue Google translate has automated at least some (the majority) of cognitive translation functions previously done professionally and every academic might short-sightedly hope mass exam marking will go the same way.

But, interestingly, this economy also creates new intensive management systems (Brynjolfsson and McAfee 2016). These management systems are related to the development of new elites (Head 2014). We can see 'elites' emerging in professional services like law, accounting, or academia. Central here are the organisational shifts that accompany these technological advances (Brynjolfsson and McAfee 2016). These shifts include greater 'real time' forms of electronic control of all employees' day-to-day routines which today further empower management at the expense of employee discretion, thereby making control of labour more effective. For example, the University of Texas has developed a business system that allows it to drill down into its data and ascertain, among other things, how successful an individual professor is at attracting students to the classroom, how many high-fee paying students take his or her modules, how many drop out, and the cost to benefit ratio of their employment status (Head 2014). Here, as with the globalised economy more generally (Baldwin 2016), management of professions is: (1) intensified; (2) homogenised – as these professorial ratings have much in common with the billable hours and income generation of lawyers (or the performance-related pay for the many); and (3) individualised – as a professor who is amenable to high-fee students will probably receive a salary increase in contrast to a professor who stresses the pursuit of knowledge as a good in its own right and hence demands 'too much' from fee-paying students. The last assertion assumes such a simple binary exists in the eyes of student-customers – although increasingly the customer is invoked as another element in disciplining labour (Head 2014). In this case we can see organisational change undermining professional solidarity even further than the undermining highlighted in the earlier part of the chapter – after all, what does a high street solicitor have in common with a successful Slaughter and May equity partner?

A recent PwC report estimated that fully 26 per cent of professional employment in the United Kingdom will be automated (BBC 2017). In addition, elites will keep their positions and so too will those others where trust, co-presence and the non-routine are essential – as, for example, in the spaces of the 'concierge economy' of the super-rich and the organisationally powerful in a city like London (Head 2016). These elites will also act as the managers overseeing large international organisations engaged in unique, expert, and routine work. There is a spatial dimension to this elitism so that increasingly large swathes of the United Kingdom will be irrelevant to non-public sector funded professional working life. The position of cities like London, New York, Shanghai and Tokyo will be strengthened in terms of their concentration of elite tasks. Thus, London's undergraduate teaching may be subject to these pressures, but in all likelihood its world-class research will remain. This is because of the centrality of agglomeration effects, the importance of proximity among elite workers, and the possibility of meeting many such workers in a single overseas sabbatical or trip (Baldwin 2016). Such a process is already found in the United Kingdom class structure where a disproportion segment of the elite identified by Savage and colleagues (2013) do not just reside in London, but have been to university there too. Here we will see global professionals who have more in common with one another than they do with their national professional compatriots (Sklair 2001).

Futuristic claims like these should always be treated with caution. But in an invigorated manner these claims reflect earlier debates about the deskilling of professional work, deprofessionalisation, and the polarisation of the professions. They do seem to indicate a polarising within professional labour between elites and a larger group which faces threats of frozen public resources, globalisation, outsourcing, automation, tele-presence, and tele-robotics. They also indicate a concentration of elite tasks in fewer and fewer UK locations. And, finally, they suggest further fragmentation to the point where the question needs to be asked as to whether there is any mileage in talking about 'professionalism' as a unifying concept across service-class labour at all? Fragmentation has happened.

These tendencies or possibilities throw into sharp relief the issue of trust and class. Outside perhaps medicine, school teaching or the judiciary, the nature of 'trust' located in social service professionalism seems to have been undermined for the group loosely talked of as 'the professions'. These professional functions are all noteworthy because of their closeness to the state and state-building – although medicine, it would seem, is not inevitably tied in this regard. Fewer and fewer will be trusted to manage their own work routines, fewer and fewer will be trusted to decide what the end of their work should be, fewer and fewer will operate on the basis of need alone, more and more will be subject to intrusive real-time management, and more and more will experience practices historically experienced by the 'worker' – automation, deskilling, deprofessionalising, cost-benefit analysis, relocation of work overseas, outsourcing, and precarity. That is, trust will be trumped by profit-driven class recomposition as capitalism, red in tooth and claw, resumes after the interregnum of the Fordist period with its accompanying working-class driven social service professionalism. Hence quite probably many of the United Kingdom's declining established professional middle class will have children in the growing class of 'emergent service workers' who have degrees from good universities, cultural capital, but modest earnings, rent and/or are located in the expanding category of the 'precariat'. In the wider global class transforming economy, whether or not social service or commercialised professionalism is dominant seems somewhat parochial because the answer to the question is derived from much wider class struggles. Professionalism is dead, long live professionalism.

References

Baldwin, R (2016) *The Great Convergence: Information Technology and the New Globalisation*, London: The Belnap Press of Harvard.
BBC (2017) Available at: www.bbc.co.uk/news/business-39377353
Beck, U. (1992) *Risk Society: Towards a New Modernity*, London: Sage.
Brynjolfsson, B. and McAfee, A. (2016) *The Second Machine Age: Work, Progress and Prosperity in a Time of Brilliant Technologies*, New York: W. W. Norton and Company.
Chertkovskaya, E. and Loacker, B. (2016) 'Work and consumption: Entangled', *Ephemera* 16(3): 1–20.
Fröbel, F., Heinrichs, J. and Krevet, O. (1978) 'The new international division of labour', *Social Science Information* 17(1): 123–42.
Hanlon, G. (1998) 'Professionalism as enterprise: Service class politics and the redefinition of professionalism', *Sociology* 32(1): 43–63.
Hanlon, G. (2015) *The Dark Side of Management: A Secret History of Management Theory*, London: Routledge.
Hanlon, G. (2016) 'The first neo-liberal science: Management and neo-liberalism' *Sociology*. Available at: http://journals.sagepub.com/doi/abs/10.1177/0038038516655260
Head, S. (2014) *Mindless – Why Smart Machines Are Making Humans Dumber*, New York: Basic Books.
Mirowski, P. (2013) *Never Let a Serious Crisis Go to Waste: How Neo-liberalism Survived the Financial Meltdown*, London: Verso.
Nolan, P. (2012) *Is China Buying the World?*, London: Polity Press.
Quan, H. L. T. (2014) *Growth against Democracy: Savage Developmentalism in the Modern World*, Maryland: Lexington Books.
Savage, M., Barlow, J., Dickens, P. and Fielding, T. (1992) *Property, Bureaucracy, Culture*, London: Routledge.
Savage, M., Devine, F., Cunningham, N., Taylor, M., Li Yaojun, Hjellbrekke, J., Le Roux, B., Friedman, S. and Miles, A. (2013) 'A new model of social class? Findings from the BBC's Great British Class Survey Experiment', *Sociology* 47(2): 219–50.
Scheper, C. (2015) 'From naming and shaming to knowing and showing: Human rights and the power of corporate practice', *International Journal of Human Rights* 19(6): 737–56.
Sklair, L. (2001) *The Transnational Capitalist Class*, Oxford: Blackwell.
Steger, M. B. (2017) *Globalization*, Oxford: Oxford University Press.

6 Enterprise, hybrid professionalism and the public sector

Mirko Noordegraaf

Introduction

The public sector is highly dependent upon professions, professionals and professional work. Medical doctors, nurses, police, public persecutors, judges, teachers, social workers – they all provide essential public services, which implies treating individual cases (such as patients, pupils or criminals) in the light of public objectives and formalised policy programmes. Public professionals, in other words, treat cases in order to serve generic public or societal ambitions – such as public health and safety – as well as more specific policy programmes that have been formally agreed upon in order to realise such ambitions.

In that sense, public professionalism was never 'pure' (Noordegraaf 2007). Public professionals feel the dependencies and were never 'free' and autonomous. Public sectors are dependent upon professionals, and professionals are embedded within public sector regimes. Their leeway was always constrained and will always be constrained, by policy ambitions and regulations, as well as bureaucratic parameters and requirements. Since the 1980s, however, these constraints have intensified. In the 'era of enterprise' public professionals have been immersed – many would say 'captured' – by neo-liberal regimes, managerial ideologies and well-organised sets of instruments that belong to the so-called 'New Public Management' (see, for instance, Enteman 1993; Hood 1991; Pollitt and Bouckaert 2004). Their purity has therefore further eroded. In addition to constraints that come from policy and bureaucratic surroundings, they face managerial and organisational constraints, with strong businesslike, consumer and market overtones. Professional services not only have to implement substantive objectives like fairness, equity and accessibility and procedural goals like legality and uniformity. They also have to perform, establish outputs and outcomes, and account for their actions. They have to be managed and organised, with a stress on efficient, effective, innovative and customer-focused action.

This has generated widespread and much-debated conflicts between a professional logic on the one hand, and bureaucratic and organisational logics on the other (see, for example, Hood 1991; Noordegraaf 2015; Reay and Hinings, 2009). It has also generated analyses of how public services and professionals respond to, and deal with, such conflicts. There are three ideal typical responses. First, conflicting logics remain *separate* and a separate professional logic is maintained and protected. Second, the logics interact and can be *combined* so that professionals can act and organisations can perform. Third, the logics are interwoven and professionalism becomes *hybrid*, so that professionals start to perform in new ways. In this chapter, these responses will be elaborated, in order to assess the state of professional services in the public sector in the era of enterprise. The third response – professional action as a hybrid phenomenon – will be especially accentuated, as it represents the most realistic and hopeful response. Entrepreneurial realities cannot be taken away, and well-organised action might enhance instead of harm the quality of services. This, in turn, needs a thorough understanding of what 'well-organised' means. We will argue that this is a matter of *organising*, much more than of 'organisations', let alone 'corporate' organisations that act in 'businesslike' and 'entrepreneurial' ways. This enables us to go beyond hybrid professionalism and portray public professionals as agents who do not merely treat cases, but who *co-organise* service provision, in order to be more effective and innovative, both for (multiple) cases as well as society at large. We will argue that public service enterprises find ways to enhance collective professional action which serves multiple instead of singular performance criteria.

Conflicting logics

A few professions are strong professions, representing classic or 'pure' professionalism (Noordegraaf 2007) – such as medical doctors, lawyers, accountants and engineers (see, for instance, Krause 1996; Larson 1977; Reed 1992). They have managed to establish strong associations and regulative mechanisms, backed by the state and universities (Burrage and Torstendahl 1990; Muzio *et al.* 2011) that enable them to regulate their own occupational fields and practices. This means they have institutionalised autonomies and much discretion as well as independence when they treat cases. Other professions might strive towards this ideal typical – and ideal – conception of occupational self-control, but they have not really attained this. They are part of 'weaker' professional fields, with less forceful regulative mechanisms, and they face many external demands and constraints – such as nurses, teachers, police officers and social workers. But even judges, who are seen as 'strong' professionals, are more embedded professionals than medical doctors, as they are part of the legal systems and law courts, which have to secure certain legal, programmatic and bureaucratic standards that do not really come from within professional fields. Obviously, medical doctors must respect the law, follow rules, and can be held accountable, but many rules and regulations come 'from within'. These other professions face rules and regulations that come from 'the outside'.

Many of these professionals are public professionals, or public professional workers. This is understandable, as public professionals might be part of professional fields, but they are also tied to political and policy programs, as well as bureaucratic systems. According to authors like Clarke and Newman (1997) they are part of 'bureau-professional regimes'. They have to contribute to higher-order societal objectives, such as public health and safety, *and* they have to implement formal policies, such as health care, educational and safety policies, *and* they have to follow procedural standards, in order to guarantee uniform, reliable and legal (client) treatment. Even pure professionals who have become part of public systems – such as medical doctors in publicly organised and funded health care systems – face such demands and constraints, and their purity is reduced.

These programmatic and especially policy standards as well as bureaucratic constraints are rather traditional, and they have become more important with the rise and extension of welfare states. In the 1980s this started to change. Welfare states were 'restructured' (Klenk and Pavolini 2015). With the rise of neo-liberalism in countries like the United States and the United Kingdom (but also many other Western countries), the *era of enterprise* entered public domains. The 'market', 'corporations' and 'entrepreneurship' became crucial images for organising public sectors, and the New Public Management offered new businesslike tools for running public organisations (see Clarke and Newman 1997; Hood 1991; Noordegraaf 2015; Pollitt and Bouckaert 2004). More practically this implied a stress on measurable results and outputs, economic yardsticks (economy, efficiency and effectiveness), transparency, innovation, customer focus, and clear lines of accountability. At first sight, new organisational and managerial models and regimes started to replace programmatic and bureaucratic regimes, aimed at optimising such a performance logic (Noordegraaf 2015). Public organisations and even sectors were designed as if they were corporations, with strategic apexes, production units or divisions, and output standardisation (Mintzberg 1983). Public executives and managers started to work along the lines of planning and control cycles with much stress on 'plan, do, check, act' (PDCA). They started to use monitoring systems, quality control and customer satisfaction ratings, with lots of emphasis on clear facts and figures, or 'management by measurement' (Noordegraaf and Abma 2003). They started to unleash 'entrepreneurial spirits' (Osborne and Gaebler 1992).

This new logic, a performance logic – alternatively called businesslike logic, organisational logic, managerial logic, entrepreneurial logic, commercial logic – put much pressure upon a professional logic, as the main thrust of performing more effectively runs against the main thrust of acting professionally (see, for example, Exworthy and Halford 1999; Noordegraaf 2015; O'Reilly and Reed 2011; Waring and Currie 2009). Instead of quality, a performance logic puts much stress on quantity. Instead of autonomy, much stress is put upon control. Instead of tacit knowledge and expertise, much stress is put upon codified information, and so on. But things are actually even more complicated, as more traditional programmatic and bureaucratic regimes have not dissolved. Professional action is not only influenced or captured by organisational and managerial regimes, but also by policy programmes and bureaucratic standards. These regimes have become *bureau-managerial-professional regimes*. Conflicts and clashes between (multiple) logics are no surprise – in fact, they are to be expected. Conflicts are part of the performance logic itself, for example as corporate optimisation clashes with entrepreneurial innovation (see, for instance, Hood 1991), but more importantly, the performance logic clashes with complex professional work in contested policy environments.

Many authors have underscored the importance of these conflicts, at various levels. Some authors have stressed conflicts at the level of public/private values (as illustrated by Hood 1991), ideologies (as exemplified by Clarke and Newman 1997; Evetts 2003; Jacobs 1992) and identities (as indicated by Thomas and Davies 2005). Others have stressed conflict at the level of institutionalised practices in systems that are both businesslike and professional (such as Reay and Hinings 2009) as well as organisational actions that represent different institutional logics (for example, Becharov and Smith 2014; Skelcher and Smith 2015). Some authors have stressed conflict at the level of professional work and actions in businesslike environments (for instance, Numerato, Salvatore and Fattore 2012; Waring and Currie 2009) and professional motivation that is weakened by businesslike pressures (for example, Tummers 2013; van Loon 2016). Irrespective of how we see and value the rise of an era of enterprise, we have entered a conflict-ridden era which calls for appropriate political, organisational and professional responses.

Responses to conflicting logics

Although conflicts are unavoidable, almost 'objectively' given and certainly subjectively experienced, we must be careful not to exaggerate the presence and effects of conflicts. First of all, conflicts might occur with less or more *intensity*, depending on broader circumstances. The New Public Management, for example, has affected different countries in different ways (Pollitt and Bouckaert 2004). In some countries, especially Anglo-Saxon countries, the New Public Management has been implemented in strong and sometimes radical ways. In continental European countries, this has taken on much more moderate forms, with the Netherlands and Nordic countries in-between Anglo-Saxon countries and France, Germany, and other Southern and Eastern countries.

Second, conflicts might be *productive*, that is, an emphasis upon results and transparency is not a bad thing in itself. Public policies and services might be improved, when performance pressures are exerted. An emphasis on more tangible results or more efficiency, for instance, is not bad as such. Not wasting public money or improving 'delivery' might also be valuable from a public or societal point of view. Whether conflicts are productive depends partly on the circumstances. In settings with less ambiguity and contestation, it is easier to focus on outputs and outcomes. This is especially so when there is lots of technical and ethical contestation – when ideas, interests and emotions clash, it is difficult to work with strict performance systems (Hofstede 1981; Hoppe 2011; Noordegraaf 2015; Noordegraaf and Abma 2003). For example, when medical interventions are new or highly complex, or when they are ethically contested, or when policing methods to trace drug trafficking or cybercrime are far-reaching, it is logical that strictly managing performances is of limited value. In addition, whether conflicts are productive also partly depends upon how they are managed. Even in ambiguous or contested circumstances, interventions might be made transparent and measured, but only productively when managers do this in smart and subtle ways – when they keep performance measurements active and lively, when they limit (financial) consequences and sanctions, and when they turn performance management into an interactive and dialogical affair (as illustrated by De Bruijn 2007; Moynihan 2008).

Third, conflicts can be *dealt with*, and not only by managers. Even when conflicts are intense and not automatically productive, people who are affected by them – including professionals – have the means and ways to cope. In other words, not only managers but also public professionals and other staff members might have the capacity to *respond* to conflicts. They might work *against* or *with* pressures and make sure that 'good' things happen, due to or despite 'bad' influences. Professionals and others are not only passive victims, but (re)active agents as well. When they work *against* pressures, they try to defend their autonomies and ways of working, something that is often emphasised in the analysis of professionals' responses when they show passive or active resistance (for example, Thomas and Davies 2005; Tummers 2013; Waring and Currie 2009). When they work *with* pressures, they might comply and conform, or do 'something' with performance pressures in order to improve their work, while maintaining their sense of professionalism (as illustrated by Reay and Hinings 2009). Especially when professionals are able to deal with multiple (and conflicting) demands and expectations in positive ways, by performing professionally in political contexts, we see the rise of what we call 'professional capability' (see van Loon *et al.* 2016). Instead of merely protecting professional autonomies or combining professional and managerial logics, more hybridised responses are deployed. New forms of professionalism are 'enacted', also by professionals themselves, instead of 'demanded' (Evans 2011).

Multiple ways of responding to conflicting logics

Many of the authors who have discussed conflicts have examined coping responses, and many other authors investigate how professionals *actually* deal with pressures. These responses might have multiple consequences:

- Coping behaviours might protect the health and wellbeing of professionals, despite the pressures and difficulties that might be experienced.
- Coping responses might be important to maintain or improve performances, despite potential counterproductive performance pressures.
- Coping might be important to maintain legitimacy, as public services conform to public or political expectations.

How conflicts are dealt with, with *what* specific effects, is variable, however, and are far from clear in an empirical sense. In other words, we have to identify multiple types of responses, especially when we study professionals. This means we need to refine the 'working *against* or *with* pressures' line of thought. When we survey the literature on coping with conflicting logics (the literature we just mentioned, as well as Martin *et al.* 2015; Numerato, Salvatore and Fattore 2012; Oliver 1991), we see the various types of responses to which we have already hinted. In addition to (1) merely protecting professionalism; (2) professional and organisational/managerial logics might also be combined; or (3) these logics might be interwoven so that more hybrid forms of action are enacted. These three major ways of responding to conflicts, especially by public professionals, are summarised in Table 6.1 and are briefly discussed beneath it.

Protecting a professional logic

First, professionals might *protect* their professional logic, including identities and autonomies, and external pressures might be resisted, countered and kept at a distance. A performance logic is seen and experienced, but it is viewed as problematic and counterproductive. Much effort is put in reducing the effects of the New Public Management. This might be done by working against New Public Management and opposing its instruments, covertly or overtly, *or* it might be done by working along with New Public Management impulses, in order to neutralise their effects, or even to use it against managers (see, for example, Waring and Currie 2009). Responding to performance pressures in order to reduce effects might – all in all – vary from:

- *ritualising* external pressures, that is appearing to conform but actually ignoring them, via
- *neutralising* pressures, that is working with them in order to make them useless, to
- *manipulating* pressures, that is, gaming the system.

Table 6.1 Responding to conflicts between organisational and professional logics

	Protecting a professional logic	*Combining professional and organisational logics*	*Interweaving multiple logics*
Key focus	Professional resistance	Pragmatic collaboration	Hybrid professionalism
Key argument	Organisational and professional logics have a distinctive core; a professional logic will, or has to, be protected.	Multiple logics can co-exist; although different logics have their own core, they both have to be respected.	Logics can come together, in organisational and professional action; professional work can be reconfigured.
Key references	Freidson (2001); Waring and Currie (2009)	De Bruijn (2002) Reay and Hinings (2009)	Denis *et al.* (2015); Noordegraaf (2011, 2015); Waring (2014)

Apart from these modalities which can be traced empirically, there is a clear normative thrust in many contributions to this debate. Freidson (2001) for example tried to rescue a professional logic – the 'third logic' – from omnipresent managerial and consumer logics. Professional and organisational/market/ entrepreneurial actions should remain separate, and organisational/entrepreneurial action should be reduced as much as possible in the case of services like health care, welfare, safety and education. At most, organisational and managerial actions are 'custodial' (Ackroyd, Hughes and Soothill 1989), that is aimed at guarding professional leeway and discretion. This is not only academically stressed. In fact, a large part of recent political and public discourses is fuelled by comparable normative sentiments, both in a very general sense of 'rescuing the public professional sphere' (see, for instance, Jansen, van den Brink and Kole 2010) and in a more specific sense, with an eye on specific sectors such as health care or education (for example, Evers and Kneyber 2015).

Combining professional and organisational logics

Second, professional work might become part of *combinations* of logics, aimed at combining 'best of both worlds'. Reay and Hinings (2009), for instance, have shown the importance of 'pragmatic collaboration' in the Canadian health care system. They showed how professional and organisational action could be related, without producing negative feelings and effects. They identified four mechanisms for improving results *and* keeping professionals satisfied: (a) linking medical professionals to decision-making; (b) using medical professionals' expertise; (c) seeking outside enemies (the government); and (d) creating room for experimentation and innovation. De Bruijn (2002), to take another example, identified various options for managing and measuring performances along the lines of a businesslike logic, but in such a way that 'management by measurement' (Noordegraaf and Abma 2003) becomes *meaningful*. As highlighted above, he stressed the importance of variety, of keeping performance management and measurement dynamic and lively, and of organising interactions, so that measurement outcomes can be interpreted. This is comparable to other elaborations of meaningful performance measurement. As others have also shown, performance measurement does not dissolve ambiguities; complex issues can be measured and interpreted in multiple ways; and we need dialogue to make sense of performance data (Radin 2006; Moynihan 2008). Instead of seeing measurement and evidence as 'end points' in improving organisational action, it is much more fruitful to use them as starting points for dialogue and debate (Noordegraaf 2008). These dialogues might not only include professionals, but also other stakeholders.

These insights are very practical and fundamental at the same time. When professional and organisational logics clash, public service organisations might establish day-to-day mechanisms for linking organisational and professional worlds, in such a way that organisational ambitions and targets are *operationally* translated into professional action, and vice versa. These translations, at the same time, are *strategic* in that they leave the logics, as such, untouched. They assume that there is a certain essence or 'core' of organisational and professional logics, which are both needed to secure well-organised action. This essence of professionalism should not so much be protected, but respected. At the same time, this implies that multiple logics remain distinct and separate, although they are connected. Authors assume that both organisational and professional logics have a core 'essence' that deserves this respect. In their analysis of how medical professionals respond to changes, Martin et al. (2015: 378) conclude: "In systems characterised by fissures between professional groups and powerful market and managerial influences, we suggest that professionalism must interact creatively but carefully with other logics". This differs from the third type of response, in which distinctions between logics become much more fuzzy.

Interweaving professional and organisational logics

Third, and again differently, professionals might interrelate and *interweave* their logic with other logics, so that elements of logics are actually coming together in both organisational and professional practices. Professional identities and acts then embody multiplicity instead of singularity. This response has become well known in widespread debates on *hybrid* professionalism (for instance, Denis, Ferlie and van Gestel 2015; Noordegraaf 2007, 2015; Waring 2014; Skelcher and Smith 2015; Waring 2014). Instead of seeing professionalism as something distinct, separate and loose from other logics, with a distinctive core, both organisational and professional actions are seen as something that is/can be *reconfigured*. Values, identities, practical action or elements of other logics can become part of professional fields, outlooks and actions. This goes for both programmatic and bureaucratic as well as organisational and managerial logics. Professionals, for example, might still strive towards 'free' or autonomous case treatment, but also acknowledge the importance of policy guidelines and procedural justice when they treat cases, *and* acknowledge the importance of tangible outputs and client and/or stakeholder satisfaction when they treat one or multiple cases. This is called 'hybrid' because it might still feel unnatural, but at the same time it might be seen as a natural part of the job (Noordegraaf 2015).

When dealing with conflicting elements is seen as something natural, we might even go beyond hybridity, and trace forms of reconfigured professionalism in which *multiplicity* is actually preferred over singularity. Professionals might acknowledge the importance of treating multiple cases instead of one case; of dealing with multiple values, including economic ones, instead of one value such as 'quality'; and of dealing with multiple realities, including political and societal realities, instead of one reality such as the professional–client interaction. This has implications for the coping capacities of professionals – we will turn to this later – but of course this concerns much more than 'a' professional or professionals. In the case of reconfigured professionalism, it is not so much 'a' professional or individual professionals that render services. It is teams of professionals, support staff, managers, clients and stakeholders who *jointly* produce services. Service processes become much more important than individual service professionals (Noordegraaf 2015). In health care, clinical guidelines, for example, might be 'carriers of institutional change', as Adler and Kwon (2013) have shown. Clinical guidelines might support the strengthening of professional collaboration, aimed at rendering 'better' services. 'Better' then means multiple things: client-focused, effective, innovative and efficient. Since this third type of response is the newest and the least developed, we now mainly highlight hybrid professionalism. Later, we again return to protected professionalism and pragmatic collaboration.

Hybrid professionalism

We think that the third response – interweaving logics and developing hybrid forms of professionalism – is especially important, for various reasons. First, it is *realistic* as many professionals and especially public professionals cannot stick to the ideal of pure professionalism. They face (too) many constraints, due to their public status and roles, due to the era of enterprise that requires demonstrable performance, and due to the broader transitions that public services are going through, driven by changing client preferences, new technologies, transnational standards, political shifts, social media, and so on, in domains like health care (for instance, Plochg, Klazinga and Starfield 2009), education (for example, Hargreaves 2000) and law (as illustrated by Faulconbridge and Muzio 2012). Moreover, there are many real-life examples of reconfigured public professionalism in which the elements of professional action change and become plural, in the light of changing context (see, among others, Noordegraaf *et al.* 2016).

Second, developing hybrid professionalism is *optimistic*, not only because it focuses on these real-life examples, but also because it offers more forceful ways of working towards more vital professional services. This is mainly the case as hybrid professionalism neither negates nor ignores conflict nor seeks to work against conflict, but makes sure that professionals *themselves* recognise conflict and are equipped to deal with it. Instead of working with or against 'demanded professionalism', they 'enact' professionalism, as Evans (2011) has argued. Conflicts are no longer located in-between different parts of the organisation (such as managers versus professionals, each carrying different logics), but they are located inside work flows, in which professionals and others make sure that 'valuable' services are rendered. What 'valuable' means is difficult to define and delineate, so the ones that are responsible for rendering services – including professionals – should acknowledge the complexity of this responsibility and find ways to cope with this. How this is, can and should be done, is explained beneath.

From professionals to professional work flows

'A' public professional, such as 'a' medical doctor or 'a' judge is and remains important. He or she does not so much treat cases, but embodies a higher cause and calling (see, for instance, Wilensky 1964). When he or she treats a case, something bigger is involved, symbolised by the appearance, rituals and physicality that surround case treatment. This is not only done to make decisions happen – it is also done to make decisions authoritative and to signify that certain higher values are at stake, such as 'independence'. At the same time, 'a' professional is a relative thing, as services *cannot* be rendered by individual professionals. On the contrary, modern health care, judicial and educational services, especially, need multiple professionals and support staff to render services *and* to make sure that the conditions for rendering services are met, including conditions that are important to secure convincing external or public communication, to secure financial soundness, and to secure judicial back-up if necessary. All of these acts are important inservice environments that are (potentially) critical of the services rendered: politicians, journalists, clients and other stakeholders might emphasise 'mistakes' and 'errors' much more than normal and/or successful case treatment, and public services might get into trouble because of case-related communication, financial problems and judicial matters.

This implies first and foremost that the era of 'autonomous professionals' is over, as authors like Hargreaves (2000) stress, and that we have entered the era of 'collegial professionalism'. Professionals have to collaborate and work together, in teams and networks. This is also stressed by others, such as Adler, Kwon and Heckscher (2008) who stress the rise of 'collaborative communities' in health care. In addition, it implies that *work processes* and *work flows* count, that is processes and flows in which teams of professionals, as well as support staff, managers and stakeholders work together to render sound services, at various levels (Noordegraaf 2015).

Case treatment

Professionals and other staff members work together in order to realise sound case treatment, that is case treatment that is valuable, timely, efficient and satisfactory. The more complex a case, the more important is inter- and multi-professional action, including the mechanisms for realising this. One can think of multi-disciplinary meetings in health care aimed at bringing medical professionals together when a complex case – such as in oncology – is treated; or of multi-disciplinary networks for helping clients with chronic diseases in ways that cut across the clinical, ambulatory and private spheres. As indicated, formal instruments like clinical guidelines can facilitate this (as illustrated by Adler and Kwon 2013). They enable professionals and others to standardise medical action and secure quality, timeliness, innovation and efficiency.

This means that guidelines themselves have become ambiguous objects, aimed at tackling ambiguous situations. Instead of being produced by either medical professionals on the basis of medical reasoning, or by organisations or inspectorates in order to measure and account for actions, they are medical/professional and organisational/managerial at the same time. Moreover, they embody *multiple values*: they serve the patient, both in terms of high-quality as well as speedy and timely treatment, they serve the interests of other patients, for instance, by saving time, and they serve organisational and political agendas, for example, by saving money. This also reinforces the ambiguities of 'entrepreneurialism' in the era of enterprise. Instead of either favouring or limiting entrepreneurial spirits, entrepreneurialism moves in different directions at the same time: medical technologies are improved, evidence-based medicine is strengthened, value-based care is propagated, client satisfaction is measured, and stakeholder expectations are taken into account – with all aimed at moving beyond strict separations between 'cure, care, control and community' (Mintzberg 2017).

Multiple case treatment

Traditionally, professionals mainly work on one case, and then the next. They put as much time and attention in this one case as possible. In the case of hybrid professionalism, this view is problematic. Professionals and other staff members increasingly work together on determining how to treat multiple cases, including how to prioritise cases, when to treat certain cases, and how to deal with delayed or backlog cases. The more cases flow towards a public service organisation, the more important this becomes. Professionals need shared mechanisms for making *trade-offs*, especially when the number and nature of cases, including the complexity of cases, exceed capacities. This brings us back to the concept of multiplicity. In terms of yardsticks it is increasingly difficult to define and assess medical professionalism, or any other form of public professionalism. Instead of mainly saying that 'good' medical action is serving 'the' interests of 'the' patient, it is much more realistic to say that 'good' medical action serves multiple interests of multiple patients, in wider political, technological and financial contexts. This all the more means that professional action in the era of enterprise is collegial action.

Treating (multiple) case treatment

Finally, concerning these wider contexts, professionals and others not only work together to determine how cases should be treated. They do so in wider and often critical environments that expect clarity, cost control, safety and lack of risks and errors. Professionals and others will have to be able to use mechanisms and skills for dealing with such critical forces, varying from political criticism via journalistic attention to citizen claims. This – among other things – implies that they have to be aware of the risks they generate, especially when they treat sensitive cases; to acknowledge the political and/or judicial implications of their decisions; to deal with public exposure; to use or withstand social media that make services transparent in new ways; and to reflect upon how they work and whether they possess the right competencies to 'survive' and remain healthy.

Given traditional images of professionals, it is attractive to limit joint professional action to the first level, and to leave the other two levels to 'the organisation' or 'management'. From the perspective of reconfigured professionalism this is untenable. On the one hand, it reproduces the conflicts that are seen and experienced as burdensome. When a case is left to professionals, and multiple cases and contexts are left to organisations, conflicts between professionals and organisations will increase, as there are growing tensions between cases and between cases and contexts, especially when 'a' case is treated. When the treatment of a case absorbs much time (and money), other cases are negatively affected – and clients might go to journalists or lawyers about this. On the other hand, it ignores the fact that setting priorities and dealing with critical environments cannot be isolated form professional action – it is professionals who share responsibility for this, not least because they use financial, technological and organisational resources when they treat cases, and how they do this influences how many cases can be treated and whether stakeholders become active or remain silent. Trade-offs in other words are tied to their actions: the time and attention they spend on individual cases cannot be spent on other cases. Quality, then, is more than maximum or absolute 'time' or 'space'; it is *relative* time and space: time spent on one case is relative to risks as well as to time spent on other cases.

Dealing with consequences

This situation has two major consequences. First, professionals will have to acknowledge that they are *co-responsible* for *organising* service processes. Organising case treatment, based upon the deployment of resources, is not detached from their work, but *is* their work. Second, professionals need to acquire new *abilities*, or more technically, competencies and capacities, in order to deal with more complex cases and service contexts. In the text below we will briefly explore these two implications.

Organising as part of work flows

Obviously, there are many instances when 'a' professional interacts with a client. When a general practitioner speaks with one of his or her patients, when a police officer deals with a burglary, when a lecturer supervises a Masters or PhD thesis, or when a judge treats a criminal offence, there is identifiable communication between a well-trained expert and someone who wants, needs or requires a public service. But even these instances cannot be separated from the work flows required to render such services. Appointments need to be made, case treatment needs to be prepared, additional investigations might need to take place, follow-up actions might be necessary, various things need to be registered, other professionals or experts might need to take another look, or might be needed to complement professional action, and so forth. The quality of services is therefore not merely tied to a distinct communicative moment, but to the chain of events. When the professionals mentioned deal with multiple cases, this only becomes more relevant. When the flows are organised smoothly, quality – including timeliness, speed and efficiency – can be assured, even when multiple cases compete for professional attention.

In many other instances, it is even more complex than this. In the case of more advanced surgery, or treating patients with multi-morbidity, or bigger criminal investigations, or running high-quality educational programs, the communicative moment, that is the bilateral interaction between professional and client, might still be crucial, but is rather marginal, when set against the bigger picture. Multiple professionals might be active, supported by colleagues and staff members, and how their interactions are co-ordinated and routinised influences the quality of services. Time and efficiency might even be crucial indicators of quality, for example when a speedy cancer diagnosis is made possible, or when law courts prevent delays and organise timely case treatment. This implies that time is relative. There might be time for professional–client interactions, to offer quality and mitigate risks, although this will have to be restricted, not least because other cases/clients also want time and attention. But the way in which these interactions are embedded within bigger work flows, in which professionals, staff members and organisational support are aligned in such a way that clients are treated or served timely and efficiently, also generates quality. This is not only an *organisational* matter that is, a matter for the organisation, but a matter of *organising* – of how crucial participants, including professionals, co-ordinate their actions and whether they have the skills and routines for co-ordinated action. Whereas *organisations* can be kept at a distance from professional action, *organising* is part of professional action. In the case of hybrid professionalism, these various spheres are connected (see Kirkpatrick and Noordegraaf 2015; Muzio and Kirkpatrick 2011). Ideally, organisations facilitate the ways in which professionals organise (multiple) case treatment.

Capabilities to cope with complexity

The latter remarks not only stress the importance of organisational capacity, but also of capability (for example, Noordegraaf and van Loon 2014) – especially professional capability. Traditionally, professionals are equipped, trained and socialised to deal with individual cases, and not so much for the things that are discussed above. Dealing with multiple cases, prioritising cases, dealing with time and money, working innovatively, stopping case treatment, making trade-offs in the light of scarce resources and financial constraints, keeping an eye on judicial and safety implications and so on – all of these more complex tasks and events are traditionally not seen as regular parts of professional repertoires. There are signs, however, that professional repertoires are reconfigured and that new attitudes and acts are developed, for instance by way of revised educational programmes that rely upon new competency models. A good example can be found in health care, where medical education is increasingly based upon competency models like the CANMeds model (Frank *et al.* 2010), stressing the importance of communication, collaboration, advocacy and day-to-day medical leadership.

The problem with competency models, however, is that they tend to focus on individual competencies instead of work situations in which (multiple) individuals will have to act and work together. This means that capacities are not so much individual but social and relational, and they need to focus on the mechanisms for strengthening social and relational capability. This can be done, among other things, by focusing on collaborative practices and shared experiences as well as work routines, which enable multiple professionals and other organisational participants to smoothly work together, at the various levels identified above. This, in turn, means that complex tasks and events, such as setting priorities, making trade-offs, making things more efficient, are not necessarily dealt with by individual professionals. Involving others – varying from colleagues to managers – referring tasks to others, speaking up and out, these are all part of professional action. Professional agency does not merely imply maximising individual professional leeway and action, but also restricting leeway and action, if and when necessary.

Conclusion

Traditional discourses on professionalism and professionals are highly attractive. They highlight the importance of well-trained experts who treat cases and serve society, at the same time. They accentuate the importance of reliable public services, also backed up by rituals, ceremonies and symbols. They enable professionals to intervene, with authority, in complex matters such as health, safety and education. These discourses have become problematic in the era of enterprise. Businesslike and market surroundings, also in public domains, have put lots of pressure upon professional action, as the symbols, ways of working and skills of professionals are at odds with new demands – efficiency, financial soundness, innovation and outputs. This has generated lots of conflicts and clashes, which – at best – might lead to peaceful co-existence, for example when there is 'pragmatic collaboration'.

This chapter argued that we can go beyond these oppositions and dichotomies, not so much by linking conflicting logics and managing conflicts, but by renewing discourses on professionals and reconfiguring professional action. More specifically, we stressed the importance of turning case treatment and especially professional–client interactions and their quality into a *relative* phenomenon; of focusing on *work flows* in which such interactions are part of collective action; of co-ordinating *multiple* work flows, as professionals face multiple cases; of *contextualising* professional action, especially by including the judicial and political dimensions of case treatment; and of emphasizing the *multiplicity* of quality. Protecting professional work spaces as well as merely combining professional and performance logics is not enough. It might be useful to go beyond an emphasis on individual professionals, toward collegial professionalism; to go beyond images of strict performance regimes, toward the meaningful improvement of professional action; and to go beyond the assumption that performing better is an organisational matter, toward the acknowledgement that professional services are unavoidably organised. Quality resides in how *organising* takes places, on a day-to-day basis, by managers, professionals and other stakeholders.

These (mental) changes not only produce more realistic – and optimistic – images of professional action, they also turn professional action into a healthier affair, as individual professionals acquire more reasonable proportions. Public services still depend upon well-trained experts, but 'the' individual and autonomous professional is no longer seen as the grand and pure embodiment of professional public services. He/she is viewed as a crucial participant in co-organising joint professional action. This makes professional lives more interesting and more liveable – especially in the harsh and demanding era of enterprise.

Acknowledgement

Thanks are given to Evelien van Leeuwen, student-assistant at the University of Utrecht, for her editorial support.

References

Ackroyd, S., Hughes, J. A. and Soothill, K. (1989) 'Public sector services and their management', *Journal of Management Studies* 26: 603–19.

Adler, P. S. and Kwon, S. W. (2013) 'The mutation of professionalism as a contested diffusion process: Clinical guidelines as carriers of institutional change in medicine', *Journal of Management Studies* 50(5): 930–62.

Adler, P. S., Kwon, S. W. and Heckscher, C. (2008) 'Perspective – professional work: The emergence of collaborative community', *Organization Science* 19(2): 359–76.

Becharov, M. L. and Smith, W. K. (2014) 'Multiple institutional logics in organizations: Explaining their varied nature and implications', *Academy of Management Review* 39(3): 364–81.

Burrage, M. and Torstendahl, R. (eds) (1990) *Professions in Theory and History*, London: Sage.

Clarke, J. and Newman, J. (1997) *The Managerial State: Power, Politics and Ideology in the Remaking of Social Welfare*, London: Sage.

De Bruijn, H. (2002) 'Performance measurement in the public sector: Strategies to cope with the risks of performance measurement', *International Journal of Public Sector Management* 15(7): 578–94.

De Bruijn, H. (2007) *Managing Performance in the Public Sector*, Abingdon: Routledge.

Denis, J. L., Ferlie, E. and van Gestel, N. (2015) 'Understanding hybridity in public organizations', *Public Administration* 93(2): 273–89.

Enteman, W. F. (1993) *Managerialism: The Emergence of a New Ideology*, Madison, WI: University of Wisconsin Press.

Evans, L. (2011) 'The "shape" of teacher professionalism in England: Professional standards, performance management, professional development and the changes proposed in the 2010 White Paper', *British Educational Research Journal* 37(5): 851–70.

Evers, J. and Kneyber, R. (eds) (2015) *Flip the System: Changing Education from the Ground Up*, London: Routledge.

Evetts, J. (2003) 'The construction of professionalism in new and existing occupational contexts: Promoting and facilitating occupational change', *International Journal of Sociology and Social Policy* 23(4/5): 22–35.

Exworthy, M. and Halford, S. (1999) *Professionals and the New Managerialism in the Public Sector*, Buckingham: Open University Press.

Faulconbridge, J. R., and Muzio, D. (2012) 'Professions in a globalizing world: Towards a transnational sociology of the professions', *International Sociology* 27(1): 136–52.

Frank, J. R., Snell, L. S., Cate, O. T., Holmboe, E. S., Carraccio, C., Swing, S. R. et al. (2010) 'Competency-based medical education: Theory to practice', *Medical Teacher* 32(8): 638–45.

Freidson, E. (2001) *Professionalism: The Third Logic*, Cambridge: Polity Press.

Hargreaves, A. (2000) 'Four ages of professionalism and professional learning', *Teachers and Teaching: Theory and Practice* 6(2): 151–82.

Hofstede, G. (1981) 'Management control of public and not-for-profit activities', *Accounting, Organizations and Society* 6(3): 193–211.

Hood, C. (1991) 'A public management for all seasons?', *Public Administration* 69(1), 3–19.

Hoppe, R. (2011) *The Governance of Problems: Puzzling, Powering and Participation*, Bristol: Policy Press.

Jacobs, J. (1992) *Systems of Survival: A Dialogue on the Moral Foundations of Commerce and Politics*, New York: Vintage Books.

Jansen, T., van den Brink, G. and Kole, J. (2010) *Professional Pride: A Powerful Force*, Amsterdam: Boom.

Kirkpatrick, I. and Noordegraaf, M. (2015) 'Hybrid professionalism: The re-shaping of occupational and organisational logics', in Empson, L., Muzio, D., Broschak, J. and Hinings, B. (eds) *The Oxford Handbook on Professional Service Firms*, Oxford: Oxford University Press.

Klenk, T. and Pavolini, E. (2015) *Restructuring Welfare Governance: Marketization, Managerialism and Welfare State Professionalism*, Cheltenham: Edward Elgar.

Krause, E. A. (1996) *Death of the Guilds: Professions, States and the Advance of Capitalism, 1930s to the Present*, New Haven, CT: Yale University Press.

Larson, M. S. (1977) *The Rise of Professionalism*, Berkeley, CA: University of California Press.

Martin, G. P., Armstrong, N., Aveling, E. L., Herbert, G. and Dixon-Woods, M. (2015) 'Professionalism redundant, reshaped, or reinvigorated? Realizing the "third logic" in contemporary health care', *Journal of Health and Social Behavior* 56(3): 378–97.

Mintzberg, H. (1983) *Structure in Fives*, Englewood Cliffs, NJ: Prentice Hall.

Mintzberg, H. (2017) *Managing the Myths of Health Care: Bridging the Separations between Care, Cure, Control, and Community*, Oakland: Berrett-Koehler Publishers.

Moynihan, D. P. (2008) *The Dynamics of Performance Management: Constructing Information and Reform*, Washington, DC: Georgetown University Press.

Muzio, D., Hodgson, D., Faulconbridge, J., Beaverstock, J. and Hall, S. (2011) 'Towards corporate professionalization: The case of project management, management consultancy and executive search', *Current Sociology* 59(4): 443–64.

Muzio, D. and Kirkpatrick, I. (2011) 'Introduction: Professions and organizations – A conceptual framework', *Current Sociology* 95(4): 389–405.

Noordegraaf, M. (2007) 'From "pure" to "hybrid" professionalism: Present-day professionalism in ambiguous public domains', *Administration and Society* 39(6): 761–85.

Noordegraaf, M. (2008) 'Meanings of measurement: The real story behind the Rotterdam Safety Index', *Public Management Review* 10(2): 221–39.

Noordegraaf, M. (2011) 'Risky business: How professionals and professional fields (must) deal with organizational issues', *Organization Studies* 32: 1349–71.

Noordegraaf, M. (2015) 'Hybrid professionalism and beyond: (New) forms of public professionalism in changing organizational and societal contexts', *Journal of Professions and Organization* 2(2): 187–206.

Noordegraaf, M. and Abma, T. (2003) 'Management by measurement? Public management practices amidst ambiguity', *Public Administration* 81: 853–71.

Noordegraaf, M., Schneider, M. M. E., van Rensen, E. L. J. and Boselie, J. P. P. E. F. (2016) 'Cultural complementarity: Reshaping professional and organizational logics in developing frontline medical leadership', *Public Management Review* 18(8): 1111–37.

Numerato, D., Salvatore, D. and Fattore, G. (2012) 'The impact of management on medical professionalism: A review', *Sociology of Health and Illness* 34(4): 626–44.

Oliver, C. (1991) 'Strategic responses to institutional processes', *Academy of Management Review* 16(1): 145–79.

O'Reilly, D. and Reed, M. (2011) 'The grit in the oyster: Professionalism, managerialism and leaderism as discourses of UK public services modernization', *Organization Studies* 32(8): 1079–101.

Osborne, D. and Gaebler, T. (1992) *Reinventing Government: How the Entrepreneurial Spirit Is Transforming Government*, New York: Addison-Wesley.

Plochg, T., Klazinga, N. S. and Starfield, B. (2009) 'Transforming medical professionalism to fit changing health needs', *BMC Medicine* 7(1): 64.

Pollitt, C. and Bouckaert, G. (2004) *Public Management Reform: A Comparative Analysis*, Oxford: Oxford University Press.

Radin, B. (2006) *Challenging the Performance Movement: Accountability, Complexity, and Democratic Values*, Washington, DC: Georgetown University Press.

Reay, T. and Hinings, C. R. (2009) 'Managing the rivalry of competing institutional logics', *Organization Studies* 30(6): 629–52.

Reed, M. (1992) 'Experts, professions and organisations in late modernity', *Management Research News* 15(5/6): 55–6.

Skelcher, C. and Smith, S. R. (2015) 'Theorizing hybridity: Institutional logics, complex organizations, and actor identities: The case of nonprofits', *Public Administration* 93(2): 433–48.

Thomas, R. and Davies, A. (2005) 'Theorizing the micro-politics of resistance: New Public Management and managerial identities in the UK public services', *Organization Studies* 26(5): 683–706.

Tummers, L. (2013) *Policy Alienation and the Power of Professionals*, Cheltenham: Edward Elgar.

van Loon, N. M. (2016) 'Is public service motivation related to overall and dimensional work-unit performance as indicated by supervisors?', *International Public Management Journal* 19(1): 78–110.

van Loon, N. M., Heerema, M., Weggemans, M. and Noordegraaf, M. (2016) 'Speaking up and activism among frontline employees: How professional coping influences work engagement and intent to leave among teachers', *The American Review of Public Administration*. Available at: https://doi.org/10.1177/0275074016682313

van Loon, N. and Noordegraaf, M. (2014) 'Professionals onder druk of professionele tegendruk? Gebalanceerde motivatie voor de publieke zaak in professionele publieke dienstverlening', *Beleid en Maatschappij* 41(3): 205–25.

Waring, J. (2014) 'Restratification, hybridity and professional elites: Questions of power, identity and relational contingency at the points of "professional–organisational intersection"', *Sociology Compass* 8: 688–704.

Waring, J. and Currie, G. (2009) 'Managing expert knowledge: Organizational challenges and managerial futures for the UK medical profession', *Organization Studies* 30(7): 755–78.

Wilensky, H. (1964) 'The professionalization of everyone?', *American Journal of Sociology* 70: 137–58.

7 Entrepreneurship and professional service firms
The team, the firm, the ecosystem and the field

Markus Reihlen, Andreas Werr and Christoph Seckler

Introduction

Although professional services have been among the fastest growing sectors in the past decades and described as 'innovative by their nature' (Hargadon and Bechky 2006; Nikolova 2012), research on entrepreneurship and entrepreneurial renewal in professional service firms has been rather limited (see, for example, Reihlen and Werr 2012, 2015). Previous research on professional service firms indicates that these represent a unique and complex context for entrepreneurial activity. First, the motivational disposition of the professional, with its focus on interesting tasks and learning opportunities (Alvesson 2004; Løwendahl 2005), creates a fertile ground for continuous learning, innovation and individual entrepreneurial initiatives (Heusinkveld and Benders 2002). At the same time, however, professionals' strong preference for autonomy counteract the dissemination and institutionalisation of such innovations as professionals may be reluctant to adhere to corporate 'best practices' developed based on such innovations. Second, the locus for innovation in professional service firms is typically the ongoing service delivery in interaction with colleagues and clients rather than a dedicated research and development function (Fosstenløkken, Løwendahl and Revang 2003; Heusinkveld and Benders 2002; Skjølsvik et al. 2007). Solving clients' unique problems in inter-organisational and often cross-functional teams represents opportunities for innovation that are, however, not always easy to realise. Third, the relationship-based nature of professional service markets both enables and restricts the creation and exploitation of entrepreneurial opportunities. Many entrepreneurial initiatives have been enabled by close client relationships. At the same time professional service firms' embeddedness in current networks, and the costs associated with extending these networks, represent an effective barrier to entrepreneurial initiatives beyond established networks (Glückler and Armbrüster 2003; Hanlon 2004).

Against the background of these specific conditions of entrepreneurship in professional service firms, this chapter, building on and developing earlier work by the authors (Reihlen and Werr 2015), reviews the extant research at the intersection of entrepreneurship and professional service firms. Entrepreneurship is here defined as how opportunities are discovered, created and exploited to bring 'future' goods and services into existence (see Venkataraman 1997). In line with recent developments, we view entrepreneurship as closely linked to the opportunity concept, describing entrepreneurship as opportunity-seeking and opportunity-exploiting behaviour (see Ramoglou and Tsang 2016). This may be manifested in the establishment of new firms but often takes place within existing firms, where it is observable through the creation of new services, markets and processes (traditionally referred to as intrapreneurship or corporate entrepreneurship).

Following Wood and McKinley (2010), we argue from a constructivist view which understands the subjectivity of entrepreneurs and their interaction with their socio-cultural environment as an integral component of the opportunity creation process. Entrepreneurial processes couple the expanding business with new interactive socio-economic milieus as represented by new regional markets, new client industries or new segments of the talent market. Therefore, the necessary learning and innovation processes of an entrepreneurial professional service firm embrace not only the discovery of industry-specific facts and skills, but also the firm's 'embedding' itself into and 'shaping' the 'new' social context with its own local regulations and institutional practices (Muzio, Brock and Suddaby 2013; Reihlen and Apel 2007). Framing the concept of opportunity and entrepreneurship within a constructivist perspective allows us to connect dispersed research streams in the entrepreneurship field, as well as in the professional service field that have been published under various headings. In the following review we will first discuss the tension between the concepts of professionalism and entrepreneurship. This is followed by a review of extant research structured along four levels of analysis – the team, the organisation, the entrepreneurial ecosystem and the organisational field.

Entrepreneurship and professionalism – opposing concepts?

Entrepreneurship as an institution is founded on ideals such as cultural individualism and change (Brandl and Bullinger 2009). Cultural individualism encourages individuals who are considered as autonomous and uncontrolled to engage in creative and innovative activities. This autonomy of the free-willed entrepreneur is regarded as a necessary social condition for entrepreneurship to emerge. Change is then seen as the consequence of opportunity-seeking entrepreneurs. Through processes of creative destruction (Schumpeter 1942), entrepreneurs engage in rule-breaking behaviour and demonstrate their capacity to control the external world. The entrepreneurial organisation or society is one in which change becomes the norm and stability the exception.

Professionalism, on the other hand, is something quite different. Abbott (1988), for instance, emphasises that a key distinguishing feature of professional work lies in its reliance on academic knowledge that formalises and standardises the skills on which professional work proceeds. Professionalisation can be conceived as a process of cognitive standardisation. This permits, as Larson (1977: 40) points out, "a measure of uniformity and homogeneity in the 'production of producers'". Professionalism therefore is a method of controlling exclusive knowledge by the professional occupation through mechanisms of recruitment, training, socialisation and peer monitoring. As a result, professions enjoy a "sheltered position … in the marketplace, with entry to the professions usually gained through obtaining relevant higher education credentials" (Saks 2012: 4). While professional work involves fresh judgement and discretion, it is not typically a rule-breaking entrepreneurial practice (Freidson 2001). Table 7.1 juxtaposes entrepreneurship with professionalism.

To resolve some of the contradictions between entrepreneurship and professionalism, we argue to differentiate different types of professional organisations. In particular, we distinguish between classic or regulated professional service firms such as accounting or law firms and neo-professional service firms such as consulting firms or advertising agencies (von Nordenflycht 2010). While in the former case professionals belong to a classic profession with well-developed institutions of professionalism, in the latter case at least some of these institutions are missing. In particular, neo-professional service firms lack a clearly confined knowledge base. In management consultancy, for instance, very little, if any, commonly accepted knowledge standards and good professional practices exist (Groß and Kieser 2006). In contrast, in classic professional service firms these standards are well defined by professional associations and mediated through teaching programmes and credentials as a reference point for assessing professional practice. Consequently, the more the professional knowledge base is confined, the less discretionary freedom and creativity is left to the professional. Innovation is then caged within professional boundaries. This explains

Table 7.1 Opposing concepts – entrepreneurship versus professionalism

	Entrepreneurship	*Professionalism*
Value	Change and innovation.	Professional standards and discretion.
Type of authority	Entrepreneurial: based on the ability to make change happen.	Professional: based on expert power.
Primary body of knowledge	Pragmatic: anything that works.	Academic: science and technology.
Market conditions	Open and free market.	Social closure and sheltered positions in the marketplace.
Mode of organisation	Emphasises autonomy and innovation: entrepreneurial model – start-ups, corporate entrepreneurship, business incubators, innovation ecosystems.	Emphasises autonomy and self-governance: professional model – professional partnerships and professional associations.

why management consultants, lacking a clearly defined body of knowledge, can engage in more 'creative' problem-solving, while their counterparts from accounting become accused of 'cooking the books' when interpreting accounting rules in novel ways. Yet, as studies on entrepreneurship in the regulated professions show, classic professional service firms do innovate beyond professional boundaries. However, they do so by taking institutional leadership roles in professional associations, and thereby get actively involved in changing the standards of their own profession (Greenwood and Suddaby 2006). This leads on to a discussion, in turn, of the entrepreneurial team, the firm, the ecosystem and the field.

The entrepreneurial team

Professional service firms create new entrepreneurial opportunities by bringing together the knowledge and expertise of individuals, often across discipline and organisational boundaries (Hargadon 1998). This is typically realised in project-based work forms, in which professionals, often together with client representatives, form an engagement team to solve the client's problem (Handley *et al.* 2012). Previous research on the ability of teams to make use of their members' knowledge and experience in processes of learning, knowledge creation, or knowledge integration is extensive. However, only a limited portion is conducted in professional service firms that, through their specific organisational context (for instance, highly competitive career structures) and the inter-organisational nature of the work, involving the client, represents unique challenges.

Challenges to opportunity creation in engagement teams

To exploit the creativity of collectives of professionals, there must be active engagement in seeking others' knowledge as well as sharing knowledge. Professionals must also engage in the reflective reframing – joint exploitation of this diverse knowledge in social interactions – in which they 'make new sense of what they already know' (Hargadon and Bechky 2006). These processes presume that professionals are willing and able to engage in these kinds of activities, something that previous research provides several reasons to question.

First, we may question professionals' willingness to share and seek knowledge. Professionals' identity and 'value' in organisations is, to a great extent, linked to their possession of a unique set of expertise and experience (Morris 2001). Against this background, it has been argued that professionals may be reluctant to share their knowledge, as that may reduce their power in relation to the organisation (Morris 2001). In a similar vein, seeking help in highly competitive organisations may risk being perceived as an admission of ignorance, providing a threat to professionals' career chances and self-confidence (Hargadon and Bechky 2006). In addition, psychological barriers, such as fear of being ridiculed or criticised, may limit the extent to which professionals share or seek knowledge (Argyris and Schön 1978; Hargadon and Bechky 2006). Research has thus found that there is a strong tendency in groups to focus on widely shared knowledge among the participants rather than bringing up their unique knowledge, which is the knowledge that has the largest potential to contribute to innovative solutions (Edmondson 2002).

Second, research provides reason to question professionals' ability to share and seek knowledge. Previous research has shown that the differences in knowledge underlying the idea of innovation through knowledge complementarities may create communication boundaries (Carlile 2002; Ringberg and Reihlen 2008). A focus on homogeneity of people and strong personal bonds – both within professional service firms and in relations with clients – are thus common. While they may limit the innovative capacity of professional service firms they increase efficiency in communication (Nikolova 2012; Nikolova, Möllering and Reihlen 2015).

Third, research questions professionals' willingness and ability to engage in reflective reframing as this may be related to considerable psychological risks. These are especially salient in the relationship between the professional and their clients. As argued by Schön (1983), this relationship is often carried out within an 'expert framework' where any doubts and uncertainties by the professional are suppressed in order not to compromise the client's confidence in the professional or threaten the professional's self-esteem. It has also been argued that the asymmetry of the relation may be the other way around (Niewiem and Richter 2004), with the client dictating what the professional should do or think, which equally limits the potential for innovation in the engagement team (Nikolova 2012; Skjølsvik et al. 2007).

Attributes and processes of the opportunity creating engagement team

While realising the entrepreneurial opportunities of the engagement team may be challenging, previous research has looked extensively at how these barriers may be overcome. Research on knowledge sharing and knowledge integration in teams highlights the importance of the possibility for direct interaction between individuals as it enables the sharing of tacit and experience-based knowledge as well as the reflective reframing through which existing knowledge may be revaluated and made relevant (or irrelevant) and new solutions may be found (Hargadon 1998; Hargadon and Bechky 2006). However, opportunities for direct interaction will not necessarily create entrepreneurial opportunities. In order for these to emerge, interaction needs to take place in a climate that encourages knowledge sharing and reflection.

In order for individuals to engage in knowledge sharing and reflection, the social environment needs to be perceived as safe by those acting in it. Edmondson (1999) shows that 'psychological safety' – "a shared belief that the team is safe for interpersonal risk taking … a sense of confidence that the team will not embarrass, reject or punish someone for speaking up" (Edmondson 1999: 354) – is related to a group's ability to reflect and learn. Psychological safety is supported by clear and shared understandings of the task. Additional characteristics of groups in which knowledge sharing is enabled include having fun (Dougherty and Takacs 2004) and communicating in approving rather than disapproving terms (Losada and Heaphy 2004). An interactive climate supporting knowledge sharing and innovation is further supported by relatively egalitarian power structures (Edmondson 2002; Hargadon and Bechky 2006).

Furthermore, previous research has emphasised the importance of professionals' understandings of their roles and responsibilities in performing the joint task. These shape the extent to which knowledge is actively shared and exploited in joint reflection as they set the boundaries of which individuals may have relevant competence and to what extent they may legitimately seek or contribute to this knowledge and which aspects of the task are open for reflection and reframing and which are not (Dougherty and Takacs 2004; Hargadon and Bechky 2006). Broad representations, creating redundancy and overlap between individual professionals' perceived responsibilities, support knowledge integration as they make it legitimate for actors to step into each other's domains (Dougherty and Takacs 2004; Swart and Kinnie 2003; Werr 2012; Werr and Runsten 2013).

The entrepreneurial firm

As the size and importance of professional service firms have grown, interest in the entrepreneurial strategies these firms employ to develop their service portfolios and market positions has increased. Still, research on the entrepreneurial strategies of professional service firms is rather limited, as the professional service firm has been attributed a less important role in entrepreneurial activity than either the profession or the professional. Three main approaches to investigating the entrepreneurial professional service firm may be identified: new venture management processes, the development and embedding of new practices in professional service firms, and the governance of entrepreneurial firms.

New venture management

One of the core research areas in entrepreneurship is new venture creation or start-up management (Cooper 1981; Gartner 1985). There are a number of general factors influencing the management of start-ups, such as active entrepreneurial cognitions (Mitchell et al. 2007), actions (Frese 2009), personal networks (Ostgaard and Birley 1996), and venture team dynamics (Ensleya, Pearson and Amasonc 2002), as well as environmental conditions including industry competition (Sandberg and Hofer 1987), capital availability (Cooper, Gimeno-Gascon and Woo 1994), legitimacy (Zimmerman and Zeitz 2002), and regulation (Capelleras et al. 2008). We can assume that these factors also play an important role for venture creation of professional service firms, but it is surprising how little empirical research has been conducted in this field.

The little empirical work that exists is mainly based on qualitative case studies. In a study of a small consulting firm, for instance, Ram (1999) explores the emergence of the firm and analyses three related processes: the hiring process of consultants, the client relationship management, and the dynamics of project management. Ram's findings suggest that small professional service firms operate under unstable co-operation conditions among their key constituencies, making it particularly challenging to manage the tension between the need to increase organisational efficiency and the pressure for continuous entrepreneurship. The study of Clarysse and Moray (2004) investigates the constitution of the entrepreneurial team of a university spin-off and explores how the team deals with and learns from a crisis situation during the start-up phase. The authors argue that the crisis in the entrepreneurial team co-evolves with disturbances in the development of the business. More recently, Günther (2012) studied the start-up and early growth stages of two successful corporate law firm spin-offs. He shows that these firms orchestrated a number of different strategies that helped them to mimic standards of large corporate law firms by high involvement service delivery and distinctive people development and to create a degree of uniqueness by particular client strategies and a strong cultural alignment. Furthermore, in a longitudinal study of law firms in Silicon Valley, California, Phillips (2002, 2005) analysed the consequences of "organizational life chances when a member of an existing firm leaves to found a new firm" (Phillips 2002: 474). His study highlights a number of consequences when resources and routines are transferred from the parent firm to the newly founded spin-off. As he shows, resource transfer increases life chances for off-springs, but decreases life chances for parents (Phillips 2002). Furthermore, he shows that in the newly founded firm gender inequality is likely to be reproduced (Phillips 2005). Overall, existing studies on new ventures provided scattered evidence. So far, they emphasise that venture success rests on a number of factors such as the firm's ability to learn quickly, including learning from crisis and learning through new hires, the creation of legitimacy and reputation, and leveraging social capital for new venture management.

The process of new practice creation

Recent research has further investigated the process of new practice development, which is typically the outcome of exploiting new opportunities, leading to new service offerings. Exploiting new knowledge areas and opportunities is highly contested in professional service firms and new ideas for service offerings are not necessarily welcomed by managers or professionals (Anand, Gardner and Morris 2007; Gardner, Anand and Morris 2008; Heusinkveld and Benders 2005; Heusinkveld, Benders and van den Berg 2009). While new practice areas may originate from new client needs, lateral hires, or from within the pool of professionals, they can also challenge individual and departmental interests and power positions as well as established client relations and reputation (Heusinkveld and Benders 2005). This highlights the need to not only identify entrepreneurial opportunities but create legitimacy around them internally as an important aspect of entrepreneurship in professional service firms (Gardner, Anand and Morris

2008). Anand, Gardner and Morris (2007) identify four prerequisites for the successful establishment of a new practice area. The first prerequisite is *agency* – the existence of a champion with a desire to create and develop a new practice area. In large professional service firms, this desire is driven by the career system and its focus on reputation and the establishment of a distinct area of expertise. Second, new practice areas are built on an *expertise,* which is sufficiently differentiated from existing practice areas to be perceived as distinct, but similar enough not to become too alien. Nevertheless, new expertise areas were often highly contested by representatives of existing core areas of expertise who felt their individual and organisational positions to be threatened (Gardner, Anand and Morris 2008; Heusinkveld and Benders 2005). Third, new practice areas required the establishment of a *defensible turf,* that is the establishment of clear territorial boundaries around the new practice area both internally toward other practice areas and externally in relation to clients. The development of a client pool was identified as an important resource in establishing internal legitimacy and thus a defensible turf. Fourth, *organisational support* in terms of resources and political sponsorship was required.

Entrepreneurial governance

The question of governance of the entrepreneurial professional service firm has been a largely neglected area of research. Previous research has focused on a dichotomous view on governance of professional service firms, in which firms choose between professional partnerships and corporations (Empson 2007; Empson and Chapman 2006; Greenwood and Empson 2003), between collegial clan control (Greenwood, Hinings and Brown 1990; Starbuck 1993) and corporate hierarchy (Brown *et al.* 1996), or between professional bureaucracy and adhocracy (Mintzberg 1979). As Empson (2012) argues, a good deal of governance systems and practices cannot be captured by these dichotomised models. We argue that especially the specific type of entrepreneurial governance has been largely overlooked by mainstream governance research on professional service firms. This is surprising since prominent empirical examples such as Greenberg Traurig LLP, a fast-growing Miami-based law firm (Kolz 2007), or the large advertising conglomerate WPP (Grabher 2001), do not seem to be explained well by either partnership or corporate models of governance.

Following some more recent work that builds upon configuration theory (Harlacher 2010; Harlacher and Reihlen 2014), we suggest that entrepreneurial governance is a distinctive form that attempts to maximise entrepreneurial opportunity seeking of organisational members by expanding individual autonomy. Contrary to managerial governance that strives to create firm-wide consistency in approaches, services, markets or partnership governance that attempts to reach consensus on strategic matters, entrepreneurial governance captures the benefits of market opportunities by encouraging its members to engage in entrepreneurship – seeking out new market opportunities. This governance form is reflected in its structure, culture and management systems. The governance structure is more decentralised and its culture favours entrepreneurial values emphasising personal autonomy (for their individual commercial gain) and thus opposing the formalisation and standardisation usually associated with becoming more 'corporate' (Empson and Chapman 2006). Furthermore, remuneration incentivises individual performance (for instance, 'eat what you kill' philosophies) and de-emphasises seniority-based remuneration (for example, lockstep).

The entrepreneurial ecosystem

Previous research at the team and firm level has neglected to integrate systematically external stakeholders (besides the client) into theory building on entrepreneurship in the professional service firm context. We therefore suggest broadening the perspective on entrepreneurship and professional service firms by taking an entrepreneurial ecosystems perspective (Moore 1993; Spigel 2015; van der Borgh, Cloodt and Romme 2012). This perspective has been proposed as an insightful lens mainly in the field of entrepreneurship, strategic management and innovation. The general idea of an entrepreneurial ecosystem is that it is a network of multiple actors (for example, suppliers, clients, entrepreneurial professional service firms and venture capital firms), which co-evolves in the creation and exploitation of an opportunity (Moore 1993). Similar to the biological concept of an ecosystem, each member of an entrepreneurial ecosystem depends on the network and also shares its fate as a whole regardless of the individual organisation's apparent strength (Ceccagnoli *et al.* 2012; Iansiti and Levien 2004). The attractiveness of the entrepreneurial ecosystem perspective lies in its ability to provide a fresh view on the interdependencies of the co-creation and co-evolution of entrepreneurial ventures (Adner and Kapoor 2010; Moore 1993). As such, it offers the opportunity to move the focus in understanding entrepreneurship from the focal entrepreneurial professional service firm towards the wider entrepreneurial ecosystem. In the following, we make an attempt to describe key aspects of an entrepreneurial ecosystem in the professional service firm context (see also Reihlen, Seckler and Werr 2017). The ecosystem perspective stresses the role of a variety of different actors, the network relationships as well as governance aspects of such networks, as shown in Figure 7.1.

Actors in entrepreneurial ecosystems

Various actors interact in the identification, creation and exploitation of opportunities (Adner and Kapoor 2010). Drawing on the professional service firm literature, we suggest that the actors within professional service firm ecosystems can mainly be distinguished as five groups: entrepreneurial professional service firms, lead clients, complementors, universities, and external stakeholders (the public, professional associations and the state).

Entrepreneurial *professional service firms* play a twofold role in the entrepreneurial ecosystem. First, they may play the role of an initiator. The motivation to initiate co-operation is to deepen and extend client relationships, build and

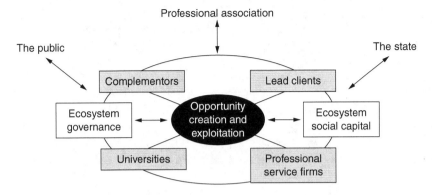

Figure 7.1 Framework of an entrepreneurial ecosystem in professional services.

maintain a reputation of thought leadership, and explore and exploit opportunities which may open up through, for instance, technological or regulatory changes. Second, by being engaged in explicitly entrepreneurial contexts, such as entrepreneurial ecosystems, professional service firms may gain both access to important knowledge and maintain a reputation of being dedicated to knowledge development.

Lead clients in professional entrepreneurial ecosystems play key roles in initiating, developing and legitimating service innovations. Client challenges often indicate opportunities for novel services. These novel services are developed in close collaboration with lead clients. Thus, lead clients provide a productive context for entrepreneurship (Fosstenløkken, Løwendahl and Revang 2003; Skjølsvik et al. 2007). Furthermore, lead clients may serve as legitimisers of the innovative services. Without the legitimation from a wider range of clients purchasing new services, service innovation will not take place (Anand, Gardner and Morris 2007).

Complementors offer products or services, which combine with existing products to yield superior value in combination (Jacobides, Knudsen and Augier 2006). As such, complementors are development partners whose resources such as specific expertise, network ties, financial capital and/or reputation become necessary ingredients in the entrepreneurial process and increase the likelihood of success. For example, IT firms may become important complementors in the ecosystem of accounting firms in order to explore and exploit opportunities related to big data analytics. In addition, venture capital firms may provide seed, start-up, and bridge-stage funding – and other professional service firms such as law or advertising agencies may provide complementary expertise and services within the ecosystem. Opinion leaders such as gurus, industry analysts and leading investment bankers also play complementary roles in successful entrepreneurial ventures.

Universities have an important role in knowledge-intensive ecosystems as the producers of academic knowledge. Academic knowledge accomplishes two main functions in a venturing process for professional service firms (Abbott 1988). First, the academic knowledge is the result of research activities potentially relevant for entrepreneurial ventures. Research is conducted in professional communities often hosted within universities or networks of innovations. Second, academic knowledge is a source of legitimacy of the professionals' claim of having esoteric knowledge that goes beyond the ordinary and is, in a fundamental sense, the source of authority of professionals as experts. As Rueschemeyer (1964) pointed out, however, we would be mistaken to accept the idea that the professional body of knowledge is always scientific in character. Legitimate expert authority is certainly gained in the name of science, but many professional services such as legal services or advertising are only loosely connected, if at all, with science.

External stakeholders are, finally, located in the contextual environment of the entrepreneurial professional service firm and comprise, besides the public and the state, the professional associations. These define qualification standards and limit the supply of professionals, and public policy supports, tolerates or restricts professional activities (Swan and Newell 1995). The professional community in highly institutionalised professions such as accounting or law also has a regulatory function by adjusting directions of professional practices. This regulatory function, however, is not only performed top-down from the community to the individual firm or practitioner. The institutionalised practices of the community are also subject to changes initiated bottom-up by individual professional service firms mediated by regulatory agencies. As Greenwood, Hinings and Suddaby (2002: 61) point out: "professional associations ... are arenas through which organizations interact and collectively represent themselves to themselves".

Network relations in ecosystems

The entrepreneurial ecosystem perspective puts an emphasis on the network relationships between the various actors (Adner and Kapoor 2010; Jacobides, Knudsen and Augier 2006; Moore 1993). The general idea of these relationships is that they are dynamic and evolving over time. This idea also separates the ecosystem idea from more linear conceptions of value creation such as value chains and supply chains (Hearn and Pace 2006). These dynamic and evolving relationships play a critical role in the entrepreneurial ecosystem perspective because resources for an entrepreneurial venture may be accessed and mobilised through a network of social relations (Hoang and Antoncic 2003). As Stuart and Sorenson (2007: 211) point out: "It is not an exaggeration to claim that existing empirical findings point to the centrality of networks in every aspect of the entrepreneurial process". Professional service firms may search for additional expertise, further network ties that help them to bridge into a new service field, symbolic capital to increase the legitimacy of the venture by collaborating with reputable partners, or financial resources, especially for more capital-intensive ventures. The seeking of resources through social networks usually goes beyond the start-up phase of the venture.

Since the entrepreneurial ecosystem literature is surprisingly silent about the characteristics of the relationships between the actors, we draw on social capital theory to distinguish between three dimensions of the social relations: structural, relational and cognitive (Nahapiet and Ghoshal 1998). First, the structural dimension describes with which actors new partnerships are formed. The creation of new ties with new members provides knowledge and other resources that would otherwise not be available to the actors within the entrepreneurial ecosystem. Second, social capital has a relational dimension, which implies a type of social relationship between individuals. This may be relations between actors as described through friendship, reciprocity, trust and shared norms of engagement shaping actors' behaviour. Third, social capital reflects shared cognitions within a community. This is especially the case when repeated work relations create shared mental models, recipes and identities in making sense of information and drawing joint conclusions for action. This may result in a certain architecture of the entrepreneurial ecosystem, which 'defines the terms of the division of labour' (Jacobides, Knudsen and Augier 2006).

Based on this specification of the dimensions of the social relationships within entrepreneurial ecosystems, we suggest that the dynamism of an entrepreneurial ecosystem may actually be rather fragile. To make this fragility more explicit we distinguish between dynamic and static entrepreneurial ecosystems. *Dynamic* entrepreneurial ecosystems foster the three dimensions of social relationships. They allow for the seeking of new partnerships and the development of relationships that are characterised by trust, reciprocity and shared cognition. However, fostering these three dimensions of social relationships may also reach a tipping point. There is an increasing body of literature that highlights the negative aspects associated with social capital (for example, Adler and Kwon 2002; Warren 2008). Maurer and Ebers (2006) found in their study of biotech ventures that social capital can unfold inertial forces based on a relational and cognitive lock-in. A relational lock-in emerges through overemphasising bonding social relations, which undermines the search for novelty and learning. Cognitive lock-in appeared when actors largely shared the same cognitive schemes and identities and engaged intensively with each other. Not surprisingly, actors may learn very little new things from similarly minded people. Based on these two sides of the same coin of social capital, we argue that the dynamism of entrepreneurial ecosystems is rather fragile and over embedding a firm within a network of relations may show its gloomy side (Granovetter 1985; Hagedoorn and Frankort 2008). Yet greater positivity may be secured – as shown in the study by Maurer and Ebers (2006) – through careful relationship management that sometimes breaks up strong and overly cohesive relations, establishes new ties, and encourages the learning of novel cognitive schemes in new partnerships.

Ecosystem governance

The importance of successful relationship management raises the question of the governance of the entrepreneurial ecosystem. The professional service firm literature has emphasised different forms of firm-level governance ranging from collegial and managerial to entrepreneurial (see, for instance, Grabher 2001; Greenwood and Empson 2003; Harlacher and Reihlen 2014). Yet the governance of alliances of professional service firms and ecosystems has not been subject to much research. Drawing on the literature on alliance governance, we follow Albers (2010: 205) account and define ecosystem governance "as the set of formal and informal arrangements used to manage, organise, and regulate an alliance".

Drawing on alliance governance literature, we can distinguish two main ideal types of ecosystem governance that seem to be equally applicable to the professional service firm context: *hub-firm ecosystems* and *distributed firm ecosystems*. The *hub-firm ecosystem* (Nambisan and Baron 2013), also referred to as the orchestra model (Nambisan and Sawhney 2008), the keystone model (Iansiti and Levien 2004) or the platform-based network model (Gawer and Cusumano 2002), assumes one dominant organisation. This dominant firm is the architect and conductor taking responsibility in selecting members, establishing, maintaining, changing and co-ordinating the ecosystem. An example from a knowledge-intensive industry is, for instance, a university which actively creates university-centred incubators to develop an entrepreneurial ecosystem in its region (OECD 2015). In contrast, the *distributed firm ecosystem*, also referred to as participant governed form, "is governed by the network members themselves with no separate and unique governance entity" (Provan and Kenis 2007: 234). A good example from the personal service firm context is Technical and Computer Graphics (TCG) as reported by Miles and Snow (1995). TCG is a highly interactive network of twenty-four knowledge-intensive firms located in Sydney, Australia. TCG is governed by shared responsibilities for managing internal and external network relations. Yet, co-ordination is triggered by specific client requests leading towards a client-driven project organisation.

The organisational field and institutional entrepreneurship

Over the last decades, an institutionalist turn has taken place across social science disciplines (see, among others, Greenwood *et al.* 2008). Complementary to the ecosystem perspective, institutionalists shifted attention outward to examine how the external environment influences organisations. In particular, teams, firms, and ecosystems are embedded in social institutions that define the 'rules of the game' and represent the 'routinised, taken for granted sets of ideas, beliefs and actions used in society' (Jennings *et al.* 2013). Institutionalists initially focused on explaining convergent change in response to isomorphic pressures within organisational fields (for example, DiMaggio and Powell 1983; Meyer and Rowan 1977; Scott 1987; Tolbert and Zucker 1983; Zucker 1977, 1983). As such, collective actors such as firms or networks of firms (like ecosystems) draw on normative, cognitive, and regulative institutional elements that provide them with templates of legitimate strategies, structures and practices. The overemphasis on the social environment imposing upon – rather than also emerging from – human interaction, however, produced increasing dissatisfaction with the inability of institutionalists to conceptualise divergent change (for instance, Barley and Tolbert 1997; DiMaggio and Powell 1991; Greenwood and Hinings 1996; Hirsch and Lounsbury 1997; Oliver 1991). In response, institutionalist scholars re-focused on explaining the role of interest and agency in divergent institutional change and, following the early lead of DiMaggio (1988), subsumed their efforts under the concept of 'institutional entrepreneurship'. This initial framing informed subsequent research in two ways. First, it pointed to the centrality of interest, agency and resources for explaining institutionalisation as a process rather than a state (as illustrated by Barley and Tolbert 1997; Greenwood and Hinings 1996). Second, it opened institutional arguments to ideas from the co-evolving entrepreneurship literature (as exemplified by Aldrich and Fiol 1994; Aldrich and Martinez 2001). The core argument of the institutional entrepreneurship literature, therefore, centres on the conditions and mechanisms that enable entrepreneurs to actively shape their institutional environment from within (Battilana, Leca and Boxenbaum 2009).

Institutional entrepreneurship has become an emerging and increasingly important research area in the field of professional services. More specifically, professions exercise 'normative, coercive, and mimetic pressures' (Muzio, Brock and Suddaby 2013) and therefore define the rules of the game in a particular professional field. Initially, institutional entrepreneurship was associated with disadvantaged actors located in the periphery of mature fields or within emerging fields, while entrepreneurial action by central, elite participants in mature fields has only been conceptualised relatively late as 'the toughest example of embedded action' (Greenwood and Suddaby 2006). In the following we review major streams and show how different empirical foci correspond to different phases of theory development, and explain how this correspondence shaped our understanding of institutional entrepreneurship in professional service firms.

Institutional entrepreneurship in emerging fields

Emerging fields are still relatively under-organised domains, characterised by weakly entrenched, relatively localised 'proto-institutions' (Lawrence, Hardy and Phillips 2002). Their constituents recognise some degree of mutual interest, but interact sporadically rather than through a structured system of social positions. Hence, actors lack clearly delineated reference groups of peer organisations whose isomorphic demands they would have to observe. This ambiguity provides considerable opportunity and motivation for institutional entrepreneurs to act strategically, shape emerging institutional arrangements to their interests, and secure for themselves a central and resourceful position in the emerging field (Garud, Jain and Kumaraswamy 2002; Maguire, Hardy and Lawrence 2004). Previous studies have investigated institutional entrepreneurship in emerging technological fields such as sponsorship strategies in setting common technological standards (Garud, Jain and Kumaraswamy 2002) or HIV/AIDS treatment advocacy in Canada (Maguire, Hardy and Lawrence 2004). These examples deal with specific types of knowledge-intensive organisational fields composed of technology developers that are not considered yet to have gained full professional status. As a result, the concept of institutional entrepreneurship has predominantly been developed from cases of strong agency, but weak embeddedness such as Sun Microsystems sponsoring the Java standard. This empirical one-sidedness has been reflected in theory development as critics note that the resultant understanding of agency is overly voluntaristic, individualistic and disembedded (see, for example, Lawrence, Suddaby and Leca 2009; Seo and Creed 2002). Disadvantaged actors may be more motivated to initiate and plan change, but they are also less equipped to make it stick. However, while the importance of mobilising coalitions and socio-political resources has been recognised, the focus largely remained on the skills and characteristics of mobilising actors (Garud, Jain and Kumaraswamy 2002; Maguire, Hardy and Lawrence 2004), rather than the activities of a collective. Accounts promote the image of 'a single organisation acting innovatively' (Greenwood and Suddaby 2006) or a heroic or 'hypermuscular' activist leading a movement of less empowered followers (Lawrence, Suddaby and Leca 2009), suggesting that this early research is more about entrepreneurs than entrepreneurship.

Institutional entrepreneurship in mature and maturing fields

Empirical work in this stream of research rediscovers classic professions such as accounting, health care and law as fruitful research settings, exemplifying highly institutionalised fields. The apparent stability and strength of institutional structures in professional contexts, as well as the recognised role of professionals as institutionalised and institutionalising actors (DiMaggio and Powell 1983; Scott 2008) make professional contexts an appropriate empirical setting for studying embedded motivated action. Instead of the professions *per se*, however, institutionalists now attend to professional service firms as elite actors in mature fields. For instance, Greenwood and colleagues published a series of papers on the efforts of the 'Big Five' global accounting firms to legitimise multi-disciplinary practice as an appropriate organisational form (Greenwood, Hinings and Suddaby 2002; Greenwood and Suddaby 2006; Suddaby and Greenwood 2005). Covaleski, Dirsmith and Rittenberg (2003) have also written on new work practices in the 'Big Five', while Sherer and Lee (2002) studied the career system in elite law firms in the United States and Reay, Golden-Biddle and Germann (2006) examined new work roles in health care.

What has remained surprisingly underexplored in this swing from emerging to mature fields, however, are those proto-professions and proto-professional firms whose institutional projects have made some progress, but whose organisational forms, practices and logics cannot yet be considered fully institutionalised. These arenas, which can be described as 'maturing' fields (Smets and Reihlen 2012), combining characteristics of emerging and mature fields, may hold particular conditions for institutional entrepreneurship. Typical cases of maturing fields are advertising or management consulting. Drawing on illustrative data from the German management consulting field, Reihlen, Smets and Veit (2010) explore those conditions and identify a portfolio of strategies such as co-option, lobbyism, membership, standardisation and influence that institutional entrepreneurs in the consulting industry employ and show how these strategies serve a dual purpose of creating individual competitive advantage and enhancing individual or collective institutional capital. This interplay of competitive and institutional strategy has previously received little attention.

Conclusion

Traditional conceptions of 'professionalism' have focused more on how professionals' knowledge base and behaviours are constrained and streamlined than on how they are challenged and developed, which has limited research in the intersection of entrepreneurship and professional services. Based on the review of existing research we conclude that professional service firms are rich in opportunity for entrepreneurial activity, but also provide a unique context for this. Aspects such as the specific motivational set-up of the professional, the ongoing micro-innovations in day-to-day service delivery, and the embedded nature of professional service work all shape the context for entrepreneurship in professional service firms.

The discussion of previous research has been structured around four levels of analysis – the entrepreneurial team, the entrepreneurial firm, the entrepreneurial ecosystem, and the organisational field. Different themes in relation to entrepreneurial activity emerged on the different levels of analysis. On a *team* level, the role of client projects and the engagement of the team as a locus for the creation and exploitation of entrepreneurial opportunities in professional service firms were important themes. The nature and quality of communication and interaction in this setting was found to be an important enabler of opportunity creation, and aspects such as the power distribution and actors' understandings of the situation and their roles in it were identified as shaping the conditions for this interaction. Future research may expand on the situated nature of team-level entrepreneurial processes by attending more systematically to differences in organisational and professional context and how these interact with the character of entrepreneurial processes. In particular, the ambiguous nature of power in the engagement team and beyond and its consequences for entrepreneurial activity deserve further attention.

Moving to the *firm* level of analysis, a first theme has been the management of new ventures of professional service firms. Although research in this area is limited, it points at a number of important enablers including the ability to learn quickly from experience or new hires, to create legitimacy and reputation and to develop and exploit social capital. A second theme dealt with entrepreneurial activity in the context of established professional service firms where it generally took the form of the establishment of new practices or services. This was shown to be a highly contested political process. While entrepreneurial opportunities are repeatedly created in ongoing client work, their exploitation through new institutionalised service offerings is challenged by a need to gain both internal and external legitimacy and support for these new services. Finally, research on the governance of entrepreneurial professional service firms suggested governance structures and processes that would give professionals a high level of autonomy and reward them for their individual achievements. Future research on the firm level may investigate further the entrepreneurial strategies of professional service firms and how these are related to different professional contexts. Additional research opportunities include the relationship between governance forms and the identification, seizing and realisation of entrepreneurial initiatives in professional service firms. Again, the role of power in these processes remains underexplored.

By drawing on the entrepreneurial *ecosystem* literature, we discussed key actors in the entrepreneurial ecosystems in the professional service firm context. Furthermore, social ties within the entrepreneurial ecosystem may enable or hinder ecosystem dynamism. Finally, we drew on the alliance governance literature to discuss governance aspects in ecosystems to distinguish between hub-firm ecosystems and distributed firm ecosystem. Previous research taking an ecosystem view of entrepreneurship in professional services has been largely lacking. This perspective thus provides multiple opportunities for future research including the nature and structure of professional service ecosystems, the enablers of collaboration with other actors than clients in professional service entrepreneurial ventures, and the character and consequences of different ecosystem governance structures.

Finally, on the *field* level, the review of current research reveals that the term 'entrepreneurship' in relation to professional service firms has been closely related to a research stream on 'institutional entrepreneurship'. This may be explained by the institutional embeddedness of especially the classical professional services and the ongoing struggles of the neo-professions to institutionalise. Entrepreneurship under these conditions requires changes not only of individual firm practices, but of institutionalised rules of the game, thus making especially the classical professional services suitable objects of study of this interplay between firm and institutional environment. Future research may specifically address the context of maturing fields, as opposed to the better researched emerging and mature fields, as many professional service fields may be characterised as such. The specific context of maturing fields further calls for a more nuanced investigation into the interplay between agency and structure in entrepreneurship in professional services. In addition, many professional service firms became diversified global players operating as multi-disciplinary practices across different national jurisdictions and cultures (see, for instance, Klimkeit and Reihlen 2016; Muzio and Faulconbridge 2013). Further research on how entrepreneurial professional service firms deal with institutional contradictions between home- and host-country structures and practices would enhance our understanding of managing internationalising professional service firms.

References

Abbott, A. (1988) *The System of Professions: An Essay on the Division of Expert Labor*, Chicago, IL: University of Chicago Press.

Adler, P. S. and Kwon, S. (2002) 'Social capital: Prospects for a new concept', *Academy of Management Review* 27(1): 17–40.

Adner, R. and Kapoor, R. (2010) 'Value creation in innovation ecosystems: How the structure of technological interdependence affects firm performance in new technology generations', *Strategic Management Journal* 30(3): 306–33.

Albers, S. (2010) 'Configurations of alliance governance systems', *Schmalenbach Business Review* 62: 204–33.

Aldrich, H. E. and Fiol, C. M. (1994) 'Fools rush in? The institutional context of industry creation', *Academy of Management Review* 19(4): 645–70.

Aldrich, H. E. and Martinez, M. A. (2001) 'Many are called, but few are chosen: An evolutionary perspective for the study of entrepreneurship', *Entrepreneurship Theory and Practice* 25(4): 41–57.

Alvesson, M. (2004) *Knowledge Work and Knowledge-intensive Firms*, Oxford: Oxford University Press.

Anand, N., Gardner, H. K. and Morris, T. (2007) 'Knowledge-based innovation: Emergence and embedding of new practice areas in management consulting firms', *Academy of Management Journal* 50(2): 406–28.

Argyris, C. and Schön, D. (1978) *Organizational Learning: A Theory of Action Perspective*, Reading, MA: Addison-Wesley.

Barley, S. R. and Tolbert, P. S. (1997) 'Institutionalization and structuration: Studying the links between action and institution', *Organization Studies* 18(1): 93–117.

Battilana, J., Leca, B. and Boxenbaum, E. (2009) 'How actors change institutions: Towards a theory of institutional entrepreneurship', *Academy of Management Annals* 3(1): 65–107.

Brandl, J. and Bullinger, B. (2009) 'Reflections on the societal conditions for the pervasiveness of entrepreneurial behavior in Western societies', *Journal of Management Inquiry* 18: 159–73.

Brown, J. L., Cooper, D. J., Greenwood, R. and Hinings, C. R. (1996) 'Strategic alliances within a Big Six accounting firm: A case study', *International Studies of Management and Organization* 26(2): 59–79.

Capelleras, J., Mole, K. F., Greene, F. J. and Storey, D. J. (2008) 'Do more heavily regulated economies have poorer performing new ventures? Evidence from Britain and Spain', *Journal of International Business Studies* 39: 688–704.

Carlile, P. R. (2002) 'A pragmatic view of knowledge and boundaries: Boundary objects in new product development', *Organization Science* 13(4): 442–55.

Ceccagnoli, M., Forman, C., Huang, P. and Wu, D. J. (2012) 'Co-creation of value in a platform ecosystem: The case of enterprise software', *MIS Quarterly* 36(1): 263–90.

Clarysse, B. and Moray, N. (2004) 'A process study of entrepreneurial team formation: The case of a research-based spin-off', *Journal of Business Venturing* 19(1): 55–79.

Cooper, A. C. (1981) 'Strategic management: New ventures and small business', *Long Range Planning* 14(5): 39–45.

Cooper, A. C., Gimeno-Gascon, F. J. and Woo, C. Y. (1994) 'Initial human and financial capital as predictors of new venture performance', *Journal of Business Venturing* 9(5): 371–95.

Covaleski, M. A., Dirsmith, M. W. and Rittenberg, L. (2003) 'Jurisdictional disputes over professional work: The institutionalization of the global knowledge expert', *Accounting, Organizations and Society* 28(4): 323–55.

DiMaggio, P. (1988) 'Interest and agency in institutional theory', in Zucker, L. G. (ed.) *Institutional Patterns and Organizations: Culture and Environment*, Cambridge, MA: Ballinger.

DiMaggio, P. and Powell, W. W. (1983) 'The iron cage revisited: Institutional isomorphism and collective rationality in organizational fields', *American Sociological Review* 48(2): 147–60.

DiMaggio, P. and Powell, W. W. (1991) 'Introduction', in Powell, W. W. and DiMaggio, P. (eds) *The New Institutionalism in Organizational Analysis*, Chicago, IL: University of Chicago Press.

Dougherty, D. and Takacs, C. H. (2004) 'Team play: Heedful interrelating as the boundary for innovation', *Long Range Planning* 37: 569–90.

Edmondson, A. C. (1999) 'Psychological safety and learning behaviour in work teams', *Administrative Science Quarterly* 44(2): 350–83.

Edmondson, A. C. (2002) 'The local and variegated nature of learning in organizations: A group level perspective', *Organization Science* 13(2): 128–46.

Empson, L. (2007) 'Your partnership. Surviving and thriving in a changing world: The special nature of partnership', in Empson, L. (ed.) *Managing the Modern Law Firm*, Oxford: Oxford University Press.

Empson, L. (2012) 'Beyond dichotomies: A multi-stage model of governance in professional service firms', in Reihlen, M. and Werr, A. (eds) *Handbook of Research on Entrepreneurship in Professional Services*, Cheltenham: Edward Elgar.

Empson, L. and Chapman, C. (2006) 'Partnership versus corporation: Implications of alternative forms of governance in professional service firms', *Research in the Sociology of Organizations* 24: 139–70.

Ensleya, M. D., Pearson, A. W. and Amasonc, A. C. (2002) 'Understanding the dynamics of new venture top management teams: Cohesion, conflict, and new venture performance', *Journal of Business Venturing* 17: 365–86.

Fosstenløkken, S. M., Løwendahl, B. R. and Revang, Ö. (2003) 'Knowledge development through client interaction: A comparative study', *Organization Studies* 24(6): 859–79.

Freidson, E. (2001) *Professionalism: The Third Logic*, Cambridge: Polity Press.

Frese, M. (2009) 'Toward a psychology of entrepreneurship – an action theory perspective', *Foundations and Trends in Entrepreneurship* 5(6): 437–96.

Gardner, H. K., Anand, N. and Morris, T. (2008) 'Chartering new territory: Diversification, legitimacy, and practice area creation in professional service firms', *Journal of Organizational Behavior* 29: 1101–21.

Gartner, W. B. (1985) 'A conceptual framework for describing the phenomenon of new venture creation', *Academy of Management Review* 10(4): 696–706.

Garud, R., Jain, S. and Kumaraswamy, A. (2002) 'Institutional entrepreneurship in the sponsorship of common technological standards: The case of Sun Microsystems and Java', *Academy of Management Journal* 45(1): 196–214.

Gawer, A. and Cusumano, M. (2002) *Platform Leadership: How Intel, Microsoft, and Cisco Drive Industry Innovation*, Cambridge, MA: Harvard Business School Press.

Glückler, J. and Armbrüster, T. (2003) 'Bridging uncertainty in management consulting: The mechanisms of trust and networked reputation', *Organization Studies* 24(2): 269–97.

Grabher, G. (2001) 'Ecologies of creativity: The Village, the Group, and the heterarchic organisation of the British advertising industry', *Environment and Planning* 33(2): 351–74.

Granovetter, M. S. (1985) 'Economic action and social structure – The problem of embeddedness', *American Journal of Sociology* 91(3): 481–510.

Greenwood, R. and Empson, L. (2003) 'The professional partnership: Relic or exemplary form of governance?', *Organization Studies* 24(6): 909–33.

Greenwood, R. and Hinings, C. R. (1996) 'Understanding radical organizational change: Bringing together the old and the new institutionalism', *Academy of Management Review* 21(4): 1022–54.

Greenwood, R., Hinings, C. R. and Brown, J. (1990) '"P²-form" strategic managment: Corporate practices in professional partnerships', *Academy of Management Journal* 33(4): 725–55.

Greenwood, R., Hinings, C. R. and Suddaby, R. (2002) 'Theorizing change: The role of professional associations in the transformation of institutionalized fields', *Academy of Management Journal* 45(1): 58–80.

Greenwood, R., Oliver, C., Sahlin, K. and Suddaby, R. (2008) 'Introduction', in Greenwood, R., Oliver, C., Suddaby, R. and Sahlin, K. (eds) *The Sage Handbook of Organizational Institutionalism*, Los Angeles: Sage.

Greenwood, R. and Suddaby, R. (2006) 'Institutional entrepreneurship in mature fields: The Big Five accounting firms', *Academy of Management Journal* 49(1): 27–48.

Groß, C. and Kieser, A. (2006) 'Consultants on the way to professionalization?', *Research in the Sociology of Organizations* 24: 69–100.

Günther, A. (2012) *Entrepreneurial Strategies of Professional Service Firms: An Analysis of Commercial Law Firm Spin-offs in Germany*, Cologne: Kölner Wissenschaftsverlag.

Hagedoorn, J. and Frankort, H. T. (2008) 'The gloomy side of embeddedness: The effects of overembeddedness on inter-firm partnership formation', in Baum, J. A. C. and Rowley, T. J. (eds) *Network Strategy*, Bingley: Emerald Press.

Handley, K., Sturdy, A., Fincham, R. and Clark, T. (2012) 'A space for learning? Physical, relational and agential space in a strategy consultancy project', in Reihlen, M. and Werr, A. (eds) *Handbook of Research on Entrepreneurship in Professional Services*, Cheltenham: Edward Elgar.

Hanlon, G. (2004) 'Institutional forms and organizational structures: Homology, trust and reputational capital in professional service firms', *Organization* 11(2): 187–210.

Hargadon, A. B. (1998) 'Firms as knowledge brokers: Lessons in pursuing continuous innovation', *California Management Review* 40(3): 209–27.

Hargadon, A. B. and Bechky, B. A. (2006) 'When collections of creatives become creative collectives: A field study of problem solving at work', *Organization Science* 17(4): 484–500.

Harlacher, D. (2010) *The Governance of Professional Service Firms*, Cologne: Kölner Wissenschaftsverlag.

Harlacher, D. and Reihlen, M. (2014) 'Governance of professional service firms: A configurational approach', *Business Research* 7(1): 125–60.

Hearn, G. and Pace, C. (2006) 'Value-creating ecologies: Understanding next generation business systems', *Foresight* 8(1): 55–65.

Heusinkveld, S. and Benders, J. (2002) 'Between professional dedication and corporate design – Exploring forms of new concept development in consultancies', *International Studies of Management and Organization* 32(4): 104–22.

Heusinkveld, S. and Benders, J. (2005) 'Contested commodification: Consultancies and their struggle with new concept development', *Human Relations* 58(3): 283–310.

Heusinkveld, S., Benders, J. and van den Berg, R. (2009) 'From market sensing to new concept development in consultancies: The role of information processing and organizational capabilities', *Technovation* 29(8): 509–16.

Hirsch, P. M. and Lounsbury, M. (1997) 'Ending the family quarrel: Toward a reconciliation of "old" and "new" institutionalisms', *American Behavioral Scientist* 40(4): 406–18.

Hoang, H. and Antoncic, B. (2003) 'Network-based research in entrepreneurship: A critical review', *Journal of Business Venturing* 18(2): 165–87.

Iansiti, M. and Levien, R. (2004) *The Keystone Advantage*, Boston, MA: Harvard Business School Press.

Jacobides, M. G., Knudsen, T. and Augier, M. (2006) 'Benefiting from innovation: Value creation, value appropriation and the role of industry architectures', *Research Policy* 35(8): 1200–21.

Jennings, P. D., Greenwood, R., Lounsbury, M. D. and Suddaby, R. (2013) 'Institutions, entrepreneurs, and communities: A special issue on entrepreneurship', *Journal of Business Venturing* 28(1): 1–9.

Klimkeit, D. and Reihlen, M. (2016) 'Local responses to global integration in a transnational professional service firm', *Journal of Professions and Organization* 3: 9–61.

Kolz, A. (2007) 'To Miami's Greenberg Traurig, culture is no vice', *Legal Times* 5 March.

Larson, M. S. (1977) *The Rise of Professionalism*, Berkely, CA: University of California Press.

Lawrence, T. B., Hardy, C. and Phillips, N. (2002) 'Institutional effects of interorganizational collaboration: The emergence of proto-institutions', *Academy of Management Journal* 45(1): 281–90.

Lawrence, T. B., Suddaby, R. and Leca, B. (2009) 'Introduction: Theorizing and studying institutional work', in Lawrence, T., Suddaby, R. and Leca, B. (eds) *Institutional Work: Actors and Agency in Institutional Studies of Organizations*, Cambridge: Cambridge University Press.

Losada, M. and Heaphy, E. (2004) 'The role of positivity and connectivity in the performance of business teams: A nonlinear dynamics model', *American Behavioral Scientist* 47(6): 740–64.

Lowendahl, B. R. (2005) *Strategic Management of Professional Service Firms*, Copenhagen: Copenhagen Business School Press, 3rd edition.

Maguire, S., Hardy, C. and Lawrence, T. B. (2004) 'Institutional entrepreneurship in emerging fields: HIV/AIDS treatment advocacy in Canada', *Academy of Management Journal* 47(5): 657–79.

Maurer, I. and Ebers, M. (2006) 'Dynamics of social capital and their performance implications: Lessons from biotechnology start-ups', *Administrative Science Quarterly* 51(2): 262–92.

Meyer, J. W. and Rowan, B. (1977) 'Institutionalized organizations: Formal structure as myth and ceremony', *American Journal of Sociology* 83(2): 340–63.

Miles, R. E. and Snow, C. C. (1995) 'The new network firm: A spherical structure built on a human investment philosophy', *Organizational Dynamics* 24(4): 5–18.

Mintzberg, H. (1979) *The Structuring of Organizations*, Englewood Cliffs, NJ: Prentice-Hall.

Mitchell, R. K., Busenitz, L. W., Bird, B., Gaglio, C. M., McMullen, J. S., Morse, E. A. and Smith, J. B. (2007) 'The central question in entrepreneurial cognition research 2007', *Entrepreneurship Theory and Practice* 31(1): 1–27.

Moore, J. F. (1993) 'Predators and prey: A new ecology of competition', *Harvard Business Review* 71: 75–86.

Morris, T. (2001) 'Asserting property rights: Knowledge codification in the professional service firm', *Human Relations* 54(7): 819–38.

Muzio, D., Brock, D. M. and Suddaby, R. (2013) 'Professions and institutional change: Towards an institutionalist sociology of the professions', *Journal of Management Studies* 50(5): 699–721.

Muzio, D. and Faulconbridge, J. (2013) 'The global professional service firm: "One firm" models versus (Italian) distant institutionalized practices', *Organization Studies* 34(7): 897–925.

Nahapiet, J. and Ghoshal, S. (1998) 'Social capital, intellectual capital, and the organizational advantage', *Academy of Management Review* 23(2): 242–66.

Nambisan, S. and Baron, R. A. (2013) 'Entrepreneurship in innovation ecosystems: Entrepreneurs' self-regulatory processes and their implications for new venture success', *Entrepreneurship Theory and Practice* 37(5): 1071–97.

Nambisan, S. and Sawhney, M. (2008) *The Global Brain: Your Roadmap for Innovating Faster and Smarter in a Networked World*, Upper Saddle River, NJ: Wharton School Publishing.

Niewiem, S. and Richter, A. (2004) 'The changing balance of power in the consulting market', *Business Strategy Review* 15(1): 8–13.

Nikolova, N. (2012) 'Innovating through Clients', in Reihlen, M. and Werr, A. (eds) *Handbook of Research on Entrepreneurship in Professional Service Firms*, Cheltenham: Edward Elgar.

Nikolova, N., Möllering, G. and Reihlen, M. (2015) 'Trusting as a "leap of faith": Trust-building practices in client-consultant relationships', *Scandinavian Journal of Management* 31(2): 232–45.

OECD. (2015) *Lessons Learned from the Lüneburg Innovation Incubator: Case Study Report*, Paris: Organization for Economic Co-Operation and Development.

Oliver, C. (1991) 'Strategic responses to institutional processes', *Academy of Management Review* 16(1): 145–79.

Ostgaard, T. A. and Birley, S. (1996) 'New venture growth and personal networks', *Journal of Business Research* 36: 37–50.

Phillips, D. J. (2002) 'A genealogical approach to organizational life chances: The parent-progeny transfer among Silicon Valley law firms, 1946–1996', *Administrative Science Quarterly* 47: 474–506.

Phillips, D. J. (2005) 'Organizational genealogies and the persistence of gender inequality: The case of Silicon Valley law firms', *Administrative Science Quarterly* 50: 440–72.

Provan, K. G. and Kenis, P. (2007) 'Modes of network governance: Structure, management, and effectiveness', *Journal of Public Administration Research and Theory* 18: 229–52.

Ram, M. (1999) 'Managing consultants in a small firm: A case study', *Journal of Management Studies* 36(6): 875–97.

Ramoglou, S. and Tsang, E. (2016) 'A realist perspective of entrepreneurship: Opportunities as propensities', *Academy of Management Review* 41(3): 410–34.

Reay, T., Golden-Biddle, K. and Germann, K. (2006) 'Legitimizing a new role: Small wins and micorprocesses of change', *Academy of Management Journal* 49(5): 977–98.

Reihlen, M. and Apel, B. A. (2007) 'Internationalization of professional service firms as learning – a constructivist approach', *International Journal of Service Industry Management* 18(2): 140–51.

Reihlen, M., Seckler, C. and Werr, A. (2017) 'Entrepreneurial ecosystems: A conceptual framework and research agenda for the professional service field', Paper presented at the Academy of Management Best Paper Proceedings, Atlanta.

Reihlen, M., Smets, M. and Veit, A. (2010) 'Management consultancies as institutional agents: Strategies for creating and sustaining institutional capital', *Schmalenbach Business Review* 62(3): 318–40.

Reihlen, M. and Werr, A. (eds) (2012) *Handbook of Research on Entrepreneurship in Professional Services*, Cheltenham: Edward Elgar.

Reihlen, M. and Werr, A. (2015) 'Entrepreneurship and professional service firms', in Empson, L., Muzio, D., Broschak, J. P. and Hinings, B. (eds) *The Oxford Handbook of Professional Service Firms*, Oxford: Oxford University Press.

Ringberg, T. and Reihlen, M. (2008) 'Towards a socio-cognitive approach to knowledge transfer', *Journal of Management Studies* 45(5): 912–35.

Rueschemeyer, D. (1964) 'Doctors and lawyers: A comment on the theory of professions', *Canadian Journal of Sociology and Anthropology* 1: 17–30.

Saks, M. (2012) 'Defining a profession: The role of knowledge and expertise', *Professions and Professionalism* 2(1): 1–10.

Sandberg, W. R. and Hofer, C. (1987) 'Improving new venture performance: The role of strategy, industry structure, and the entrepreneur', *Journal of Business Venturing* 2: 5–28.

Schön, D. (1983) *The Reflective Practitioner – How Professionals Think in Action*, Aldershot: Avebury.

Schumpeter, J. A. (1942) *Capitalism, Socialism, Democracy*, New York: Harper & Brothers.

Scott, W. R. (1987) 'The adolescence of institutional theory', *Administrative Science Quarterly* 32(4): 493–512.

Scott, W. R. (2008) 'Lords of the dance: Professionals as institutional agents', *Organization Studies* 29(2): 219–38.

Seo, M. and Creed, W. E. D. (2002) 'Institutional contradictions, praxis, and institutional change: A dialectical perspective', *Academy of Management Review* 27(2): 222–47.

Sherer, P. D. and Lee, K. (2002) 'Institutional change in large law firms: A resource dependency and institutional perspective', *Academy of Management Journal* 45(1): 102–30.

Skjølsvik, T., Løwendahl, B. R., Kvålshaugen, R. and Fosstenløkken, S. M. (2007) 'Choosing to learn and learning to choose: Strategies for client co-production and knowledge development', *California Management Review* 49(3): 110–27.

Smets, M. and Reihlen, M. (2012) 'Institutional entrepreneurship: A literature review and analysis of the maturing consulting field', in Reihlen, M. and Werr, A. (eds) *Handbook of Research on Entrepreneurship in Professional Service Firms*, Cheltenham: Edward Elgar.

Spigel, B. (2015) 'The relational organization of entrepreneurial ecosystems', *Entrepreneurship Theory and Practice*, June. Available at: http://dx.doi.org/10.1111/etap.12167.

Starbuck, W. H. (1993) 'Keeping a butterfly and an elephant in a house of cards: The elements of exceptional success', *Journal of Management Studies* 30(6): 885–97.

Stuart, T. E. and Sorenson, O. (2007) 'Strategic networks and entrepreneurial ventures', *Strategic Entrepreneurship Journal* 1(3/4): 211–27.

Suddaby, R. and Greenwood, R. (2005) 'Rhetorical strategies of legitimacy', *Administrative Science Quarterly* 50(1): 35–67.

Swan, J. A. and Newell, S. (1995) 'The role of professional associations in technology diffusion', *Organization Studies* 16(5): 847–74.

Swart, J. and Kinnie, N. (2003) 'Sharing knowledge in knowledge-intensive firms', *Human Resource Management Journal* 13(2): 60–75.

Tolbert, P. S. and Zucker, L. G. (1983) 'Institutional sources of change in the formal structure of organizations: The diffusion of civil service reform, 1880–1935', *Administrative Science Quarterly* 28(1): 22–39.

van der Borgh, M., Cloodt, M. and Romme, A. G. L. (2012) 'Value creation by knowledge-based ecosystems: Evidence from a field study', *R&D Management* 42(2): 150–69.

Venkataraman, S. (1997) 'The distinctive domain of entrepreneurship research: An editor's perspective', in Katz, J. A. and Brockhaus, R. (eds) *Advances in Entrepreneurship, Firm Emergence and Growth: Volume 3*, Greenwich, CT: JAI Press.

von Nordenflycht, A. (2010) 'What is a professional service firm? Towards a theory and taxonomy of knowledge intensive firms', *Academy of Management Review* 35(1): 155–74.

Warren, M. E. (2008) 'The natural and logic of bad social capital', in Castiglione, D., van Deth, J. W. and Wolleb, G. (eds) *The Handbook of Social Capital*, Oxford: Oxford University Press.

Werr, A. (2012) 'Knowledge integration as heedful interrelating: Towards a behavioral approach to knowledge management in professional service firms', in Reihlen, M. and Werr, A. (eds) *Handbook of Research on Entrepreneurship in Professional Service Firms*, Cheltenham: Edward Elgar.

Werr, A. and Runsten, P. (2013) 'Understanding the role of representation in interorganizational knowledge integration – A case study of an IT outsourcing project', *The Learning Organization* 20(2): 118–33.

Wood, M. S. and McKinley, W. (2010) 'The production of entrepreneurial opportunity: A constructivist perspective', *Strategic Entrepreneurship* 4: 66–84.

Zimmerman, M. A. and Zeitz, G. J. (2002) 'Beyond survival: Achieving vew venture growth by building legitimacy', *Academy of Management Review* 27(3): 414–31.

Zucker, L. G. (1977) 'The role of institutionalization in cultural persistence', *American Sociological Review* 47(5): 726–43.

Zucker, L. G. (1983) 'Organizations as institutions', *Research in the Sociology of Organizations*, Greenwich: JAI Press.

Part III
Key issues related to professions and professional service firms

8 The implications for gender of work in professional service firms
The case of law and accountancy

Hilary Sommerlad and Louise Ashley

Introduction

Over the past forty years, the gender composition of many professions has changed dramatically. For instance, within the legal profession of England and Wales, women's representation has grown tenfold since the mid-1980s, and from 1992 onwards female entry to the profession has exceeded male entry. As a result, over the past twenty years the number of female admissions has grown by 50.6 per cent, compared to 6 per cent for men over the equivalent period, and by 2015 women represented 48.8 per cent of all solicitors (Law Society 2016). The entry of women has then been a key factor in the profession's expansion by almost 70 per cent between 1995 and 2015. These patterns are mirrored both in other jurisdictions and other professions. For instance, in the Australian legal profession there is a close to even split between males (51.5 per cent) and females (48.5 per cent) and female entrants (+19.3 per cent) outnumber males (+5.4 per cent) (Urbis 2015). In the United States women represent 45 per cent of associates in private practice (American Bar Association 2017). Accountancy has also seen a steady growth in female practitioners: in the United Kingdom the number of qualified female accountants rose from 30 per cent to 34 per cent between 2006 and 2011 (Financial Reporting Council 2015), and in the United States in 2015 63 per cent of all accountants and auditors were women (Bureau of Labor Statistics 2015), while in Canada women represent 50.5 per cent of all auditors, accountants and investment professionals (Statistics Canada 2015).

However, the statistics also reveal that the mass entry of women has produced occupations which are horizontally and vertically segregated on gender lines. Compared to their male counterparts, women are less likely to be partners, more likely to be working in specialisms which are 'female typed' and which are also less prestigious, and to be paid less; for instance, in the English legal profession there is a gender pay gap which starts early in women's careers and increases in line with their progression, such that female legal professionals are paid on average 10.3 per cent less than their male colleagues. In the accountancy profession in the United Kingdom in 2016 a female accountant's average basic salary was worth 83 per cent of that awarded to a man. This pay gap is still more evident with regard to bonuses, where women in 2016 earned an average of

£8,260, which is 36.9 per cent less than the amount received by men (Kirton 2016). In the United States women working as accountants or auditors earned a weekly median salary of $999 in 2014, compared to the weekly median salary of $1,236 earned by men in the same fields.

Further, while there was some progress towards gender equality within both professions from the late 1980s through to the turn of the century, this has stalled in the last fifteen years. For example, between 1989 and 2012 the percentage of female partners in American accountancy firms rose from 1 per cent to 19 per cent, an increase of 1,800 per cent; however today, while 47 per cent of all professional staff at Certified Public Accountancy firms are female, women make up just 22 per cent of partners and principals (American Institute of Certified Public Accountants 2015). In England and Wales, the proportion of women solicitors who occupy senior positions has hardly changed over the past ten years; in 2015 under 30 per cent of partners were women, and a higher proportion of men (48 per cent) than women (22 per cent) were partners, irrespective of experience (Law Society 2016). Moreover, women are more likely to be salaried partners than to have equity, and it seems that the more prestigious the law firm, the lower the numbers of female partners: the overall percentage of female partners for the top 100 firms was 24 per cent in 2014, and reduces to just over 18 per cent for the most prestigious 'magic circle' law firms (Chambers Student 2014). The statistics indicate too that the intersection of gender with other diversity strands generally compounds its negative effects. For example, the Black, Asian, Minority Ethnic (BAME) female solicitor is more likely to be a solo practitioner than their white peer and to be working in low-status and less profitable sectors of the profession (Law Society 2016).

Our discussion of these issues will be situated in the (changing) wider socio-economic context, and will focus on the corporate sectors of law and accountancy in England and Wales and the United States. While the two professions are distinct in terms of their regulatory framework and boundaries, they are broadly comparable in that both were formerly exclusively male, and, as the above statistics indicate, have followed a similar pattern in their subsequent inclusion of women. Further, there are parallels in the ways in which, over the course of the last thirty years, they have restructured their models of practice based on a commercial or capitalist logic or rationality (Hanlon 1998; Suddaby, Gendron and Lam 2009). There is also a direct relationship between this commercialisation of their professional ethos and practices, their massive expansion and the dramatic increase in female participation in the corporate sectors of both professions (Sommerlad and Ashley 2015). These intertwined developments are related to two major socio-economic revolutions which took place in both the United Kingdom and the United States from, roughly, the 1960s onwards: first, the (partial) modernisation and democratisation of society (Burrage 2010), including higher education and professional labour markets, and, second, the socio-economic, political and cultural restructuring which resulted from the development of neo-liberal global capitalism from the mid-1970s onwards. These and other factors underpinning the changes will now be explored further.

Explaining the gender shift in law and accountancy

For both social democratic and economic reasons, the post-war Keynesian interventionist states oversaw an expansion and opening up of higher education (Willemse and de Beer 2012), while the cultural and political changes generated by the civil rights movements of the 1960s (such as Second Wave Feminism) facilitated women's mass move into higher education, and generated equal opportunities policies and anti-discrimination laws which supported their participation in formerly male-dominated labour markets. From extremely low levels of participation in both professions following the lifting of formal barriers to entry in the 1920s, these developments resulted, from the 1970s onwards, in a rapid increase in the numbers of women lawyers and accountants. Thus, in 1973 the admission of 222 women into the English legal profession tripled their numbers, and by 1979 34 per cent of all US accountants and auditors were women.

The second cause of the rise in the numbers of female accountants and lawyers was the dramatic expansion which both professions began to undergo in the late 1970s. Here the neo-liberal global economic order, with its deregulated capital markets and lowered trade barriers (the result of the ending of the dominance of the Keynesian paradigm following the oil crisis and stagflation of the 1970s), clearly placed law and accountancy centre stage (Cohen 2002). The need for new financial instruments and forms of legal regulation, both national and international, produced an extraordinary boom in corporate business, stimulating the emergence of large multinational firms of lawyers and accountants (Lee 1992), dramatically accentuating the division between these firms and other sectors of their professions, and eroding the power of the professional association. The central role played by the new 'professional entrepreneurs' (Dezalay 1995a) in building the cultures of global capitalism, entailed a restructuring of their sectors for the international market (Flood 1995); this transnational deal making and regulation building resulted in their penetration by the discourses of entrepreneurialism (Boon 2014; Sommerlad 2011), inserting a neo-liberal logic so that commercialism came to constitute their primary rationale, rendering obsolete traditional models of professionalisation (Lee 1992; Olgiati 1995). This 'commercialised professionalism' (Hanlon 1998) therefore not only generated structural changes in the (highly bureaucratised) corporate law and accountancy firms, but also, as market rationality, financialisation and the use of new technology became increasingly dominant characteristics, in their working practices, habitus and logic. The related shifting of the centre of power and control from the professional association to large professional service firms (Cooper and Robson 2006) accelerated the process of isomorphism between these firms and corporate organisations (Mueller, Carter and Ross-Smith 2011). This process was then furthered by the growing dominance of powerful clients, generating significant downward pressures on cost, an increasingly aggressive drive to maximise profits and an intensification of the work ethic, producing a 'hypercompetitive professional ideology' (Epstein *et al.* 1999; Hanlon 1999; Wald 2010).

Clearly the move to an industrial mode of production (Flood 2007), which this capitalist model of professionalism required, entailed the de-composition and re-constitution of legal work and elongation of professional structures, so that standardised, specialised part work could be assigned to different hierarchies of legal 'professionals' (Sandefur 2007; Susskind 2008). This horizontal segregation and wholesale internal rationalisation of labour processes therefore depended on the introduction of a new stratum of lower cost expert labour (Derber 1982; Larson 1977); that is 'adjunct employees' (Hagan and Kay 1995) who were effectively technicians (Dezelay 1995b). There was an intricate reciprocal relationship between this need for both more and low-level labour (accentuated by the high rates of attrition in both professions) and the burgeoning numbers of female law and accountancy graduates, rapidly overcoming firms' former reluctance to employ women (Bolton and Muzio 2007). However, there is a further, complex interplay between this process of stratification and the cultural resilience in these traditionally patriarchal fields of the archaic discourses of femininity, and particularly motherhood, previously used to justify women's exclusion. This discourse marked female professionals as inherently unsuited to full professional status, and certainly to partnership, rationalising their allocation to the new, sub-professional, less well remunerated, transient roles which the corporate sectors of both professions required. Women thus represented the disposable (sub-professional) resource which rendered possible the commercialised professionalism of professional service firms.

The version of complexity theory of Sylvia Walby (2007) offers a useful tool for understanding the inter-relationship outlined above between gender and the reconfiguration of the systems of organisation and governance, and occupational cultures, which together comprise the professional field (Bourdieu 1977; Bourdieu and Wacquant 1992). Walby conceptualises the social order as a series of systems, each of which exists within a wider environment comprising all the other systems with which it is connected. While these systems are not determined by each other, they are nevertheless causally related, and can thus be understood as enmeshed in a series of self-reproducing relationships. A number of features of complexity theory make it particularly relevant in the current context. These include its reminder that the speed and pace of change is not uniform between systems and that a system may adapt to changes in its environment either to restore equilibrium (which Walby terms self-equilibration), or through more radical transformation enabling dominant elites to insulate themselves against threats to their power (see Beaverstock, Hubbard and Short 2004). Ongoing gendered inequalities can therefore be conceptualised in terms of the relationships between complex systems such as public and private patriarchy, neo-liberal globalised capitalism and the professions themselves, and the co-evolution of these systems across time and space. Elite domination of the path of this co-evolution ensures the persistence of patriarchal elements of the professions. This is despite both women's demands for equal inclusion and the displacement of traditional craft and kinship cultures, with their explicit reliance on ascriptive criteria in selection and promotion (Burrage 1996), by an ostensibly meritocratic, commercialised professionalism, characterised by bureaucratic recruitment and promotion processes grounded in objective criteria which discourage direct discrimination.

Further, the complex interaction between these different systems is exemplified by the double-edged nature of bureaucratisation, which, in its vindication of the neo-liberal discourse of the intrinsic rationality and hence fairness of labour markets has rationalised the displacement of the equal opportunities policies of the 1960s and 1970s by the diversity and inclusion agenda (Ashley 2010; Braithwaite 2010). The refusal of this agenda to recognise the socio-cultural context of women's experiences, and particularly the persistence of traditional gendered divisions of labour in the private domain which constrain agentic choice (Walkerdine, Lucey and Melody 2001), justifies its individualised, depoliticised approach to diversification – thereby, in practice, also facilitating the persistence of patron–client relationships, and hence cloning (Kanter 1977).

In summary, while the dramatic and ongoing increases from the 1970s onwards in the numbers of women accountants and lawyers are symptomatic of increased gender equality in terms of women's mass participation in public life, their inclusion has been articulated with the persistence of archaic structures and discourses around gender, and, as we discuss below, may even, in some respects, have accentuated these. In other words, the experience of women accountants and lawyers can be narrated as a story of continuity and change, or, following complexity theory, of the professions' adaptation to environmental changes by channelling the possibilities generated by women's mass entry into the professions into a path of development characterised both by work intensification and subservience to the client *and* pre-modern patriarchal practices, thereby insulating the system from any substantive re-working of the gender order.

In the following section, we take up these arguments to reflect further on the relationship between the profession's patriarchal culture and the progressive embedding of a capitalist logic at both the occupational and organisational level, and in particular the demand for 'total commitment' (Sommerlad and Sanderson 1998) enforced through the tournament. We explore the tension between this demand, gender stereotypes and their relationship to women's unpaid role in social reproduction, and the significance of this (historical) role in maintaining patriarchal culture. In the subsequent section, we discuss how the resulting ambivalence surrounding the concept of a woman professional is both accentuated by (and causative of) ongoing sexual stereotyping and overtly misogynistic and exclusionary practices. Finally, we return to complexity theory to consider, briefly, likely future trends, including those related to the recent resurgence in populist, anti-feminist discourse.

Patriarchal capitalism, separate spheres and commitment

The two spheres

An understanding of the complex relationship between continuity and change within the professions must start with an analysis of role and effect of the ideology of separate, gendered, public and private spheres (Walby 1997). A key dimension of classical liberal theory, separate spheres ideology is embedded within the structural parameters of nineteenth century patriarchal capitalism, which was in turn crucial in shaping the modern professions of accountancy and law (Witz 1990). Its postulation of an absolute divide between the public and the private was the basis for the construction of the archetypal legal subject as a free and equal individual who is rational, autonomous, and self-sufficient – that is unencumbered. As feminist theorists have pointed out, this construct was therefore gendered male, and presupposed the existence of a (house) wife to take care of his daily needs (Pateman 1988), thereby naturalising male dominance in the public sphere and restricting (middle class) women to the home, with responsibility for social reproduction. For Pateman (1988), the implication of both spheres in each other was effected through a 'sexual contract' which established the private realm as an extra-legal space, where men *were* the law, while also reserving the public sphere for them. The ideology of separate spheres (crucial to which is the ideology of motherhood) was thus a key component of both private and public patriarchy from the early nineteenth century onwards.

These ideological assumptions about the distinct, gendered, responsibilities and capacities which the public and private spheres generate and require, exemplify what Bourdieu (2001: viii) described in his discussion of masculine domination as "long reified ways of thinking, feeling, and acting" which – despite being historical constructs – appear natural, 'eternal'. As a result, these ideologies are able to remain active properties of the field of power (and hence of multinational capitalism and the professions), for, following Bourdieu, the habitus of the professional field is history embodied and incorporated (Bourdieu and Wacquant 1992). Contemporary commonsense discourses about gender are therefore grounded in these archaic ideologies and discourses, which thus form the basis for ostensibly modernising theories such as human capital and rational choice. Men therefore continue to be assumed to possess a range of qualities, such as objectivity, rationality and competitiveness, which fit them for public life, while women's supposed natural affinity with care still tends to position them as emotional and irrational. The resulting synergy between masculinity and professional identity is then reinforced in the everyday practices and structures of contemporary labour markets. Recognition that in practice there is an intimate relationship between work – paid and unpaid, formal and informal – undertaken in diverse socio-economic spaces (Glucksmann 1995) would place pressure on employers to assume some responsibility for the costs of social reproduction. However, the fiction is that the private sphere is entirely separate and the primary domain of woman can justify both the devaluation of her labour and the retention of indirectly discriminatory structures and practices (Crompton and Sanderson 1990; Fraser 2016).

Long hours

One such discriminatory practice, grounded in the separate spheres ideology, is the requirement to work excessively long hours. Men's irresponsibility for social reproduction and hence the male breadwinner discourse, together with the fuzzy boundary between their homosocial activities and work, made long days a traditional part of professional life. As Sugarman (1996) shows, the role of nineteenth-century professionals in public life, as pillars of the community, and 'heroic' mythologies of work marathons produced a conceptualisation of professional service as open ended.

However, the relationship between time and professionalism is of course not static, but has been profoundly affected both by the entry of women and ongoing developments in globalised capitalism, technological innovations and the relationship with the corporate client. Long working days are therefore not only presented as part of an honourable professional tradition; their increasingly open-ended nature is also a key component of the cultural logic of neo-liberal flexible capitalism (Sennett 1998). A major factor in the inexorable expansion of the working day is the increased power of the client (Hanlon 1998), and the pressures that corporate clients – subject to their own commercial imperatives – have exerted on costs. Concurrently, the total service which technological innovations have made it possible to offer global clients and the consequent increase in client demands, function as one of the profession's primary disciplinary mechanisms (Anderson-Gough, Grey and Robson 2000), naturalising the longstanding association between professionalism and long hours and total commitment (Fournier 1999) and reinforcing the supposed independence of the world of work from the private sphere. We can also understand the increase in the working day and resistance to alternative forms of working as a form of 'boundary practice' (Parker 2006), which is a common response to female encroachment on male territory (Cockburn 1991). Presenteeism thus becomes a source of cultural capital, the value of which turns on the devaluation of non-work time and life and the construction of 'absentees' as the 'other', 'lacking commitment' (Kornberger, Carter and Ross-Smith 2010; Sommerlad and Sanderson 1998) – reinforcing the ideal professional as flexible, totally committed, and unencumbered by domestic responsibilities (Meriläinen et al. 2004).

The difficulties that women either do have, or are assumed to have, in offering such an infinitely responsive service confirms their unsuitability for the highest levels of professional practice (Krause 1999). Consequently, although new technologies have, in principle, the capacity to liberate professionals from the workplace and hence facilitate the performance of both paid work and caring responsibilities, in an illustration of the capacity of elites to channel this potential for change in particular directions, these technologies have instead been deployed to colonise the private sphere as a new site of productivity (Thornton 2016). Further, the value of presenteeism as a sign of 'competence and ambition' (Saab-Fortney 2006) – a "symbolic measure of loyalty, 24/7 commitment, and near-instant responsiveness" (Wald 2010: 2283) – has increased. As a result, the 'boundedness' of working time has been virtually extinguished (Kay, Alarie and Adjei 2013; Moen, Kelly and Hill 2011), increasing the need for domestic servicing, yet reinforcing the supposed separateness of the two spheres. The fact that this ongoing intensification of work represents a significant material barrier to women's career progression as a result of the difficulties it poses to a family life is therefore of secondary importance. More significant is the way in which the interplay between temporal regulation and constructions of professionalism normalise traditional masculine work culture and, by extension, the separate spheres of ideology and hence traditional gender roles. The same phenomenon is apparent in the medical profession (Ozbilgin, Tsouroufli and Smith 2011).

Tournament and the field

This equation of professionalism with preparedness to offer open-ended commitment is most apparent in the 'tournament' (Galanter and Palay 1991). In fact, contemporary understandings and practices of professionalism could be said to converge in the tournament: the perfect 'training for hierarchy' (Kennedy 1998), it inculcates professional values, including the human capital view of the profession as essentially rational and fair, thereby legitimising the dominance of the few, and is a highly effective mechanism for extracting surplus value. The effectiveness of these disciplinary functions has been enhanced by the shift in the locus of socialisation and power from the professional association to the professional service firm (Muzio, Brock and Suddaby 2013) and the restructuring of working practices and hierarchies, since these changes stretched the 'up or out' model of professional career trajectories by generating an increasingly 'hypercompetitive professional ideology' (Wald 2010). From the moment of entry as a trainee, professionals are in a competition for promotion, and, generally, those who do not progress, or who have limited prospects, are asked to leave (or may choose to do so). Nevertheless, the highly competitive tournament system depends on most members of the bottom layer of the profession entering with a belief that it is fair and hence the expectation that they have an equal chance of progress (Thornton 2016). But the minimum requirement for promotion is that they exceed their billable hours' targets, and engage in the aggressive pursuit of profits by firms (Hanlon 1999) and by individual partners (since partners' profits, and their security, depend on their associates' billable hours) (Bruck and Canter 2008). This has produced a 'billable hours derby' (Saab-Fortney 2006). As a result, profits per equity partner within the English corporate legal sector grew by over 155 per cent between 1993 and 2008 (Muzio and Flood 2012), and associate lawyers working in large commercial law firms in the City of London are now required to achieve upwards of 1,800 billable hours in a year, while reports suggest that corporate and financial lawyers in some firms regularly record 3,000 or more (see, for example, Law Society 2000).

In practice, applying a Bourdieusian conceptualisation of the field functioning as a 'game' and the need for participants to have a feel for its rules, the tournament is an engine for establishing the value of different forms of capital, and, as our statistical snapshot indicates, thereby reinforces the 'natural' hierarchies of gender, class and 'race'. As a result, the distribution of rewards is based not only on billable hours, but also on a range of other factors which include pre-existing conceptualisations of what partnership material looks like (Sommerlad 2012, 2015; Sommerlad *et al.* 2013). However, through its meritocratic gloss, the system normalises the social Darwinist culture of firms and, correspondingly, the domination of the pyramid by a small number of overwhelmingly white males, while also operating as a highly effective form of surveillance.

In summary, the transition towards commercialised professionalism has rested on a deep change in the meaning of professionalism and the structure of professional work. As already noted, complexity theory's notion of path-dependency suggests that where such changes occur, a number of potential paths for development may emerge, with the possibility that small influences may produce major transformation. Yet this exists alongside the phenomenon of 'lock-in', within which powerful social and political institutions ensure that possibilities are channelled into one path of development thereby safeguarding their power (Walby 2007). With respect to professional service firms, we argue that transformational change extending to gender roles is both exploited as the female labour force becomes ever more essential to corporate professionalism, and yet also resisted through the sustenance of patriarchal structures and ideologies. As a result, women as a category are confined to sub-professional roles, thereby supporting the massive increase in profits, by, for instance, facilitating the setting of huge billable targets, lengthening the working day and rationalising gendered differences in pay, thereby reproducing women's role as primary caregiver (Asher 2011).

Culture, clients and careers

The persistence of patriarchal ideologies revealed by the gendered patterns of horizontal and vertical segregation which characterise both accountancy and law is not only reinforced by, and manifest in, the practice of long hours and the tournament. As indicated above, the assumptions which pervade these ideologies about the 'natural' aptitudes of men and women continue to support the 'misrecognition' (Sommerlad 2012, 2015) of women's potential for roles and specialisms other than those that have become feminised (less prestigious and less well paid – and therefore also less likely to lead to partnership), discouraging their entry into highly masculinised specialisms. A further dimension of the articulation of professional service firms' hyper-masculine culture (Bolton and Muzio 2007) with the broader patriarchal culture of global capitalism is the significance placed on women's bodies.

Traditional professionalism, grounded in the ideology of its detachment from social divisions and politics, produced an archetype whose neutrality was signalled by its supposed disembodiment, bleached of all physical and socio-economic characteristics (Collier 2013; Levinson 1993). Consequently, women's corporeality – however masked by dark, masculine attire – is an immediate signal of a lack of professionalism, so that they can never quite 'fit' and are literally 'out of place' (Puwar 2004). The work by Haynes (2008) on embodiment and accountancy highlights how differences in perceptions, categorisations and valuations of women's and men's bodies play an important role in legitimising and reproducing gendered inequalities within the professions. This is most evident in the sphere of relationship building, which remains a key part of a successful career, necessary both within the firm and externally with clients, through business development – exemplified by the advice to aspiring lawyers that they need a 'winning mentality', and to play 'a role in business development' to contribute to the financial wellbeing of their firm and to build the sustainability of their own career (Harvey 2010). This requirement, and the general pan-promotionalism (Moor 2008) and sexualisation of contemporary culture, means that women's bodies can represent highly valued forms of capital. Women are therefore urged to recognise the market value of "erotic capital ... in the sexualised culture of affluent modern societies" (Hakim 2010: 499) and to deploy it to their advantage.

Thus, it is not only that business development is another activity that further extends the working day. The problems it poses for women also reside in the attention it brings to their corporeality and in particular the roles it requires them to play, which can be explicitly sexualised. The conduct of much of this work in social arenas involving the consumption of large amounts of alcohol, in which practitioners are exhorted to 'schmooze' clients, can entail the commodification of women as 'sexualised saleswomen' (Sommerlad 2016). Evidently, there is a deep contradiction between this type of sexualised work and the ideal type of professionalism. The tensions produced by this contradiction for female professional identity (Witz 1997) were illustrated in the 'advice' recently circulated by the magic circle law firm Clifford Chance to women lawyers to 'lower the pitch' of their voice, 'lose the quirky mannerisms' and 'practice hard words,' and not to 'giggle', 'squirm' or 'tilt your head' (Stowe 2013).

As noted above, the contemporary emphasis on business development and networking is not confined to external clients. Personal bonds between colleagues were a feature of traditional professionalism, a way in which succession – or cloning – occurred (Kanter 1977). This practice, which we refer to as patron–client relations, has persisted in the new form of professionalism, since professional service firms now function as markets in which diverse entrepreneurs of the self come together to advance both their individual interests and those of the organisation. Thus, a further form of the presenteeism, which professional life demands, entails marketisation of the self within the professional service firm, and this is a key activity for achieving success in the tournament for partnership. In addition to this internal networking, participation in 'after work' social activities, demonstrating a willingness to 'work hard and play hard', is also vital. Such activities and the spaces where they occur represent a crystallisation of the social relations, processes, experiences and understandings characteristic of the field, leading Massey (1994) to describe them as articulated moments of power, spatialised sites of social reproduction. Her argument is exemplified by the type of 'heroic masculinity', defined by the homo-sociality, competitiveness and heavy drinking that these activities tend to involve, and which require of women, in turn, a performance of acceptable femininity (Collier 2013;

Sommerlad 2003). Further, as noted in our discussion of the tournament, the low valuation of the capital that outsiders bring to a field makes self-promotion even more essential – but also more problematic – for the female lawyer (see Kumra and Vinnicombe 2008; Rhode 2011).

Moreover, in order to be able to engage in successful self-promotion, the practitioner needs access to good quality work, underlining the key significance of mentoring in career development. However, the tendency for powerful (white) men to act as patrons to younger versions of themselves, ensures that they have the sort of access to clients which can support partnership applications. The corresponding disinclination to mentor those who, by virtue of their gender, class and/or ethnicity, lack valuable capital and are therefore not recognised as partnership potential, prompted David Wilkins and Mitu Gulati (1996: 565) to argue in their study of black lawyers in top firms in the United States that, "from the moment they enter a firm, the career destiny of the majority of non-normative lawyers is fixed and will entail drowning in 'a sea of routine paperwork'".

Finally, the importance of client development, the value placed on women's 'erotic capital' in this work and the highly gendered nature of firm social events encourage and normalise everyday micro aggressions such as sexist 'jokes' (Essed 1991). This use of 'humour' allows the perpetrator not only to deflect criticism (Benwell 2007), but also to caricature the unamused target as a humourless feminist. In this way, the 'joke' simultaneously establishes men's ownership of public space, and disciplines those who dare to speak out (Sommerlad 2016). The circulation by male employees at PwC in Ireland of an email with an invitation to rate the photos of their female colleagues is exemplary (Singh 2010).

The diversity policy realm

The foregoing discussion is based on a conceptualisation of men and women as situated in a system of complex gender inequality (Walby 2007), determined by historically constructed hegemonic masculine identities produced and performed in the professional arena, which in turn are predicated on the construction of women professionals as primarily domestic, but also productive, meticulous, anxious and sexual. This is not, however, to suggest that women are devoid of agency. Over the past fifteen years, a number of industry associations and pressure groups have been established, including for example in England and Wales, the Association of Women Solicitors, which aims to protect and support women's interests in the legal profession. The increasing numbers of these networking and affinity groups within leading professional service firms form part of the expanding diversity and inclusion agenda. As discussed above, this agenda is informed by a neo-liberal, market discourse which has translated the democratic and ethical equal opportunities case for opening up the professions into economistic terms. Nevertheless, a focus of this business case for diversity and inclusion has been the commercial need to attract and retain talent regardless of gender (Sommerlad and Ashley 2015). The policies it has generated, however, focus on the supply side, and aim to remedy women's 'deficit' by, for instance, assertiveness training or coaching and mentoring. To the extent that structural dimensions of the workplace feature as possible impediments to women's progress, the main concern is with the pressure of long hours, which is situated in a discourse of female 'difference' and choice. For instance, in 2007 the Law Society's Gender Equality Scheme framed the overwhelming evidence of gendered patterns of inclusion in such a way as to suggest the need for optimism, in terms of there still being some way to go before there is equality of representation between women and men at the senior levels of the profession. Prominent in their subsequent discussion of the explanatory factors they advanced for this situation were 'women's decisions related to work-life balance'. More recently, the finding of research conducted by a leading London-headquartered firm that 77 per cent of male respondents aspired to partnership compared to 57 per cent of female respondents, of whom only 34 per cent thought that law was a career for life, prompted a senior law firm leader to explain that "Women are sometimes motivated by different things; top jobs and titles may not be as important as they are to men" (Binham 2014).

This explanation for the professions' segmentation and segregation is clearly informed by human capital theory's reduction of society to agentic individuals operating in free (that is neutral) markets, so that persistent differentials in status and income between the genders are attributed to women's individual choices rather than to systemic inequalities (Hakim 2002). This representation of gendered differentials as the product of women's decision to invest in the home, causing deficits in, for example, education and ambition also tends to inform popular literature. For instance, Sheryl Sandberg (2013), although acknowledging institutional barriers to equality, encourages women to address the 'internal voices' which she argues cause them to self-select out of opportunities for career progression. This perspective entails similarly attributing the high rates of female attrition from both law and accountancy to female difference (and fundamental incompatibility with the needs of the profession), thereby further reinforcing the cultural stereotype of the woman as primarily a homemaker (Wald 2010). While Fortune's *100 Best Companies to Work For* had a turnover rate of 2–3 per cent (Shanker 2013), American firms with over 250 attorneys lost a much higher proportion of their associates during the period 2008 to 2011 (Leipold and Collens 2016), and historically a higher percentage of those exiting their firm have been women (Ribeiro, Bosch and Becker 2016). A similar pattern is to be found in England and Wales, where 60 per cent of women solicitors, compared with 27 per cent of males, leave within ten years of qualification (Nada-Arfa 2010).

More recently, however, there has been some recognition of the limitations of this 'deficit' model of diversity, encouraging firms to address demand-side barriers to equality through, for instance, unconscious bias training which, despite limited evidence of efficacy in terms of outcomes, has become ubiquitous in large professional service firms (see, for example, Meyer 2016). Equally widespread now are policies aimed at mitigating the impact of both the structure and culture of long hours and the problem of attrition, especially through the provision of 'flexible work' (Bacik and Drew 2006; Sommerlad and Ashley 2015). These initiatives have, though, done little to displace the normativity of extreme hours, since, as one senior member of the legal profession recently acknowledged, these generate huge profits: "It's many different aspects of the way we do our business, which over years and years has been hugely profitable. Therefore people hang on to a traditional model" (Binham 2014). However, as noted above, the deeper significance of long hours lies in the support they give to the ideology of separate spheres and hence traditional gender roles – with the consequence that the professional who does take advantage of alternative forms of working is pathologised (Thornton and Bagust 2007). And, as previously mentioned, it is precisely the invocation of women's 'difference' – recognised for its potential to deliver profit, efficiency and growth (Prügl 2011) – that assures their sub-professional role. As a result, despite the mobilisation by professional service firms engaged in diversity and inclusion of a positive discourse of change, they have in fact been 'busy doing nothing' (Kumra 2014). Diversity and inclusion policies must therefore be understood as representing token or gestural engagements with women's subordination.

Conclusion

We have suggested in this chapter that, following Walby (2007), there is a dynamic and mutually adaptive relationship between gender and reconfigured professional labour markets, systems of organisation and governance, and occupational cultures. The implications of gender for work in professional service firms of this complex interplay converge in the reconfiguration of the meaning of professionalism. As complexity theory's construct of co-evolution would suggest, the professional fields into which women were gaining access from the late 1970s were already adapting to an environment which was being transformed as a result of neo-liberal assaults on the market shelters that had created them. The traditional professions were consequently well on the way to becoming very different to those from which women had previously been excluded. In the corporate sector, the dramatic expansion generated by neo-liberal globalisation, and the consequent financialisation of large corporate professional service firms (Faulconbridge and Muzio 2009) and the decomposition of work and its reconstitution into routine and specialist tasks, generated a need for large numbers of a new type of worker who, while still called professional, would be characterised by few of the traditional traits associated with professionalism.

These developments then interacted with the system of gender, which remained imbued with the historical understandings expressed in the ideology or discourse of separate spheres. In Bourdieusian terms, this is a discourse of familiarity, which includes all those presuppositions taken for granted by the historical agent, which are themselves provided by the habitus and are therefore not capable of being rationalised. This persistence of the common sense meaning of gender meant that women remained defined by their connection with the imperative of reproduction, rendering them unsuitable for full professional status. As a result, as has occurred in other elite professions, the influx of woman has been accommodated through the establishment of a clear division between "prestige jobs ... and a new class of more routinised, poorly paid jobs with little autonomy and which are unconnected by promotion ladders to the prestige jobs" (Carter and Boslego 1981: 478) – jobs which, of course, were essential to the industrial mode of production developing in professional service firms. At the same time, this segregation of sub-professionals reinforces the status and power of 'true professionals' (namely the equity partners), and many of the profession's practices – such as long hours, social activities, and rituals – remained inflected with their nineteenth century patriarchal past. The pre-existing sexual division of labour has thus formed the basis for the new forms of classification (for example, of roles and spatial divisions) which order the new professionalism. These new systems of classification then work to naturalise the 'arbitrariness' of the new social order of the professions (Bourdieu 1977). The fragility of woman's professional status is thus also functional to the total social organisation of labour, and the mechanisms – such as sexualisation – which de-professionalise her simultaneously underscore men's ownership of public spaces (McLaughlin, Uggen and Blackstone 2012), while also serving the commercial needs of the profession. In other words, neo-liberal and neo-conservative rationalities in both society at large and in the profession are working together to position women as sexualised saleswomen and technicians with a short shelf life. We might therefore describe the new professionalism as an articulation of 'neo-liberalism with neo-patriarchy' (Campbell 2017).

Even while this reinforcement of gendered inequalities is fundamental to the profit levels of professional service firms, it may be that its ultimate sustainability is uncertain, due to what Fraser (2016) identifies as a significant 'crisis of care' embedded within the structural conditions of financialised capitalism. Fraser argues that the reliance of economic production upon the provision of social reproduction as though it were free, while, through its drive for unlimited accumulation, destabilising the very reproductive processes that capitalism and individuals need, is producing a significant 'care deficit' (Fraser 2016). Women professionals seek to manage the conflict between the two spheres by, for example, foregoing marriage and/or family altogether (Bacik and Drew 2006; Schneer and Reitman 2002), or delaying childbirth to fit a male model of work (Blair-Loy 2009), or attempting to 'cheat biology' by submitting to technological interventions of dubious efficacy, as evidenced by the availability of egg-freezing as an additional benefit to female staff (see, for instance, O'Hara 2015). Within the system of gender, these scientific advances illustrate the constant tension between progress and cultural lag, and can be read as, on the one hand, representing women's emancipation from the restrictions of biology, and, on the other, the near total subsumption of professional labour to market demands. Yet, the economic dividend which capitalism in general and the professions in particular earn from free social reproduction together with the internalisation of discourses which naturalise women's position suggest that changes in the nature and structure of work are unlikely to be imminent.

References

American Institute of Certified Public Accountants (2015) 'Percentage of women partners is highest at smaller firms, AICPA Survey finds'. Available at: www.aicpa.org/press/pressreleases/2015/pages/percentage-of-women-partners-is-highest-at-smaller-firms.aspx

American Bar Association (2017) *A Current Glance at Women in the Law*, ABA: Chicago.

Anderson-Gough, F., Grey, C. and Robson, K. (2000) 'In the name of the client: The service ethic in two professional services firms', *Human Relations* 53(9): 1151–74.

Asher, R. (2011) *Shattered: Modern Motherhood and the Illusion of Equality*, London: Vintage Books.

Ashley, L. (2010) 'Making a difference? The use (and abuse) of diversity management at the UK's elite law firms', *Work, Employment and Society* 24(4): 711–27.

Bacik, I. and Drew, E. (2006) 'Struggling with juggling: Gender and work/life balance in the legal professions', *Women's Studies International Forum* 29(2): 136–46.

Beaverstock, J., Hubbard, P. and Short, J. R. (2004) 'Getting away with it? Exposing the geographies of the super-rich', *Geoforum* 35: 401–7.

Benwell, B. (2007) 'New sexism?', *Journalism Studies* 8(4): 539–49.

Binham, C. (2014) 'Law firms try female leadership', *Financial Times* 10 March.

Blair-Loy, M. (2009) *Competing Devotions: Career and Family among Women Executives*, Cambridge, MA: Harvard University Press.

Bolton, S. C. and Muzio, D. (2007) 'Can't live with 'Em; Can't live without 'Em: Gendered segmentation in the legal profession', *Sociology* 41(1): 47–64.

Boon, A. (2014) *The Ethics and Conduct of Lawyers in England and Wales*, Oxford: Hart, 3rd edition.

Bourdieu, P. (1977) *Outline of a Theory of Practice*, Cambridge: Cambridge University Press.

Bourdieu, P. (2001) *Masculine Domination*, Stanford, CA: Stanford University Press.

Bourdieu, P. and Wacquant, L. (1992) *An Invitation to Reflexive Sociology*, Chicago, IL: University of Chicago Press.

Braithwaite, J. P. (2010) 'The strategic use of demand-side diversity pressure in the solicitors' profession', *Journal of Law and Society* 37(3): 442–65.

Bruck, A. and Canter, A. (2008) 'Supply, demand and the changing economics of large law firms', *Stanford Law Review* 60: 2087–130.

Bureau of Labor Statistics (2015) *Current Population Survey*, Washington, DC: BLS.

Burrage, M. (1996) 'From a gentlemen's to a public profession: Status and politics in the history of English solicitors', *International Journal of the Legal Profession* 3(1/2): 45–80.

Burrage, M. (2010) *Martin Trow: Twentieth Century Education – Elite to Mass to Universal*, Baltimore, MD: The John Hopkins University Press.

Campbell, B. (2017) 'Football and feminism: Memories of Doreen Massey', *Soundings* 65: 116–17.

Carter, M. and Boslego, C. S. (1981) 'Women's recent progress in the professions or women get a ticket to ride after the gravy train has left the station', *Feminist Studies* 7(3): 476–504.

Chambers Student (2014) *2014 Gender in the Law Survey*. Available at: www.chambers student.co.uk/where-to-start/newsletter/2014-gender-in-the-law-survey

Cockburn, C. (1991) *In the Way of Women: Men's Resistance to Sex Equality in Organisations*, London: Macmillan Press.

Cohen, E. (2002) *Allocating Power and Wealth in the Global Economy: The Role of Private Law and Legal Agents*, Working Paper No. 101, University of Warwick Centre for the Study of Globalisation and Regionalisation.

Collier, R. (2013) 'Rethinking men and masculinities in the contemporary legal profession: The example of fatherhood, transnational business masculinities, and work-life balance in large law firms', *Nevada Law Journal* 32(2): 101–30.

Cooper, D. J. and Robson, K. (2006) 'Accounting, professions and regulation: Locating the sites of professionalization', *Accounting, Organizations and Society* 31(4): 415–44.

Crompton, R. and Sanderson, K. (1990) *Gendered Jobs and Social Change*, London: Unwin.

Derber, C. (1982) 'The proletarianisation of the professional: A review essay', in Derber, C. (ed.) *Professionals as Workers: Mental Labour in Advanced Capitalism*, Boston, MA: G. K. Hall.

Dezalay, Y (1995a) '"Turf battles" or "class struggles": The internationalization of the market for expertise in the "professional society"', *Accounting, Organizations and Society* 20(5): 331–44.

Dezalay, Y. (1995b) 'Introduction: Professional competition and the social construction of transnational markets', in Dezalay, Y. and Sugarman, D. (eds) *Professional Competition and Professional Power: Lawyers, Accountants and the Social Construction of Markets*, London: Routledge.

Epstein, C. F., Seron, C., Oglensky, B. and Saute, R. (1999) *The Part-time Paradox: Time Norms, Professional Life, Family and Gender*, New York: Routledge.

Essed, P. (1991) *Understanding Everyday Racism: An Interdisciplinary Theory*, London: Sage.

Faulconbridge, J. and Muzio, D. (2009) 'Legal education, globalization, and cultures of professional practice', *Georgetown Journal of Legal Ethics* 21: 1335–59.

Financial Reporting Council (2015) *Key Facts and Trends in the Accountancy Profession*. Available at: www.frc.org.uk/Our-Work/Publications/Professional-Oversight/Key-Facts-and-Trends-in-the-Accountancy-Profes-(1).pdf

Flood, J. (1995) 'The cultures of globalization: Professional restructuring for the international market', in Dezalay, Y. and Sugarman, D. (eds) *Professional Competition and Professional Power: Lawyers, Accountants and the Social Construction of Markets*, London: Routledge.

Flood, J. (2007) 'Law Firms', in Clark, D. S. (ed.) *Encyclopaedia of Law and Society: American and Global Perspectives*, Los Angeles, CA: Sage.

Fournier, V. (1999) 'The appeal to "professionalism" as a disciplinary mechanism', *Sociological Review* 47(2): 280–307.

Fraser, N. (2016) 'Contradictions of capital and care', *New Left Review* 100: 99–117.

Galanter, M. and Palay, T. (1991) *Tournament of Lawyers: The Transformation of the Big Law Firms*, Chicago, IL: University of Chicago Press.

Glucksmann, M. A. (1995) 'Why "work"? Gender and the total social organization of labour', *Gender, Work and Organization* 2(2): 63–75.

Hagan, J. and Kay, F. (1995) *Gender in Practice: A Study of Lawyers' Lives*, New York: Oxford University Press.

Hakim, C. (2002) 'Lifestyle preferences as determinants of women's differentiated labor market careers', *Work and Occupations* 29(4): 428–59.

Hakim, C. (2010) 'Erotic capital', *European Sociological Review* 26(5): 499–518.

Hanlon, G. (1998) 'Professionalism as enterprise: Service class politics and the redefinition of professionalism', *Sociology* 32(1): 43–63.

Hanlon, G. (1999) *Flexible Accumulation and the Emergence of the 'Commercialised Professional' Lawyers, the State and the Market*, Basingstoke: Palgrave Macmillan.

Harvey, D. (2010) 'Friendly advice', *Lawyer* 9 December. Available at: http://l2b.the lawyer.com/friendly-advice/1006372.article.

Haynes, K. (2008) '(Re)figuring accounting and maternal bodies: The gendered embodiment of accounting professionals', *Accounting, Organizations and Society* 33(4): 328–48.

Kanter, R. (1977) *Men and Women of the Corporation*, New York: Basic Books.

Kay, F., Alarie, S. and Adjei, J. (2013) 'Leaving private practice: How organizational context, time pressures, and structural inflexibilities shape departures from private law practice', *Indiana Journal of Global Legal Studies* 20(2): 1223–60.

Kennedy, D. (1998) 'Legal education as training for hierarchy', in Kairys, D. (ed.) *The Politics of Law: A Progressive Critique*, New York: Basic Books.

Kirton, H. (2016) 'Female accountants beware: Women in the profession take home an average £17,000 less a year than their male counterparts, but the gap is getting narrower', *CityAM*. Available at: www.cityam.com/235653/female-accountants-beware-women-in-the-profession-take-home-on-average-17000-less-a-year-than-their-male-counterparts-but-the-gap-is-getting-narrower

Kornberger, M., Carter, C. and Ross-Smith, A. (2010) 'Changing gender domination in a Big Four accounting firm: Flexibility, performance and client service in practice', *Accounting, Organizations and Society* 35(8): 775–91.

Krause, E. A. (1996) *Death of the Guilds: Professions, States, and the Advance of Capitalism, 1930 to the Present*, New Haven, CT: Yale University Press.

Kumra, S. (2014) 'Busy doing nothing: An exploration of the disconnect between gender equity issues faced by large law firms in the United Kingdom and the diversity management initiatives devised to address them', *Fordham Law Review* 83: 2277–99.

Kumra, S. and Vinnicombe, S. (2008) 'A study of the promotion to partner process in a professional services firm: How women are disadvantaged', *British Journal of Management* 19.

Larson, M. S. (1977) *The Rise of Professionalism: A Sociological Analysis*, Berkeley, CA: University of California Press.

Law Society (2000) 'Paying the price – as City Firms raise their assistants' salaries, billing targets are going in the same direction', *Law Society Gazette* 9 November.

Law Society (2007) *The Law Society Gender Equality Scheme*, London: Law Society.

Law Society (2016) *Diversity Profile of the Solicitors' Profession 2015*, London: Law Society.

Lee, R. (1992) 'From profession to business: The rise and rise of the City law firm', *Journal of Law and Society* 19: 31–48.

Leipold, J. G. and Collens, J. N. (2016) 'The stories behind the numbers: Jobs for new grads over more than two decades', *NALP Bulletin* December.

Levinson, S. (1993) 'Identifying the Jewish lawyer: Reflections on the construction of professional identity', *Cardozo Law Review* 14: 1577–1612.

McLaughlin, H., Uggen, C. and Blackstone, A. (2012) 'Sexual harassment, workplace authority and the paradox of power', *American Sociological Review* 77(4): 625–47.

Massey, D. (1994) *Space, Place and Gender*, Minneapolis: University of Minnesota Press.

Meriläinen, S., Tienari, J., Thomas, R. and Davies, A. (2004) 'Management consultant talk: A cross-cultural comparison of normalizing discourse and resistance', *Organization* 11(4): 539–64.

Meyer, C. (2016) 'How CPA firms can counter unconscious bias', *Journal of Accountancy* 7 March. Available at: www.journalofaccountancy.com/newsletters/2016/mar/counteract-unconscious-bias.html

Moen, P., Kelly, E. and Hill, R. (2011) 'Does enhancing work-time control and flexibility reduce turnover? A naturally occurring experiment', *Social Problems* 58(1): 69–98.

Moor, L. (2008) 'Neo-liberalism and promotional culture', *Soundings* 38.

Mueller, F., Carter, C. and Ross-Smith, A. (2011) 'Making sense of career in a Big Four accounting firm', *Current Sociology* 59(4): 551–67.

Muzio, D., Brock, D. M. and Suddaby, R. (2013) 'Professions and institutional change: Towards an institutionalist sociology of the professions', *Journal of Management Studies* 50(5): 699–721.

Muzio, D. and Flood, J. (2012) 'Entrepreneurship, managerialism and professionalism in action: The case of the legal profession in England and Wales', in Reihlen, M. and Werr, A. (eds) *Handbook of Research on Entrepreneurship in Professional Services*, Cheltenham: Edward Elgar.

Nada-Arfa, S. (2010) 'Female solicitors in UK private practice', *Women in Law* 22 December.

NALP (2003) *Keeping the Keepers II – Mobility and Management of Associates*, Dallas: National Association for Legal Professionals Foundation.

O'Hara, M. (2015) 'Egg freezing promises to liberate women – but creepy corporatism looms', *Guardian* 3 August.

Olgiati, V. (1995) 'Process and policy of legal professionalism in Europe: The deconstruction of normative order', in Dezalay, Y. and Sugarman, D. (eds) *Professional Competition and Professional Power: Lawyers, Accountants and the Social Construction of Markets*, London: Routledge.

Ozbilgin, M., Tsouroufli, M. and Smith, M. (2011) 'Understanding the interplay of time, gender and professionalism in hospital medicine in the UK', *Social Science and Medicine* 72(10): 1588–94.

Parker, A. (2006) 'Lifelong learning to labour: Apprenticeship, masculinity and communities of practice', *British Educational Research Journal* 32(5): 687–701.

Pateman, C. (1988) *The Sexual Contract*, Cambridge: Polity Press.

Prügl, E. (2011) 'Diversity management and gender mainstreaming as technologies of government', *Politics and Gender* 7(1): 71–89.

Puwar, N. (2004) *Space Invaders: Race, Gender and Bodies out of Place*, Oxford: Berg.

Rhode, D. L. (2011) 'From platitudes to priorities: Diversity and gender equity in law firms', *Georgetown Journal of Legal Ethics* 24: 1041–77.

Ribeiro, S., Bosch, A. and Becker, J. (2016) 'Retention of women accountants: The interaction of job demands and job resources: Original research', *South African Journal of Human Resource Management* 14(1): 1–11.

Saab-Fortney, S. (2006) 'The billable hours derby: Empirical data on the problems and pressure points', *Fordham Urban Law Journal* 33(1): 171–92.

Sandberg, S. (2013) *Lean In: Women, Work, and the Will to Lead*, New York: Random House.

Sandefur, R. (2007) 'Staying power: The persistence of social inequality in shaping lawyer stratification and lawyers' persistence in the profession', *Southwestern Law Review* 36(3): 539–56.

Schneer, J. A. and Reitman, F. (2002) 'Managerial life without a wife: Family structure and managerial career success', *Journal of Business Ethics* 37(1): 25–38.

Sennett, R. (1998) *Corrosion of Character: The Personal Consequences of Work in the New Capitalism*, New York: W. W. Norton.

Shanker, D (2013) 'Why are lawyers such terrible managers?', *Fortune* 11 January. Available at: http://fortune.com/2013/01/11/why-are-lawyers-such-terrible-managers/

Singh, R. (2010) 'PwC sexual harassment victims given voice', *Accountancy Age* 22 November. Available at: www.accountancyage.com/aa/news/1899588/pwc-sexual-harassment-victims-voice

Sommerlad, H. (2003) 'Women solicitors in a fractured profession: Intersections of gender and professionalism in England and Wales', *International Journal of the Legal Profession* 10(1): 213–34.

Sommerlad, H. (2011) 'The commercialisation of law and the enterprising legal practitioner: Continuity and change', *International Journal of the Legal Profession* 18(1/2): 73–108.

Sommerlad, H. (2012) 'Minorities, merit, and misrecognition in the globalized profession', *Fordham Law Review* 80: 2482–512.

Sommerlad, H. (2015) 'The "social magic" of merit: Diversity, equity and inclusion in the English and Welsh Legal Profession', *Fordham Law Review* 83: 2325–47.

Sommerlad, H. (2016) '"A pit to put women in": Professionalism, work intensification, sexualisation and work – life balance in the legal profession in England and Wales', *International Journal of the Legal Profession* 23(1): 61–82.

Sommerlad, H. and Ashley, L. (2015) 'Equality, diversity and inclusion', in Empson, L., Muzio, D., Broschak, J. and Hinings, B. (eds) *Oxford Handbook of Professional Service Firms*, Oxford: Oxford University Press.

Sommerlad, H. and Sanderson, P. (1998) *Gender, Choice and Commitment: Women Solicitors in England and Wales and the Struggle for Equal Status*, Aldershot: Dartmouth Publishing Company.

Sommerlad, H., Webley, L., Muzio, D., Tomlinson, J. and Duff, L. (2013) *Diversity in the Legal Profession in England and Wales: A Qualitative Study of Barriers and Individual Choices*, London: University of Westminster Law Press.

Statistics Canada (2015) *Household Survey: Data Tables*, Ottawa: StatsCan.

Stowe, M. (2013) 'Patronising, sexist and wrong. Law firm issues note on how to dress', *Guardian* 11 November.

Suddaby, R., Gendron, Y. and Lam, H. (2009) 'The organizational context of professionalism in accounting', *Accounting, Organizations and Society* 34(3): 409–27.

Sugarman, D. (1996) 'Bourgeois collectivism, professional power and the boundaries of the state: The private and public life of the Law Society, 1825–1914', *International Journal of the Legal Profession* 3(1/2): 81–135.

Susskind, R. (2008) *The End of Lawyers. Rethinking the Nature of Legal Services*, Oxford: Oxford University Press.

Thornton, M. (2016) 'The flexible cyborg: Work-life balance in legal practice', *Sydney Law Review* 38(1): 1–21.

Thornton, M. and Bagust, J. (2007) 'The gender trap: Flexible work in corporate legal practice', *Osgoode Hall Law Journal* 45(4): 773–811.

Urbis (2015) *Law Society National Profile 2014: Final Report*. Available at: www.lawsociety.com.au/cs/groups/public/documents/internetcontent/1005660.pdf

Walby, S. (1997) *Gender Transformations*, Hove: Psychology Press.

Walby, S. (2007) 'Complexity theory, systems theory, and multiple intersecting social inequalities', *Philosophy of the Social Sciences* 37(4): 449–70.

Wald, E. (2010) 'Glass ceilings and dead ends: Professional ideologies, gender stereotypes, and the future of women lawyers at large law firms', *Fordham Law Review* 78(5): 2245–88.

Walkerdine, V., Lucey, H. and Melody, J. (2001) *Growing Up Girl: Psycho-Social Explorations of Class and Gender*, Basingstoke: Palgrave Macmillan.

Wilkins, D. and Gulati, G. M. (1996) 'Why are there so few black lawyers in corporate law firms? An institutional analysis', *California Law Review* 84: 493–625.

Willemse, N. and de Beer, P. (2012) 'Three worlds of educational welfare states? A comparative study of higher education systems across welfare states', *Journal of European Social Policy* 22(2): 105–17.

Witz, A. (1990) *Professions and Patriarchy*, London: Routledge.

Witz, A. (1997) 'Patriarchy and professions: The gendered politics of occupational closure', *Sociology* 24(4): 675–90.

9 Regulation and governance of the professions

Institutional work and the demise of 'delegated' self-regulation of the accounting profession

Mary Canning and Brendan O'Dwyer

Introduction

While professions are now widely viewed as primary societal institutional agents (Scott 2008) assuming central roles in creating, disrupting and maintaining prevailing institutions (Currie *et al*. 2012; Lawrence and Suddaby 2006; Lawrence, Suddaby and Leca 2009, 2011; Suddaby and Viale 2011), they are also often the *object*s of institutional change efforts, especially regarding how they are regulated. Nowhere has this change been more profound than in the accounting profession. In the last fifteen years as the profession has evolved to embrace and serve globalised enterprise, it has come under increased scrutiny. This is especially evident in the steady imposition of independent oversight bodies established to supervise key aspects of its governance. This represents a major disruption to a regulatory regime that prevailed for almost a century in several Western-European jurisdictions (Canning and O'Dwyer 2013; Caramanis, Dedoulis and Leventis 2015; Hazgui and Gendron 2015; Malsch and Gendron 2011; Quack and Schubler 2017).

Shifting institutional logics[1] underpinning the rationales and actions prevalent in the regulatory field of accounting have both shaped and been shaped by the institutional work enrolled by various regulatory actors seeking to activate altered regulatory oversight of professional accountants (see also Empson, Cleaver and Allen 2013; Gawer and Phillips 2013; Marquis and Lounsbury 2007; Thornton 2004). Institutional work[2] refers to the practices and processes associated with these actors' effort to develop, dismantle, expand and contain the regulatory institutions overseeing the accounting profession, as well as magnifying or suppressing the effects of these institutions (Hampel, Lawrence and Tracey 2017; Lawrence and Suddaby 2006). Different forms of interrelated institutional work have underpinned a shift away from a self-regulatory logic relating to the rationales and practices surrounding the regulation of accountants towards an oversight logic advocating greater interference in the profession's affairs. There is, however, some debate as to the effectiveness of this change effort, with recent evidence suggesting that change has been minimal in many contexts as a result of enterprising efforts by the accounting profession to assimilate the 'new' oversight logic within the pre-existing self-regulatory logic (Caramanis, Dedoulis and Leventis 2015; Hazgui and Gendron 2015; Malsch and Gendron 2011; Quack and Schubler 2017). Such debate is to be expected given that prevailing logics can promote conformity (Tracey, Phillips and Jarvis 2011) and thereby restrict the possibility of institutional work instigating substantive change. This chapter explores the nature of the extensive efforts to reconfigure the regulation of the accounting profession. Drawing on over a decade studying regulatory change in the Irish context, it illuminates how the state, and in particular its supporting agencies, has engaged in forms of institutional work in its interactions with the accounting profession in order to legitimise and implement radical changes to the profession's governance.

The chapter is organised as follows. We first outline the nature of regulation of the accounting profession and explore the process through which the demise of self-regulation and public oversight has unfolded. We then contest the widespread view that transnational development in oversight has been readily translated to the national level while simultaneously exploring the role that the 'Big N' professional services firms have played as the sites of governance have shifted. Drawing on the case of Ireland, we outline how the accounting profession has strategically responded to efforts to interfere in its governance by engaging in enterprising efforts to obstruct change aimed at making it more accountable to the public interest it claims to serve. We present a process model drawn from an analysis of this context to depict the interrelated institutional work required by nascent regulators seeking to introduce, legitimise and implement oversight of the accounting profession in order to dismantle self-regulatory regimes and make them more publicly accountable.

Governing without interference: the 'public interest' underpinnings of self-regulation

A defining characteristic of a profession is its commitment to serve and protect the public interest (Abbott 1988). This ability to subordinate or at least assuage self-interest in the service of the public interest (Canning and O'Dwyer 2001; Lee 1995) has traditionally been used by sociologists to distinguish professions from other occupations (Suddaby and Muzio 2017; Willmott 1990). While there is little agreement on what is meant by the public interest or how to measure it (see, for instance, Saks 1995), the public interest legitimation of professions is a key reason they have historically been granted the privilege to regulate themselves with minimal government or outside interference. Failure to grasp the public interest basis for the social contract that underpins self-regulation (Robson, Willmott, Cooper and Puxty 1994) has resulted in the gradual demise of the self-regulatory model for the accounting profession in many jurisdictions (Canning and O'Dwyer, 2013, 2016; Caramanis, Dedoulis and Leventis 2015; Hazgui, Lesage and Pochet 2011; O'Regan and Killian 2014; Quack and Schubler 2017). In its place a regulatory environment comprising a broad mix of independent oversight bodies has emerged whose role has been to enhance and restore public confidence in corporate financial reporting and auditing (Catasus, Hellman and Humphrey 2013; Humphrey, Loft and Woods 2009; Quack and Schubler 2017) in the face of recurring crises.

The gradual demise of 'delegated' self-regulation

The notion of self-regulation within the accounting profession has long been problematic. In the United Kingdom and Ireland, for example, a more precise term is 'delegated' self-regulation because professional accounting bodies were traditionally recognised and supervised by government ministers under statutory powers set out in various pieces of Companies legislation. As such, they were considered part of the modern capitalist state schema operating as quasi-state regulators, a relationship that was seen to be of benefit to both the state (politicians) and the accounting profession (Quack and Schubler 2017). For example, the state saved on the cost of regulation by passing it off to the private sector (Willmott, Cooper and Puxty 1993) but it was also allegedly able to benefit from the profession's knowledge and expertise (Sikka and Willmott 1995), as well as distancing itself from the downside of any accounting failures by being able to blame the profession instead. In return, the state granted the accounting profession a monopoly over the provision of audits and the setting and enforcing of auditing and accounting standards on the assumption that the profession continued to demonstrate its ability "to responsibly and reliably regulate the quality of its services" (Willmott 1986: 558). In many jurisdictions, there was a widespread belief that leaving the profession to regulate itself worked "infinitely better than a statutory regime managed by civil servants" (Suiter 1997: 15).

Professional bodies have continually drawn on their knowledge-based resources to maintain the self-regulatory logic traditionally underpinning the governance of professions. In doing so, they seek to protect their own professional interests by endorsing or seeking to construct rule systems that become part of the institutional fabric of the regulatory field. These rules are constructed in such a manner that the profession can lay claim to being the only parties with the necessary expertise and legitimacy to interpret and apply them (Humphrey, O'Dwyer and Unerman 2017; Suddaby and Viale 2011). For example, the accounting profession's disciplinary rules are purportedly designed in the broader social interest, but largely operate to consolidate the power and status of the profession (Canning and O'Dwyer 2001, 2003; Muzio, Brock and Suddaby 2013) with their application often shrouded in mystery. However, when the rules have been exposed to external scrutiny, they have frequently been found to be wanting (Canning and O'Dwyer 2001, 2003) – thereby instigating attacks on the continuation of the profession's self-regulatory status.

In the Irish context that we have studied extensively over the past sixteen years, evidence of extensive frauds incriminating members of the Irish accounting profession in the late 1990s led to a public outcry as the profession failed to take disciplinary measures against implicated members, including a former Prime Minister. Public and political support for delegated self-regulation diminished, eventually leading to the formation of an oversight body following the stages set out in Box 9.1 below (Canning and O'Dwyer 2013; O'Regan and Killian 2014). After the subsequent high profile corporate collapses of Enron and WorldCom in the United States, efforts to restore confidence in financial audit and reporting also led to the establishment of independent oversight bodies in other jurisdictions, such the Public Company Accounting Oversight Board (PCAOB) in the United States, the Professional Oversight Board (POB) in the United Kingdom and other umbrella organisations such as the International Forum of Independent Audit Regulators (IFIAR). Subsequent mimetic and isomorphic pressures led to many other jurisdictions dismantling their self-regulatory regimes and replacing them with greater state oversight of core elements of the accounting profession's activities (Caramanis, Dedoulis and Leventis 2010; Hazgui, Lesage and Pochet 2011; Humphrey 2008; Humphrey et al. 2011; Malsch and Gendron 2011).

Box 9.1 Key events leading to regulatory change in the Irish accounting profession

Events leading to the proposal to remove self-regulation and the setting up of an oversight supervisory body:

- Three major public inquiries implicating accountants in malpractice and accusing accounting profession of a weak disciplinary process:
    1. Inquiry into the beef processing industry which found Irish accountants involved in the setting up of illegal tax avoidance schemes (Beef Tribunal Inquiry 1994).
    2. Revelations about the operation of a complex tax evasion scheme by various accountants, to benefit among others, a former Prime Minister (McCracken Report 1997).
    3. Investigative media reports revealing the setting up by accountants of bogus non-resident bank accounts to facilitate the widespread evasion of deposit interest retention tax (Bougen, Young and Cahill 1999).
- The Irish Government expresses concern and establishes the Review Group on Auditing (RGA) to investigate the effectiveness of self-regulation of the accounting profession (O'Regan 2009).
- Extensive lobbying by professional accounting bodies and the then 'Big Five' professional services firms for the maintenance of self-regulation (submissions to Department of Enterprise Trade and Employment and to RGA, see Canning and O'Dwyer 2013).
- RGA reported in 2000 and proposed the removal of self-regulation of the accounting profession and the setting up of an oversight supervisory body (RGA 2000).
- Interim oversight body, Irish Auditing and Accounting Supervisory, was set up in April 2001.
- Continued resistance to oversight by the professional accounting bodies using manipulation and offers of help to draft legislation (Canning and O'Dwyer 2013).

- The manipulation was resisted and the Irish Auditing and Accounting Supervisory Authority (IAASA) was established on a statutory footing in December 2005 (see Canning and O'Dwyer 2013).

Events leading to the move from an oversight supervisory body to an oversight interventionist body:

- International accounting-related scandals (for example, Enron, WorldCom) led to the setting up of oversight bodies with direct interventionist powers while IAASA (the Irish Auditing and Accounting Supervisory Authority) remained with oversight supervisory powers (Canning and O'Dwyer 2013).
- In 2008, the European Union Commission recommended direct inspection of public interest entities (Erwin 2012).
- The global financial crisis resulted in regulators being interrogated as to how the crisis could have occurred 'on their watch' (Canning and O'Dwyer 2016).
- IAASA was called in front of the Irish Parliament in 2009 to face questioning. IAASA responded by seeking direct interventionist powers similar to its international contemporaries (Erwin 2009).
- Responsibility for direct inspection was given to IAASA on 17 June 2016 (Canning and O'Dwyer 2016).

Translating global governance trends to the local level: sedimentation as opposed to synergy

Accounting practice is increasingly global and frequently requires oversight at a global level as the gaze and reach of national regulators can be increasingly compromised (Muzio *et al.* 2016). However, it is misleading and somewhat naïve to assume that local regulators operate as regulatory dopes easily enacting mandates emanating from the global arena. While acknowledging that local regulatory sites do not exist in a vacuum (Djelic and Sahlin 2009; Humphrey, Kokkali and Samsonova 2010; Humphrey, Loft and Woods 2009; Loft, Humphrey and Turley 2006; Malsch and Gendron 2011; Richardson 2009), a series of studies contest the ease with which global governance trends translate at the national or local level. These studies unveil numerous contextual factors that local regulators must address either in isolation or as part of their efforts to translate global regulatory trends in accounting within their national contexts (see, for example, Arnold 2005; Canning and O'Dwyer 2013, 2016; Caramanis, Dedoulis and Leventis 2010; Hazgui, Lesage and Pochet 2011; Jeppesen and Loft 2011; Malsch and Gendron 2011). Moreover, the translation of transnational regulatory oversight models within different national contexts is especially dependent on the capacity and inclination of nation-states to interfere with self-regulation among national professional accounting associations (Suddaby, Cooper and Greenwood 2007). The Big Four professional services firms also play an influential role here (Muzio *et al.* 2016). Hence, global trends in oversight, often supported by transnational actors, can confront resistance from nation-states and their professional accounting associations. In several jurisdictions a form of 'sedimentation process' has occurred (Cooper *et al*. 1996) in which transnational regulatory/oversight requirements have operated alongside national requirements and relied extensively on traditional national actors for their approval and execution (Caramanis, Dedoulis and Leventis 2010; Jeppesen and Loft 2011; Malsch and Gendron 2011). Transnational actors promulgating public oversight of the accounting profession have therefore not *dislodged* national professional associations but have instead, to varying degrees, been superimposed on them (Suddaby, Cooper and Greenwood 2007).

This variation in the embeddedness of global trends in governance of the accounting profession is especially evident in the translation of global oversight trends to the national contexts of Greece and Ireland. The study by Caramanis, Dedoulis and Leventis (2015) of the formation and operation of an oversight body for the accounting profession in Greece (see also Blavoukos, Caramanis and Dedoulis 2013) showed how the Greek oversight body remained largely dormant during its lifespan. Caramanis, Dedoulis and Leventis (2015) attributed this to acutely entrenched local socio-political influences and pressures such as the supremacy of delegative democracy in Greece, rifts within the Greek accounting profession, state control of the oversight body, and a political system where clientelism was rampant. While the Greek oversight body was restricted by its inability to operate independently of the state, Canning and O'Dwyer (2016) found that the oversight body established in Ireland was much more exercised with operating independently of the accounting profession. In Greece, political leaders sought to directly influence appointments to the oversight body (Blavoukos, Caramanis and Dedoulis 2013), but this was barely evident in Ireland. In Greece, state control and widespread apathy inhibited the transformation of domestic policy making. In contrast, socio-political factors in the Irish context, such as the legislation underpinning the oversight body's formation, sheltered it from government intrusion. Unlike Ireland, in Greece the oversight body was denied basic resources such as office space, manpower, and expertise (where these were available) and was established in a vague legal environment. This contrasting evolution of two oversight bodies supports the claim by Caramanis, Dedoulis and Leventis (2015) that the efficacy of oversight bodies in governing the accounting profession should not be taken for granted given the different historical, social, cultural and economic traditions into which they are introduced. It also sustains their claim that globally inspired institutional reforms of governance of the accounting profession do not necessarily translate readily to the local level where their operationalisation can "often [be] ... a mere facade" (Blavoukos, Caramanis and Dedoulis 2013: 151; see also Hazgui and Gendron 2015). Hence, domestic political and institutional settings continue to represent important 'intervening variables' that shape the national response to global institutional pressures to govern the accounting profession in a particular manner.

Shifting sites of governance of the accounting profession: the fluctuating role of the 'Big N' professional service firms

While significant research attention has been afforded to the role of new regulators in shifting governance of the accounting profession, it is also widely argued that the Big Four professional service firms have become the site and not the subject of (global and local) regulation, including that related to the accounting profession (Cooper and Robson 2006; Humphrey, Loft and Woods 2009; Malsch and Gendron 2011; Muzio et al. 2016; Suddaby, Cooper and Greenwood 2007). A significant stream of work suggests that their global size and significance offers them leverage over national regulators and influence over the design of international regulatory arrangements (Muzio et al. 2016) in which they seek to align regulations with their commercial interests (Arnold 2005, 2009; Caramanis 1999, 2002). Caramanis (2002) demonstrated this tendency when revealing the central role played by the (then) Big Five firms in initiating and co-ordinating actions by the European Union, OECD and World Trade Organisation to promote regulation aimed at opening up the local Greek audit market to international competition (see also Caramanis 1999, 2005), thereby allowing the (then) Big Five to enter this market and prosper at the expense of smaller, local Greek audit firms. Recent work, however, offers a more nuanced perspective on the process through which this influence may arise and suggests that the nature of these regulatory alliances may be contingent on the stage of the regulatory change process. For example, in the Irish context, Canning and O'Dwyer (2013) showed how the Big Four/Five firms formed an allegiance with professional accounting bodies in the early stages of a regulatory realignment of the accounting profession and opposed key regulatory oversight proposals that appeared to threaten their commercial freedom. When they realised that this battle was effectively lost, and independent oversight would occur, with or without their support, they remained silent, choosing to let the professional accounting bodies co-ordinate any further resistance to regulation on their behalf. This positioning is consistent with prior work by Clemens and Douglas (2005) and Goodstein (1994) who contend that individual organisations which are members of professional bodies may adopt less active strategic responses to interference from regulation as they believe they can rely on their 'trade associations' (in this case, the professional accounting bodies) to publicly adopt the more active, resistant strategies. The following section examines in more detail the interactions between these organisations (and their representative professional bodies) and a nascent regulator set up to modify the governance of the accounting profession.

'The most effective lies are those we believe ourselves': the profession's strategic responses to governance change

There is extensive research suggesting that the accounting profession has been highly successful in influencing the design and initial interpretation of new governance models (Malsch and Gendron 2011) with many claiming that the profession has largely diluted new governance regimes, thereby rendering them ineffective (Shapiro and Matson 2008). Prior research work also recounts how reforms in the internal management of the accounting profession have been (sometimes) inadvertently stimulated by government initiatives in contexts where heightened proximity between governments and the accounting profession has ensued (Radcliffe, Cooper and Robson 1994; Robson *et al*. 1994; Willmott, Cooper and Puxty 1993).

The ecological perspective of Muzio and colleagues (2016) on professions highlights how the projects of specific occupations are constrained, supported and generally affected by the moves of social actors adjacent to them and with whom they regularly interact, such as the state and its appointed regulators (see also Suddaby and Muzio 2017; Suddaby and Viale 2011). This interactive process has been a key feature of governance change efforts in the accounting profession. Canning and O'Dwyer (2013) and O'Regan and Killian (2014) studied the extensive interactions between an incoming regulator and the Irish accounting profession in attempts to change the governance of the profession prior to the implementation of new regulatory arrangements. In this context, the accounting profession aggressively resisted proposed changes by seeking to discredit the oversight logic underpinning the proposed changes and to dilute the powers offered to a proposed new public oversight body in the pre-implementation phase of new governance procedures.

Control of information was mobilised as a key resource by the profession to maintain its power to self-govern and, in particular, to dictate the interpretation of the proposed governance changes (Scott 2001). The profession realised that if it relinquished control of this key resource to the oversight body, its ultimate goal of non-interventionist oversight would not be attained. Hence the profession adopted defiance and manipulation strategies seeking to enforce boundaries on what the oversight body would be permitted to do (see Hancher and Moran 1989). For example, when the creation of an oversight body was initially proposed, the profession sought to limit the body's intervention powers so that it would maintain control over key information regarding its members' activities and the operation of its disciplinary processes. Allusions to the profession's extensive knowledge, expertise and organisational capacity resources permeated these resistance strategies. The profession also sought to undermine the regulatory power assigned to the oversight body by interpreting the draft legislation establishing the body in a manner that suggested the oversight body would be powerless to intervene in the profession's governance, as well as continually highlighting a lack of sufficient expertise in the body. These responses exposed tensions between a desire to present a picture of a profession keen to identify itself with a traditional public interest logic (Muzio, Brock and Suddaby 2013; Suddaby, Cooper and Greenwood 2007) and that of a commercial logic evident in its uncompromising responses.

The defiant nature of the accounting profession's response to proposed governance changes in this case illustrates how governance changes imposed from the outside can leave a profession blind to how it publicly promotes its own self-interest while enrolling public interest rhetoric. The remorseless nature of the profession's defiance sought to deflect extensively researched and widely publicised criticisms of its governance of members, in particular in the area of its complaints procedures. The profession's responses expressed disbelief that its 'self' governance was being questioned (see also Canning and O'Dwyer 2003). The blinkered nature of these responses reflected a desire to retain relevance and control at national level *at all costs*, while also unveiling the persistent problems the profession was having adjusting to a local (and global) political and social environment where automatic deference to the accounting profession was no longer guaranteed. According to Moore and colleagues (2006: 11), most professionals sense that their professional decisions are always defensible and that 'external' criticisms of their work are "overblown by ignorant or demagogic outsiders who malign them unfairly". The Irish accounting profession's complacency and implicit dismissal of international regulatory developments corresponds with this perspective. However, the extreme nature of its defiance of efforts to interfere in its governance also unveils some of the internal dynamics of 'moral seduction' within professions, where professionals become unconsciously biased and find it difficult to abandon their own self-interest even if they seek to do so (Moore *et al.* 2006). As Canning and O'Dwyer (2013) argue, it is as if the Irish profession was in denial about the authenticity of the accumulation of public concerns over an extended period which contested its previously undisputed status in the Irish social and political context. The profession failed to fully appreciate the extent to which the defiant strategies it adopted actually exhibited extreme self-interest even if the profession itself may have perceived them as reasoned and balanced. As Moore and colleagues (2006: 22) note, "the most effective lies are those we believe ourselves".

Two intriguing features of this case urge caution when seeking to construct stories of an all-powerful profession and the interventionist Big Four firms alluded to in the previous section. First, the regulator consistently repelled the efforts of the profession to neuter its proposed powers. While the regulator initially signalled a symbolic commitment to compromising with the profession to alleviate the profession's concerns, when the profession refused to back down on its demands and escalated its aggressive rhetoric, the regulator defied the profession and dismissed its concerns. This resulted in the final legislation supporting most of the power the regulator was seeking over the profession's governance. Hence, little compromise was evident as the regulatory space was altered, with the joint construction of meaning that Scott (2001) sees as central to the interpretation of initial regulatory rules rarely evident. Second, despite the widely cited influence of the Big Four professional service firms on regulation and regulators, noted in the previous section, these firms were not visible in protecting the profession's self-regulatory status. Perhaps the Big Four did not consider that increased regulation of many of their employees posted a commercial threat or, more likely, they were happy for their representatives in the interim regulatory body to make their case privately. We explore this further in the next section by unpacking the institutional work that the nascent regulator undertook to beget change that effectively dismantled the delegated self-regulation of the Irish accounting profession.

The institutional work underpinning the dismantling of self-regulation

Recent work on the professions has been keenly focused on the relationship between professions and institutions such as markets, regulators, and business practices. Aspects of this work highlight how professions are not only key mechanisms for, but are also targets of institutional change (Humphrey, O'Dwyer and Unerman 2017; Muzio, Brock and Suddaby 2013). In this section, we mobilise the theorisation by Canning and O'Dwyer (2016) of the interactive, dynamic process through which new governance oversight arrangements for the accounting profession evolve. We unveil a process of institutional work through which a nascent oversight body targeted the accounting profession as part of a process aimed at introducing interventionist public oversight of the profession. This takes aspects of the empirical dimension of our discussion of professional resistance in the previous section and postulates how the state and its proposed regulators conduct institutional work to fundamentally alter the governance of the accounting profession. We also unveil how shifting institutional logics shape and are shaped by the institutional work undertaken within this process (see also Empson, Cleaver and Allen 2013; Marquis and Lounsbury 2007; Thornton 2004; Thornton and Ocasio 1999). While the process model evolved from the contextualised longitudinal study by Canning and O'Dwyer (2016) in the Irish context, it is adapted to theorise the dynamics underpinning the aforementioned shifts in the regulation of the accounting profession from delegated self-regulation to public oversight more widely. This five-stage process is depicted in Figure 9.1. We elaborate on this figure in five separate phases below.

Figure 9.1 Institutional work and governance change in the accounting profession.
Source: adapted from Canning and O'Dwyer (2016: 8).

Notes
The direction of the arrows indicates the direction of support from one form of institutional work to another as part of the efforts by individuals in an oversight body to realise regulatory change. The key terms used can be defined as follows:

Hard advocacy work, evident in Phases 1 and 5, is defined as the use of direct, explicit, confrontational and threatening practices of social suasion which mobilise rhetoric and explicit contrasts in outlining terrible consequences. Hard advocacy work is highly insistent and impatient and can encompass scare mongering and a lack of openness to negotiation or consensus. It is focused on ensuring that advocates get exactly what they are advocating for and is aimed at creating a sense of a crisis to which there needs to be a response.

Soft advocacy work, evident in Phase 2, involves the use of subtle, largely implicit, unthreatening techniques of social suasion. It focuses on seeking consensus as opposed to conflict and mobilises gentle rhetoric while avoiding direct confrontation.

Consensual identity construction work, evident in Phase 2, involves efforts to build constructive relationships in order to be viewed as consensual and responsive.

Confrontational identity construction work, evident in Phases 3 and 4, is defined as work involving taking firm, non-negotiable, uncompromising positions in order to be viewed as conflictual and confrontational.

Self-mythologising work involves work among a community of peers designed to create and sustain myths regarding the community's history and actions in a specific domain.

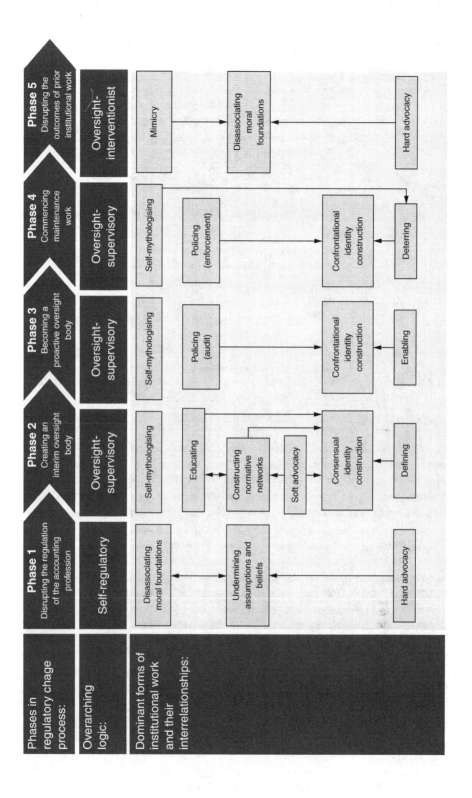

Phase 1 – Initiating institutional change in governance and disrupting a self-regulatory regime

As noted earlier, proposals to shift the governance of the accounting profession have evolved largely from the proliferation of public scandals surrounding the profession and its members. These proposals are frequently underpinned by a shift from a self-regulatory logic to an oversight-supervisory logic. The latter seeks to tentatively disrupt pre-existing governance structures surrounding the accounting profession by promoting independent oversight models that are not overly interventionist. However, given the embedded nature of the existing self-regulatory logic, the institutional work required to provoke a response from the profession often has to be confrontational. Groups seeking to promote change need to be unambiguous in their attacks on the moral foundations of existing self-regulatory regimes. Direct accusations, with supporting evidence, of the 'lack of effectiveness' of existing arrangements, often pointing to prior self-regulatory failures, are required. Campaigning individuals with broad-based credibility, such as high-profile politicians, need to mobilise 'hard' advocacy work in order to undermine widespread assumptions and beliefs supporting the efficacy of self-regulation. This can involve the unremitting mobilisation of media and political support and confrontational behaviour seeking to publicly undermine the moral foundations associated with self-regulation. Existing assumptions and beliefs must be continually undermined by pre-empting any professional concerns with the perceived risks and costs attached to close oversight. This institutional work also needs to ensure that the 'public interest' rhetoric commonly adopted by the profession is re-articulated in a manner that makes the profession look weak. In the Irish case, behind the scenes, highly direct and explicit confrontational practices were mobilised to inculcate the accounting profession's conscious obedience (Lawrence and Suddaby 2006). The combination of work comprising 'hard' advocacy and the disassociation of moral foundations underpins the core institutional work seeking to undermine assumptions and beliefs supporting the self-regulatory *status quo*. This creates a sense of crisis surrounding self-regulation which demands a response and provides the space that facilitates the introduction of interim oversight of the accounting profession in advance of full legislative reform. In this way, it legitimises the change efforts and allows an oversight-supervisory logic to prevail in discussions of the profession's governance.

Phase 2 – Establishing the structures to realise shifts in governance

Shifting regulation through establishing oversight bodies combines numerous forms of interrelated institutional work such as educating work, 'soft' advocacy work, work aimed at constructing normative networks, and defining work. Given the diverse composition of oversight bodies, which include some members of the regulated profession, educating work is crucial to ensuring that members fully and independently commit to their role as insiders in the oversight body and to its normative goals. 'Soft' advocacy work aimed at legitimising the body with legislators and public officials is essential to securing the material and intellectual resources necessary to support the body's effectiveness. This also operates to ensure that the legislation establishing the body's authority is not diluted and is passed swiftly.

The institutional work of constructing normative networks seeks to soothe the profession's concerns and pursues legitimacy using intermediaries such as consultants with professional attachments to accounting firms. This is assisted by 'soft' advocacy work involving extensive engagement with the professional bodies and Big Four firms aimed at offering reassurances and clarification. Defining work is mobilised to delineate the boundaries of the oversight body's duties. This combination of 'soft' advocacy and defining work ultimately aims to create a consensual identity for the oversight body that will enable it to regularly interact with the profession and be viewed as both consensual and responsive. A further contextual feature of the theorisation by Canning and O'Dwyer was the explicit *rejection* of mimicry work by the oversight body's Chairman and CEO which was driven by a desire not to unwittingly follow international trends and to offer a unique, locally-grounded shift in governance of the accounting profession in Ireland.

Phase 3 – Countering profession efforts at logic assimilation

While the interrelated forms of work outlined in phase 2 above seek to inculcate an oversight-supervisory logic to underpin governance of the profession, resistance from the profession is likely when governance moves from the aspirational to the implementation phase. In the Irish case, this was fuelled by a sense within the accounting profession that the oversight body sought to interfere too much in its 'private' affairs and involved a concerted effort by the profession to assimilate the oversight-supervisory logic within the previously dominant self-regulatory logic. The assimilation of logics occurs when the core elements of a prevailing logic remain – in this case, the self-regulatory logic – but new practices, such as those proposed by the oversight body, are made part of this prevalent logic (Thornton, Ocasio and Lounsbury 2012). This resistance from the profession, the nature of which was outlined in the previous section, can be countered by an oversight body adopting more confrontational forms of work such as 'audit' policing work which instructs professional bodies as to where they need to change their procedures and structures. This work needs to be supported by enabling work aimed at creating a rule system that will facilitate the oversight body's operationalisation of its mandate. Persistent resistance from the profession, however, can necessitate continual work aimed at creating a confrontational identity for the oversight body. While this is contingent on the composition of the oversight board and the extent of mutual trust therein, it also necessitates self-mythologising work to bolster the body's confidence and authority.

Phase 4 – Coercion as institutional maintenance work

The ultimate test of changes to the governance of the accounting profession arises when actions need to be taken in the face of non-compliance with regulations. Initial institutional changes now have to be maintained. This is where oversight bodies need to become coercive and impose their authority using 'enforcement' policing work while recognising that resistance from the profession can escalate. In the Irish case, a major enquiry into key aspects of one professional accounting body's handling of a high-profile complaint offered a test to the oversight body. In the face of extensive, legally backed professional body resistance involving, *inter alia*, the submission of irrelevant documentation and significant delays in presenting key evidence, deterring work was mobilised whereby the oversight body aggressively fought the profession's resistance by drawing on its own legal foundations. This combination of 'enforcement' policing work and deterring work enabled the continual construction of the oversight body's confrontational identity.

Phase 5 – Inserting the global into the local: coping with shifting logics

While we have already argued that the insertion of global shifts in the regulation of the accounting profession to the local national level cannot be presumed, global developments can be used by local regulators to support a reassessment of their role and powers. In the Irish case, while the oversight body was busy seeking to sanction the profession over an extended period (see phase 4 above), a shift from an oversight-supervisory logic to an oversight-interventionist logic occurred at the global level. This involved oversight bodies acquiring much more power to intervene in the governance of professional accounting bodies. In the Irish context, the oversight body moved swiftly to seek such powers which served to disrupt the moral foundations of the oversight regime they had spent so long establishing and implementing in phases 1 to 4 above. The body mobilised 'hard' advocacy work, in which it demanded increased powers from the Irish government in public forums, in conjunction with mimicry work seeking to imitate international trends to enable this increased intervention.

Overall, the institutional work performed by the oversight body in phases 3 and 4 sought to repel the logic assimilation efforts by the profession in phase 3 lest it succeed in neutering the oversight body's proposed powers and new practices. In the final stage above, the oversight body, recognising its relative impotence in light of this global shift, sought to mobilise the core elements of this more interventionist logic to underpin the mimicry and 'hard' advocacy work focused on gaining expanded powers and practices. In particular, the oversight-interventionist logic underpinned the rationales the oversight body's chairman constructed to shape the regulatory environment in a manner suited to the oversight body's new-found needs (see also Suddaby and Greenwood 2005; Thornton and Ocasio 2008; Tracey, Philips and Jarvis 2011).

Conclusion

This chapter has explored the nature of the efforts to reconfigure the regulation and governance of the accounting profession as it has evolved to embrace and serve globalised enterprise. Drawing on over a decade studying regulatory change in the Irish context, it illuminates how the state – and in particular its supporting agencies – engages in institutional work in its interactions with the accounting profession as it seeks to legitimise and implement changes in the governance of the profession.

Extensive examinations of the processes through which professional accounting regulation has been developed and interpreted exist in the literature (see, for example, Canning and O'Dwyer 2013; Caramanis, Dedoulis and Leventis 2015; MacDonald and Richardson 2004; Malsch and Gendron 2011; O'Regan and Killian 2014; Yee 2012; Young 1994, 1995). It is, however, also important, to explicitly examine how new regulation is implemented by studying how oversight bodies interact at the micro level with the accounting profession during dynamic processes seeking changes in the profession's governance. This can expose the "jockey[ing] for positions that [operates to] confer legitimacy on [oversight bodies] as they attempt to ensure [their] relevance and survival" (Gillis, Petty and Suddaby 2014: 897). It also unveils not only the regulatory consequences of the profession's enhanced focus on serving globalised enterprise, but also exposes the profession's own enterprising nature when responding to threats to it self-regulatory authority.

The dynamic involved in shifting the governance of the profession does not simply involve government imposition on a previously self-regulated profession (Radcliffe, Cooper and Robson 1994). Instead, movements among assorted constituencies influence the relative power of these constituencies in ways that are not evident from a standpoint that relies on a simple antagonism between a homogenous profession and the state. By focusing on individuals and their day-to-day efforts which can be "successful and not, simultaneously radical and conservative, strategic and emotional, full of compromises, and rife with unintended consequences" (Lawrence, Suddaby and Leca 2011: 52), an institutional work framing also allows researchers to connect to practical issues surrounding regulatory change, thereby increasing the practical relevance of management (and accounting) research (Alvesson and Sandberg 2011, 2013; Kieser, Nicolai and Seidl 2015).

We conclude our chapter by advising scholars not to lose sight of the local in their quests to prioritise studies of global regulatory arrangements seeking to govern professions. While we accept that such studies are important given transnational developments, they should not lead us to lose sight of the detailed processes through which these global regulations are translated at local level. Furthermore, studying the interactions between local and global regulators offers insights into how local regulatory mandates are operationalised in the presence of global pressures and highlights how regulatory shifts can be substantive in some contexts (Canning and O'Dwyer 2013, 2016) while symbolic in others

(Hazgui and Gendron 2015). This supports the importance of recognising the social and political landscape in which regulation is embedded (Caramanis, Dedoulis and Leventis 2015) and for us to continue to investigate, rather than presume, passivity on the part of local regulators (Canning and O'Dwyer 2013).

Notes

1 Institutional logics provide a link between institutions and action (Thornton and Ocasio 2008) by offering belief systems that furnish guidelines for practical action. They represent frames of reference used by actors to inform their sense making and are reflected in their vocabulary, actions and sense of self and identity (Greenwood, Diaz, Li and Lorente 2010; Thornton, Ocasio and Lounsbury 2012). They are absorbed into regulatory structures, organisational forms and social norms. They manifest themselves in the issues that are deemed relevant, the goals to be followed, the instruments to be adopted and the standards that are summoned to reflect success (Smets *et al.* 2014).
2 Institutional work considers "institutional actors as reflective, goal-oriented and capable" and prioritises the study of actors' actions in order to "capture structure, agency and their interrelations" (Lawrence, Leca and Zilber 2013: 1024). It can be categorised into the work of actors aimed at creating, maintaining and/or disrupting institutions (Lawrence and Suddaby 2006). Creation work is concerned with the establishment of rules and the construction of rewards and sanctions to enforce those rules. Maintenance work seeks to ensure conformance with existing rules and systems and entails supporting, repairing and recreating social mechanisms. Disruption work involves attacking or undermining the mechanisms that lead actors to comply with institutions (and their rule systems).

References

Abbott, A. (1988) *The System of Professions: An Essay on the Division of Expert Labor*, Chicago, IL: Chicago University Press.
Alvesson, M. and Sandberg, J. (2011) 'Generating research questions through problematization', *Academy of Management Review* 36(2): 247–71.
Alvesson, M. and Sandberg, J. (2013) *Constructing Research Questions: Doing Interesting Research*, London: Sage.
Arnold, P. (2005) 'Disciplining domestic regulation: The World Trade Organization and the market for professional services', *Accounting, Organizations and Society* 30: 299–330.
Arnold, P. (2009) 'Global financial crisis: The challenges to accounting research', *Accounting, Organizations and Society* 34(6/7): 803–9.
Beef Tribunal Inquiry (1994) *Report of the Tribunal of Inquiry into the Beef Processing Industry*, Dublin: The Stationery Office.
Blavoukos, S., Caramanis, C. and Dedoulis, E. (2013) 'Europeanisation, independent bodies and the empowerment of technology: The case of the Greek auditing oversight body', *South European Society and Politics* 18(2): 139–57.
Bougen, P. D., Young, J. J. and Cahill, E. (1999) 'Accountants and the everyday: Or what the papers said about the Irish accountant and tax evasion', *European Accounting Review* 8(3): 443–62.
Canning, M. and O'Dwyer, B. (2001) 'Professional accounting bodies' disciplinary procedures: Accountable, transparent and in the public interest', *European Accounting Review* 10(4): 725–49.

Canning, M. and O'Dwyer, B. (2003) 'A critique of the descriptive power of the private interest model of professional accounting ethics: An examination over time in the Irish context', *Accounting, Auditing and Accountability Journal* 16(2): 159–85.

Canning, M. and O'Dwyer, B. (2013) 'The dynamics of a regulatory space realignment: Strategic responses in a local context', *Accounting, Organizations and Society* 38(3): 169–94.

Canning, M. and O'Dwyer, B. (2016) 'Institutional work and regulatory change in the accounting profession', *Accounting, Organizations and Society* 56: 1–21.

Caramanis, C. (1999) 'International accounting firms versus indigenous auditors: Intra-professional conflict in the Greek auditing profession', *Critical Perspectives on Accounting* 10: 153–96.

Caramanis, C. (2002) 'The interplay between professional groups, the state and supra-national agents: Pax Americana in the age of "globalization"', *Accounting, Organizations and Society* 27: 379–408.

Caramanis, C. (2005) 'Rationalisation, charisma and accounting professionalisation: Perspectives on the intra-professional conflict in Greece, 1993–2001', *Accounting, Organizations and Society* 30(3): 195–221.

Caramanis, C., Dedoulis, E. and Leventis, S. (2010) 'The establishment of EU-inspired "independent" oversight boards: Local constraints and the elusive feat of Europeanization in Greece'. Paper presented at the European Accounting Association Annual Congress, Istanbul, April.

Caramanis, C., Dedoulis, E. and Leventis, S. (2015) 'Transplanting Anglo-American accounting oversight boards to a diverse institutional context', *Accounting, Organizations and Society* 42: 12–31.

Catasus, B., Hellman, N. and Humphrey, C. (2013) 'Thinking differently: Making audit innovation the new practice standard', in Humphrey, C., Catasus, B. and Hellman, N. *The Role of Auditing in Corporate Governance*, Stockholm: SNS Forlag.

Clemens, B. W. and Douglas, T. J. (2005) 'Understanding strategic responses to institutional pressures', *Journal of Business Research* 58: 1205–13.

Cooper, D. J., Hinings, B., Greenwood, R. and Brown, J. L. (1996) 'Sedimentation and transformation in organizational change: The case of Canadian Law firms', *Organization Studies* 17(4): 623–47.

Cooper, D. J. and Robson, K. (2006) 'Accounting, professions and regulation: Locating the sites of professionalization', *Accounting, Organizations and Society* 31(4/5): 415–44.

Currie, G., Lockett, A., Finn, R., Martin, G. and Waring, J. (2012) 'Institutional work to maintain professional power: Recreating the model of medical professionalism', *Organization Studies* 33: 937–62.

Djelic, M. L. and Sahlin, K. (2009) 'Governance and its transnational dynamics: Towards a reordering of our world', in Chapman, C., Cooper, D. J. and Miller, P. B. (eds) *Accounting, Organizations, and Institutions*, Oxford: Oxford University Press.

Empson, L. Cleaver, I. and Allen, J. (2013) 'Managing partners and management professionals: Institutional work dyads in professional partnerships', *Journal of Management Studies* 50(5): 808–44.

Erwin, K. (2009) *Joint Committee on Economic Regulatory Affairs – 31 March 2009 Role and Functions: Discussion with Irish Auditing and Accounting Supervisory Authority*. Available at: http://debates.oireachtas.ie/ERJ/2009/03/31/00003.asp

Erwin, K. (2012) *Joint Committee on Jobs, Enterprise and Innovation – 18 December 2012 Scrutiny of EU Legislative Proposals: Discussion with Irish Auditing and Accounting Supervisory Authority*. Available at: http://oireachtasdebates.oireachtas.ie/Debates%20Authoring/DebatesWebPack.nsf/committeetakes/BUJ2012121800003

Gawer, A. and Phillips, N. (2013) 'Institutional work as logics shift: The case of Intel's transformation to platform leader', *Organization Studies* 34(8): 1035–71.

Gillis, P., Petty, R. and Suddaby, R. (2014) 'The transnational regulation of accounting: Insights, gaps and an agenda for future research', *Accounting, Auditing and Accountability Journal* 27(6): 874–902.

Goodstein, J. D. (1994) 'Institutional pressures and strategic responsiveness: Employer involvement in work-family issues', *Academy Management Journal* 3: 350–82.

Greenwood, R., Diaz, A. M., Li, S. X. and Lorente, J. C. (2010) 'The multiplicity of institutional logics and the heterogeneity of organizational responses', *Organization Science* 21(2): 521–39.

Hampel, C., Lawrence, T. and Tracey, P. (2017) 'Institutional work: Taking stock and making it matter', in Greenwood, R., Lawrence, T., Oliver, C. and Meyer, R. (eds) *The Sage Handbook of Organizational Institutionalism*, London: Sage, 2nd edition.

Hancher, L. and Moran, M. (1989) 'Organizing regulatory space', in Hancher, L. and Moran, M. (eds) *Capitalism, Culture and Regulation*, Oxford: Clarendon Press.

Hazgui, M. and Gendron, Y. (2015) 'Blurred roles and elusive boundaries', *Accounting, Auditing and Accountability Journal* 28(8): 1234–62.

Hazgui, M., Lesage, C. and Pochet, C. (2011) 'Independent audit oversight: A comparative study of the United States and France'. Working paper, Paris: HEC, July.

Humphrey, C. (2008) 'Auditing research: A review across the disciplinary divide', *Accounting, Auditing and Accountability Journal* 21(2): 170–203.

Humphrey, C., Kausar, A., Loft, A. and Woods, M. (2011) 'Regulating audit beyond the crisis: A critical discussion of the EU Green Paper', *European Accounting Review* 20(3): 431–57.

Humphrey, C., Kokkali, S. and Samsonova, A. (2010) 'Debating the transnational nature of European policymaking – The case of auditor liability limitation'. Paper prepared for presentation at the Alternative Accounts conference and workshop, Toronto, April.

Humphrey, C., Loft, A. and Woods, M. (2009) 'The global audit profession and the international financial architecture: Understanding regulatory relationships at a time of financial crisis', *Accounting, Organizations and Society* 34(6/7): 810–25.

Humphrey, C., O'Dwyer, B. and Unerman, J. (2017) 'Re-theorizing the configuration of organizational fields: The IIRC and the pursuit of "enlightened" corporate reporting', *Accounting and Business Research* 47(1): 30–63.

Jeppesen, K. K. and Loft, A. (2011) 'Regulating audit in Europe: The case of the implementation of the EU Eight Directive in Denmark 1984–2006', *European Accounting Review* 20(2): 321–54.

Kieser, A., Nicolai, A. and Seidl, D. (2015) 'The practical relevance of management research: Turning the debate on relevance into a rigorous scientific research program', *Academy of Management Annals* 9(1): 143–233.

Lawrence, T. B., Leca, B. and Zilber, T. B. (2013) 'Institutional work: Research, new directions and overlooked issues', *Organization Studies* 34(8): 1023–33.

Lawrence, T. B. and Suddaby, R. (2006) 'Institutions and institutional work', in Clegg, S. R., Hardy, C. Lawrence, T. B. and Nord, W. R. (eds) *Handbook of Organization Studies*, London: Sage, 2nd edition.

Lawrence, T. B., Suddaby, R. and Leca, B. (2009) 'Introduction: Theorizing and studying institutional work', in Lawrence, T. B., Suddaby, R. and Leca, B. (eds) *Institutional Work: Actors and Agency in Institutional Studies of Organizations*, Cambridge: Cambridge University Press.

Lawrence, T. B., Suddaby, R. and Leca, B. (2011) 'Institutional work: Refocusing institutional studies of organization', *Journal of Management Inquiry* 20: 52–58.

Lee, T. A. (1995) 'The professionalization of accountancy: A history of protecting the public interest in a self-interested way', *Accounting, Auditing and Accountability Journal* 8(4): 48–69.

Loft, A., Humphrey, C. and Turley, S. (2006) 'In pursuit of global regulation: Changing governance structures at the international federation of accountants (IFAC)', *Accounting, Auditing and Accountability Journal* 19(3): 428–51.

McCracken Report (1997) *Report of the Tribunal of Inquiry (Dunnes Payments)*, Dublin: The Stationery Office.

MacDonald, L. D. and Richardson, A. J. (2004) 'Identity, appropriateness and the construction of regulatory space: The formation of the Public Accountant's Council of Ontario', *Accounting, Organizations and Society* 29(5/6): 489–524.

Malsch, B. and Gendron, Y. (2011) 'Reining in auditors: On the dynamics of power surrounding an "innovation" in the regulatory space', *Accounting, Organizations and Society* 36: 456–76.

Marquis, C. and Lounsbury, M. (2007) 'Vive la resistance: Competing logics and the consolidation of U.S. community banking', *Academy of Management Journal* 56: 799–820.

Moore, D. A., Tetlock, P. E., Tanlu, L. and Bazerman, M. H. (2006) 'Conflicts of interest and the case of auditor independence: Moral seduction and strategic issue recycling', *Academy of Management Review* 31(1): 10–29.

Muzio, D., Brock, D. M. and Suddaby, R. (2013) 'Professions and institutional change: Towards an institutionalist sociology of professions', *Journal of Management Studies* 50(5): 699–721.

Muzio, D., Faulconbridge, J., Gabbioneta, C. and Greenwood, R. (2016) 'Bad apples, bad barrels and bad cellars: A 'boundaries' perspective on professional misconduct', in Palmer, D., Smith-Crowe, K. and Greenwood, R. (eds) *Organizational Wrongdoing*, Cambridge: Cambridge University Press.

O'Regan, P. (2009) 'Regulation, the public interest and the establishment of an accounting supervisory body', *Journal of Management and Governance* 14(4): 297–312.

O'Regan, P. and Killian, S. (2014) '"Professionals who understand": Expertise, public interest and societal risk governance', *Accounting, Organizations and Society* 39(8): 615–31.

Quack, S. and Schubler, E. (2017) 'Dynamics of regulation of professional service firms: National and transnational developments', in Empson, L., Muzio, D., Broschak, J. and Hinings, B. (eds) *The Oxford Handbook of Professional Service Firms*, Oxford: Oxford University Press.

Radcliffe, V., Cooper, D. J. and Robson, K. (1994) 'The management of professional enterprises and regulatory change: British accountancy and the Financial Services Act, 1986', *Accounting, Organizations and Society* 19(7): 601–28.

Review Group on Auditing (2000) *Report of the Review Group on Auditing*, Dublin: The Stationery Office.

Richardson, A. (2009) 'Regulatory networks for accounting and auditing standards: A social network analysis of Canadian and international standard setters', *Accounting, Organizations and Society* 34(5): 571–88.

Robson, K., Willmott, H., Cooper, D. J., and Puxty, T. (1994) 'The ideology of professional regulation and the markets for accounting labour: Three episodes in the recent history of the UK accountancy profession', *Accounting Organizations and Society* 19(6): 527–53.

Saks, M. (1995) *Professions and the Public Interest: Medical Power, Altruism and Alternative Medicine*, London: Routledge.

Scott, C. (2001) 'Analysing regulatory space: Fragmented resources and institutional design', *Public Law* Summer: 329–53.

Scott, W. R. (2008) 'Lords of the dance: Professionals as institutional agents', *Organization Studies* 29: 219–38.
Shapiro, B. and Matson, D. (2008) 'Strategies of resistance to internal control regulation', *Accounting, Organizations and Society* 33(2/3): 199–228.
Sikka, P. and Willmott, H. (1995) 'Illuminating the state-profession relationship: Accountants acting as department of trade and industry investigators', *Critical Perspectives on Accounting* 6(4): 341–69.
Smets, M., Jarzabkowski, P., Spee, A. P. and Burke, G. (2014) 'Reinsurance trading in Lloyd's of London: Balancing conflicting-yet-complementary logics in practice', *Academy of Management Journal* 58(3): 932–70.
Suddaby, R., Cooper, D. J. and Greenwood, R. (2007) 'Transnational regulation of professional services: Governance dynamics of field level organizational change', *Accounting, Organizations and Society* 32(4/5): 333–62.
Suddaby, R. and Greenwood, R. (2005) 'Rhetorical strategies of legitimacy', *Administrative Science Quarterly* 50: 35–67.
Suddaby, R. and Muzio, D. (2017) 'Theoretical perspectives on the professions', in Empson, L., Muzio, D., Broschak, J. and Hinings, B. (eds) *The Oxford Handbook of Professional Service Firms*, Oxford: Oxford University Press.
Suddaby, R. and Viale, T. (2011) 'Professionals and field-level change: Institutional work and the professional project', *Current Sociology* 59: 423–42.
Suiter, J. (1997) 'Harney again asks accountants to act', *Irish Times* 11 October.
Thornton, P. H. (2004) *Markets from Culture: Institutional Logics and Organizational Decisions in Higher Education Publishing*, Stanford, CA: Stanford University Press.
Thornton, P. H. and Ocasio, W. (1999) 'Institutional logics and the historical contingency of power in organizations: Executive succession in the higher education publishing industry, 1958–1990', *American Journal of Sociology* 105: 801–43.
Thornton, P. H. and Ocasio, W. (2008) 'Institutional logics', in Greenwood, R., Oliver, C., Sahlin, K. and Dussaby, R. (eds) *The Sage Handbook of Organizational Institutionalism*, London: Sage.
Thornton, P. H., Ocasio, W. and Lounsbury, M. (2012) *The Institutional Logics Perspective*, Oxford: Oxford University Press.
Tracey, P., Philips, N. and Jarvis, O. (2011) 'Bridging institutional entrepreneurship and the creation of new organizational forms: A multilevel model', *Organization Science* 22(1): 60–80.
Willmott, H. (1986) 'Organising the profession: A theoretical and historical examination of the development of the major accounting bodies in the UK', *Accounting, Organizations and Society* 11(6): 555–80.
Willmott, H. (1990) 'Serving the public interest? A critical analysis of a professional claim', in Cooper, D. and Hopper, T. (eds) *Critical Accounts*, London: Macmillan.
Willmott, H., Cooper, D. and Puxty, T. (1993) 'Maintaining self-regulation: Making interests coincide in discourses on the governance of the ICAEW', *Accounting, Auditing and Accountability Journal* 6(4): 68–93.
Yee, H. (2012) 'Analyzing the state-accounting profession dynamic: Some insights from the professionalization experience in China', *Accounting, Organizations and Society* 37(6): 426–44.
Young, J. (1994) 'Outlining regulatory space: Agenda issues and the FASB', *Accounting, Organizations and Society* 19(1): 83–109.
Young, J. (1995) 'Getting the accounting "right": Accounting and savings and loan crisis', *Accounting, Organizations and Society* 20(1): 55–80.

10 The medical profession, enterprise and the public interest

Mike Saks

Introduction

In this chapter, the role of the medical profession is analysed in the enterprise context in which doctors work in the public and private sector – with a particular focus on the United States and Britain, albeit with brief wider international referents in the modern world. The reason for the choice of countries is that the United States and Britain, while representing species of liberal democracies in the global economy, have different political philosophies – spanning from the more privatised, relatively free market principles of the United States, which gives greater emphasis to individual liberty, to the more mixed economy in Britain, with stronger but by no means overriding state welfare principles (Saks 2015c). Both countries nonetheless in different ways have provided enterprise environments. From a neo-Weberian perspective, this chapter considers at a macro level the prevalence of altruistic professional values in medicine in each of these societies, such that the self-interests of professional groups are subordinated to the wider public interest. In this respect, it asks whether professional claims to serve collective interests are simply an ideological smokescreen to mask group self-interests in enhancing income, status and power. In so doing, it employs an interlinked neo-institutionalist approach to explore broader entrepreneurial forces that have shaped the activities of the medical profession in the wider health care division of labour in the Anglo-American context and beyond. This discussion, as will be seen, takes place in the context of the fast-changing health systems on both sides of the Atlantic – where seismic shifts in the structural frame of reference for health care have taken place, not least since the Second World War (Klein 2013; Scott *et al.* 2000). However, initially the theoretical framework underpinning this discussion will be elucidated.

Theories of the professions: medicine, enterprise and the public interest

Reference to macro theories of the professions leads us to recall that such perspectives were first and most fully developed in the United States and Britain. Up to the 1960s and 1970s in the form of the trait approach and structural functionalism these initially took a generally benevolent view of the professions – including medicine, alongside such other top ranking occupational groups with high socio-economic rewards like law. Trait writers typically defined professions by distinguishing them from other occupations in terms of a range of disparate, but desirable, characteristics – from their certified high-level expertise to codes of ethics (see, for example, Greenwood 1957; Wilensky 1964). Functionalists meanwhile adopted a more integrated positive theoretical approach based on the needs of the social system. Here it was argued that there was a functional trade-off such that professional groups like medicine gained a privileged social position for employing their esoteric knowledge of great importance to society in a non-exploitative manner (see, for instance, Barber 1963; Goode 1960). This provides a convenient link both to enterprise and to the public interest in so far as professions in this sense were generally seen as distinct from business in subordinating their self-interests to the public interest, even if more sophisticated functionalists like Parsons (1952) noted that it was not necessarily the case that professions were different from business in acting altruistically – not least because the relative conceptions were based on ideal types and the nature of their activities needed to be empirically established on an evidential basis.

Such generally sugar-coated views of professions like medicine, though, came under heavy attack in the 1960s/70s counter culture for being less than positive forces in society – as professional groups more generally were criticised for, among other things, generating illusions of progress and disempowering users of services (Roszack 1995). Indeed, it was argued that the proponents of altruism had reflexively and uncritically taken the ideologies of professions on trust and that there was little or no distinction between such professions and other occupations, including those in the business world (Hughes 1963; Roth 1974). Rather, the notion of a profession was seen as an honorific symbol used entrepreneurially in the politics of work to sustain claims for substantially higher socio-economic rewards (Becker 1962). Certainly, in terms of codes of ethics, the medical and other professions in the Anglo-American context did emphasise their service to the public – even if in Britain these codes were more heavily weighted towards a collectivity orientation than in the United States where a client focus predominantly prevailed in line with their respective neo-liberal socio-political philosophies (Saks 1995). More recent critiques of this self-proclaimed altruistic ideology of medicine and other professions at a macro theoretical level will now be outlined.

Foucauldian contributors have argued that welfare professions, including medicine, have impeded rather than facilitated societal development, thereby casting considerable doubt on their public interest credentials. The basis for this belief is largely predicated on the idea that such professional groups have been integrated into the task of governance in the modern state in a manner that has negatively affected their operation (Johnson 1995). In consequence, their commonly perceived association with rational scientific progress in terms of benefit to humankind in areas such as mental illness (Foucault 2001), obstetrics (Arney 1982) and dentistry (Nettleton 1992) has been contested as professionalisation has been seen to increase state control. However, aside from the methodological flaws of the governmentality approach based on its typically cavalier use of evidence (Jones and Porter 1994) and the lack of an analytical separation of professions and the state which makes it difficult to operationalise (Saks 2012), it does not focus in this context on the direct links between professions and enterprise, except in the most general way through the activity of making populations governable. This is a charge, though, that could not be levelled at Marxist theorists of the professions in Britain and the United States who have been concerned to tie them into the fabric of capitalism in these countries and have generally not been complimentary about their role in class-divided neo-liberal societies.

To be sure, there are debates within Marxism about how professions like medicine should be regarded under capitalism. Most writers like Ehrenreich and Ehrenreich (1979) see them as some kind of a 'professional-managerial class' engaged in surveillance and control for a capitalist class that owns the means of production or like Navarro (1986) as part of a more broadly cast capitalist class itself. However, some contributors – following the position of Braverman (1998) on the labour process – view this as a transitional role, with growing proletarianisation of the medical profession as highly skilled work is degraded with the development of capitalism (McKinlay and Arches 1985). Nonetheless, medicine and such related personal service professions as social work and counselling are typically held to be maintaining the capitalist *status quo* in the interests of the bourgeoisie. This is highlighted by Esland (1980) who argues, among other things, that the individualisation of health problems distracts attention from the enterprise-linked structural conditions under capitalism that create them and need to be addressed if they are to be resolved. Such accounts again undermine the altruistic ideologies of medicine because of the entanglement of doctors and other cognate professions in what is considered to be an oppressive capitalist system. However, they are again often methodologically flawed, particularly when based on a tautological view of the state as inevitably serving the interests of capital (Saunders 2007).

Since it sidesteps the key methodological problems of Foucauldianism and Marxism, the macro perspective adopted in this chapter on professional altruism in medicine is that of neo-Weberianism. If appropriately set up and operationalised, this framework allows professions generally to be analysed in a more open fashion than that of either of the perspectives outlined above; by simply defining professions in terms of exclusionary social closure in the market it avoids fixed assumptions about them and provides the possibility of both positive and negative outcomes regarding the self-interest versus public interest debate, following empirical investigation (Saks 1995). This is not to say that all neo-Weberians have realised the potential of the approach in practice (Saks 2016b), but there are great advantages in seeing professionalisation as restricting access to socio-economic opportunities to a limited circle of eligibles through legal monopolies underwritten by the state (Parkin 1979), whether through state-by-state licensing as in the United States or a more federalised structure as in Britain (Saks 2015b). Although this is normally seen as enhancing the interests of the group concerned in terms of occupational rewards, the tools adapted from Max Weber (1968) enable professions to be more subtly examined, including their interface with state decision making in enterprising environments. This is assisted by the complementary adoption of the neo-institutional perspective which views professions as one among several key actors competing with each other nationally and internationally in an ecology of institutional forms (Muzio, Brock and Suddaby 2013).

Saks (1995) has in fact developed a neo-Weberian methodological framework to analyse the relationship between professional self-interests and the public interest in a medical context – illustrated by a case study of the extent to which the British medical profession responded flexibly to the innovatory practice of acupuncture in an enterprise context. This is a tricky task as both the concept of interests and that of the public interest are shrouded in contention and debate (see respectively Lukes 2005; King and Chilton 2009). In the case of professional interests, Saks (1995) avoids the bear trap of seeing these as subjective preferences, not least because people can mistake their interests, and prefers to view them as being realised when benefits objectively outweigh costs in terms of income, status and power in decision making – duly taking account of the potential influence on perceptions of interest by powerful elites in society (Saks 2016a). In the case of the public interest, he similarly sidesteps such difficulties as those posed by preponderance accounts which do not always sufficiently encompass minority interests in favour of judging the public interest against the particular political parameters extant in specific societies. In the case of the United States and Britain these include their own variants of the political values underpinning liberal democracies – namely, justice, liberty and the collective welfare (Saks 2018 forthcoming). This leads neatly on to the consideration of the link between the medical profession and enterprise in the United States in terms of the balance between self-interests and the public interest.

Medicine in the United States

Medicine has for long been deeply influenced by enterprise in the United States, a society in which individual freedom has been viewed as the primary political good with charity as the main means for displaying social concern – with greater emphasis given to the 'hidden hand' of the market, alongside equality before the law (Rodwin 2011). This has meant that perhaps more than any other modern country, American medicine has been dominated by the private sector. Having said this, there has been significant state intervention in the regulation of professional practice in this wider entrepreneurial framework, in which private corporations are more powerful in the medical arena than in Britain (Moran 1999). Notwithstanding its rather different value system, though, as we shall see, the extent to which doctors meet the public interest in the United States can be challenged with reference to the negative impact of big business and private enterprise on features like co-ordination and social divisions in a system in which the medical profession is embroiled (Rosenthal 2017). This is crystallised by the fact that, while it has the most expensive health provision in the world as a proportion of gross domestic product, the United States has a poorer performance in terms of life expectancy and other health indicators than many other modern neoliberal societies (Tulchinsky and Varavikova 2009).

The impact of the competitive American market structure in a relatively *laissez-faire* economy was apparent even before the licensing of physicians on a state-by-state basis emerged at the beginning of the twentieth century, when anyone was free to practice. This may explain the vitriolic attacks on so-called 'quacks' who challenged the earnings and thereby the interests of impecunious 'regular' doctors in the marketplace in the eighteenth and nineteenth centuries, at a time when they sought to forge a group identity in a strongly anti-monopolistic culture (Stevens 1998). In this process the American Medical Association played a very important role in the serial development of medical licensing across the United States which restricted competition in the *de jure* monopoly that was established by the early twentieth century – in a predominantly fee-for-service system with high levels of physician self-employment (Berlant 1975). The position of physicians in the market was further enhanced by the 1910 Flexner reforms of medical standards which drove out homeopathic rivals with whom they had allied in their drive for professionalisation by closing down their schools, which did not meet the level set (Kaufman 1988). It was at this point that the enterprise of medicine started to be significantly affected by the rise of corporatisation.

As Starr (1982) documents, an increasing number of corporations adopted medical care schemes for workers, which – along with the growing number of private hospitals in a predominantly private market – pushed medical fees down and more generally challenged the power and status of doctors. Nonetheless, given the protection the Federal Drugs Administration offered against unlicensed practitioners and the enhanced control the medical profession gained over the supply of doctors, among other things, physicians still managed to pursue their own individual and group interests in the market frequently at the expense of the broader public good – as exemplified by the wide inequalities in geographical access to physicians that developed between more and less attractive states, and between urban and rural areas (Anderson 1989). Operating on behalf of physicians as largely independent medical entrepreneurs, the American Medical Association was also able to successfully fight against proposals for a comprehensive health insurance scheme before the Second World War, to the detriment of many citizens. However, this freedom in the so-called 'golden age of medicine' (Brandt and Gardner 2000) was not to last long as a growing number of private third-party providers came to challenge the power of physicians with the escalating costs of specialist high technology medicine – along with ever larger corporate pharmaceutical and surgical companies that also compromised medical independence in prescribing and other matters (Gabriel 2014), to the potential cost of patients (Goldacre 2013).

Doctors, especially in more prestigious areas of medicine such as heart surgery as opposed to general practice, were at first able to benefit from this position in terms of income, status and power in a health care structure where patients were free to go without referral directly to the burgeoning number of specialists who typically held co-terminous hospital appointments (Weisz 2006). This was reinforced in a fee-based marketplace by state support at federal and local level up to the mid-twentieth century for medical dominance over limited and subordinated health professions in the division of labour, including the gendered area of nursing (Roberts and Group 2001) and hitherto excluded alternative practitioner competitor groups (Johnson 2004). Thereafter, in a system which remained heavily privatised, inegalitarian, fragmented and decentralised with much expensive duplication of medical facilities and rising health expenditure, it was a long and slippery slope for physicians as a professional group. To be sure, from the mid-1960s onwards inequalities were mitigated in the public interest to some degree – if by no means completely (Ng, Harrington and Kitchener 2010) – by the federally funded Medicare programme for the elderly and the state-run Medicaid system for the poor. These schemes operated alongside company medical services, prepaid group schemes like Kaiser Permanente, individual commercial insurance schemes, and non-profit Blue Cross and Blue Shield plans (Peltz 2008). Although the public-facing developments of Medicare and Medicaid – that physicians initially fought against in a non-altruistic manner – benefited them financially (Potter 2013), the growing corporate environment increasingly weighed heavily on the otherwise powerful male-dominated medical profession (Krause 1996).

This is largely because cost containment in the public interest became a top priority in a competitive enterprise environment in both the private sector, attracting the majority of health care expenditure, and federal, state and local government settings with fewer resources (Cacace 2012). As a result of standardised fee-setting procedures through Diagnostic Related Groups (Blank and Burau 2010), doctors faced a real challenge to their income, status and power in both non-profit and for-profit hospitals. This dynamic can be illustrated in managed care where Health Maintenance Organisations (HMOs) have been favoured in providing prepaid group and hospital services over the past few decades because of their focus on cost reduction for subscribers (Starr 1982). Unfortunately, in a world of big business, they have not only driven down the reimbursement of doctors, but also been associated with high administrative costs and compromised quality in health care – leading many HMOs to be acquired, merged or bankrupted (Coombs 2005). By the same token employers have sought to reduce costs by limiting employee entitlement in private health insurance schemes. The net result has been to increase patterns of multidimensional unequal access to health care (Barr 2014) – in a situation where until recently tens of millions of Americans possessed either no or inadequate levels of health insurance (Cacace 2012).

However, after several unsuccessful attempts by a number of governments in the United States to provide more universal health insurance coverage (Starr 2013), this has now been addressed by Obamacare – which has extended provision in this area through a combination of incentivisation and political subsidies to support egalitarian health care provision in a predominantly private market, in a manner resonant with the underpinning philosophy of America's version of liberal democracy (Allhoff and Hall 2014). This might therefore be seen as advancing the public interest in the United States – despite the attempts by President Donald Trump to repeal the Obama health reforms (Nelson and Fuller 2017). Nonetheless, the American Medical Association has generally continued to oppose such reforms along with health insurance companies and employers (Haas-Wilson 2003), even if it has been prepared to compromise over aspects of Obamacare that do not involve increased quality reporting measures and decreased physician payment (Potter 2013). Although a number of factors appear to have delayed the adoption of these market-oriented egalitarian reforms (see, for instance, Hacker 2001), the main fear of physicians seems to have been interest based – namely, the extension of bureaucratic subordination to organisational administrators in a manner damaging to their power and status and the reduction of financial rewards (Ramsden 2013). Given that the United States was the only major modern capitalist democracy not to have universal health care (Starr 2013), doubt can thereby be shed on how far the professional altruism ideal in medicine has been implemented in practice at a macro level.

This is not the only time that medical self-interests have significantly been asserted in face of the public interest in this marketised neo-liberal society – which in health care paradoxically boasts the most advanced facilities globally alongside some of the highest inefficiency levels, notwithstanding recent efforts by government to augment the quality of medical care (Bradley and Taylor 2013). This is underlined by the response by doctors in the United States to increasingly successful challenges from the allied health professions (Malka 2007) and state-by-state licensing of rival alternative health care groups such as chiropractors with more oppositional philosophies to orthodox biomedicine (Saks 2015a). The attacks by medical elites on these potential interlopers in an enterprise economy when incorporation within the profession on favourable terms was not possible highlight the operation of self-interests (see, for instance, Cayleff 2016). They also suggest the subversion of the public good at a time when public demand for – and expenditure on – unorthodox therapies has been sharply rising and the voice of consumers in medicine has been expanding through legal and other mechanisms beyond market structures in the wake of the counter culture (Saks 2000). Nonetheless, the growing influence of consumers has to some degree emaciated the income, status and power of medicine in a country where the state has intervened primarily to shore up the private market. The major impact of such state positioning on trends towards medical deprofessionalisation, though, has been through national and multinational corporations – even if top end medical specialists still command high professional rewards (Saks 2015c).

Medicine in Britain

The effects of such corporatisation on the medical profession in the largely marketised American economy have not occurred so extensively in modern Britain, where stronger collective welfare and egalitarian principles underpin liberal democracy (Newton and van Deth 2010). Consequently, at a macro level, more stress has characteristically been placed on meeting basic needs than on individual liberty in its mixed economy, which lies further along the continuum from marketisation to statism (Grimmeisen and Frisina 2010). To be sure, therefore, private enterprise has thrived, but has been balanced in the contemporary context by greater public sector engagement than in the United States to ensure justice and human rights, on which the articulation of the public interest is based (Saks 1995). This is most starkly represented in medicine by the National Health Service (NHS) which was established in Britain in the mid-twentieth century, alongside a smaller, but growing, private health care system where the medical profession has been afforded greater protection by the state (Saks 2015b). In this framework health expenditure is about half that of the United States relative to gross domestic product with greater tangible benefits in terms of morbidity and mortality (Tulchinsky and Varavikova 2009). As will be seen, though, this more effective performance in a better co-ordinated and less socially divisive setting does not mean the medical profession has necessarily acted in a more altruistic manner than in America, despite its ideology.

However, it should be noted that in terms of enterprise there are parallels with medicine in the United States. In their interlinked colonial histories, there was also a pluralistic market in Britain for health care in the two centuries immediately before the profession of medicine was legally established with exclusionary closure in the mid-nineteenth century. At this time physicians, apothecaries and surgeons competed for custom with 'unofficial' practitioners such as herbalists and purveyors of patent medicine on a predominantly fee-for-service basis, cashing in on the new-found affluence of the developing capitalist economy – in which medical interests were pursued against 'irregulars' in a cutthroat commercial battle for recognition and reward (Porter 2002). Such interests were more fully realised when the various branches of medicine united to gain a *de facto* medical monopoly on a national basis through the Medical Registration Act in 1858. Aside from the federal nature of this monopoly, it differed from that in the United States because it was centred on the protection of medical title for those on a register held by the General Medical Council and did not formally prevent alternative therapists from practising under the Common Law (Berlant 1975). However, it had a similar effect as in terms of legitimacy and the state shelters that were subsequently created; in an overcrowded marketplace it put rivals at a competitive disadvantage and facilitated the upward collective social mobility of doctors, with all the associated increases in income, status and power (Parry and Parry 1976).

Following professionalisation, British doctors were not faced with quite the same array of private corporate bodies in the market as in the United States. Although health insurance schemes were provided by friendly societies, trade unions and private companies, these were mainly supplanted by state support. A landmark here was the 1911 National Health Insurance Act which enabled payment for non-hospitalised medical care for workers from the private practices of general practitioners through capitation fees derived from employees, employers and the state (Ham 2009). However, if this could be seen to advance the public interest by reducing social inequalities, as well as meeting the financial self-interests of doctors as entrepreneurs, the founding of the NHS in 1948 performed this dual function to an even greater extent – not least because of its more extensive contribution to the collective welfare, aligning with the political principles of the British variant of liberal democracy. More specifically, the NHS provided a comprehensive state health service, free at the point of delivery, with capitation pay for generalists and salaries for hospital specialists (Klein 2013). It is therefore perverse that general practitioners should have initially opposed participation to protect their economic independence and medical consultants should have needed their 'mouths stuffed with gold' to enter the service, given the benefits gained (Allsop 1995). In terms of the enterprise environment, though, it was always envisaged that the NHS would also operate alongside a private health service – a position that was to become more significant with the increasing privatisation of services in the NHS in neo-liberal Britain.

But if aspersions may be cast on the altruism of doctors because of their stance on the formation of the NHS, medical professionalisation itself in Britain which took place a century before and fifty years in advance of the United States may also have served their interests more than the wider public. This is because it occurred before major pharmacological and other advances in Western medicine, when the 'heroic' medicine mainly on offer could be very harmful and hospitals were widely seen as 'gateways to death' (Saks 2015c). Against this, though, it should be recognised that there are also occasions when medical practitioners have acted in the public interest. This clearly was the case in the campaign by the British Medical Association in the first half of the twentieth century against 'secret remedies' the often dubious, undeclared contents of which were potentially damaging to consumers on the commercial market (Saks 1992) – thus paralleling the battle for the public good waged at a similar stage by the American Medical Association against more questionable unorthodox practices (Burrow 1963). This said, such actions against alternative practitioners, who continue to operate mainly in the private sector, also accorded with doctors' own interests in asserting dominance over rivals who threaten their income, status and power – highlighting that the public interest and professional group self-interests are not always juxtaposed (Saks 1995). However, today with the growing professionalisation of, and escalating public demand for, alternative medicine in Britain the direction of the public interest might be seen in a rather different perspective (Saks 2015b). So too might the long running territorial struggle in Britain of doctors with nurses, midwives and other professions allied to medicine, particularly with the increasing specialisation and graduate status of the groups concerned in the marketplace (Allsop and Saks 2002).

In an enterprise context, these debates have shaped the content and form of the NHS, which has undergone a number of structural changes since its establishment (Klein 2013). Most significantly, it has resisted the free market drivers for fragmented and extensive mass medical specialisation – respecting the need for salaried hospital specialists working with a balanced number of general practitioners in primary care at the hub of a referral system (Ham 2009). Nonetheless, with the 1960s/1970s counter culture, pressures grew from the state for the male-dominated medical profession to be both more commercially oriented and consumer facing to improve efficiency and effectiveness in the face of resource constraints, in a manner threatening to the interests of doctors (Saks 2015c). Thus, the Conservative government in Britain from 1979 onwards sought to appoint general managers to bring greater American-style private sector principles into the NHS and to decrease the autonomy of medicine which it saw as obstructing market forces (Allsop 1995). This was coupled with encouraging greater patient use of private medicine, promoting contracting out for domestic and other services, creating an 'internal market' with a purchaser–provider split, establishing self-governing hospital and community trusts and general practitioner fundholders, and introducing a Patients' Charter setting out patient rights and standards (Levitt, Wall and Appleby 1999). Such potential public interest reforms, however, were in part subverted by the self-interests of the medical profession – because, among other things, doctors themselves colonised general manager posts (Harrison and Pollitt 1994) and helped to ensure that the principles to protect users were formalistic, limited and without mandatory force (Saks 2002).

While the notions of both competition in the market and the previous command-type structures were subsequently downplayed in British health care policy, doctors came under further challenge with New Labour from 1997 when Tony Blair attempted to modernise the NHS with a focus on service enhancement and reducing inequalities (Saks 2015c). Pivotal to this was the concept of partnership to break down market fragmentation and to increase collaboration between both health professions and service agencies. One mechanism to achieve this was to give primary care more leverage in commissioning services – which has led to the restratification of the medical profession in so far as general practitioners have as a result grown in influence and standing as compared to hospital specialists, in contrast to the United States (Calnan and Gabe 2009). Another method was to improve clinical governance and increased public engagement (Tritter *et al*. 2010), while strengthening structural and operational links between health and social care through more interprofessional working (Thomas, Pollard and Sellman 2014) and enhancing market controls over pharmaceutical companies that were potentially threatening to the effective delivery of health care (Abraham 2009). But the biggest change was to respond to a number of worrying abuse scandals in medicine, including that of the serial killing Dr Harold Shipman, by reforming the medical profession – not least by introducing regular appraisals, systematic re-accreditation, greater lay representation on the General Medical Council, independent adjudication of disciplinary cases and a regulatory oversight body with referral powers back to the medical profession (Chamberlain 2015).

A number of these reforms were enacted from 2010 onwards by the Conservative-Liberal Democratic Coalition and the subsequent Conservative government that have created a system of more devolved 'regulated self-regulation' in medicine with greater levels of collaboration – underwritten by the 2012 Health and Social Care Act (Saks 2016c). They have thereby managed to reduce the formal power of medicine in Britain, albeit in ways that accord with the public interest in protecting patients, but not on the same scale as in America in the wake of corporatisation. Having said this, while neo-liberal Britain has had a less explicit enterprise culture in medicine, it has made increased efforts to improve the synergies between the public and private sector in health care for patient benefit since the turn of the twenty-first century (Klein 2013). Despite the differences in the political underpinning of the respective health systems, Britain has also adopted similar principles to America of the New Public Management. This is based centrally on performance audits and outcome measures in increasing managerial control and driving down costs in the public sector, mirroring the steps taken in the less prevalent private sector (Dent 2015). Interestingly, though, doctors in Britain have succeeded within the protective shell of the state in ensuring that these new challenges to their position have at least partially been deflected, including through the hybridisation of medical managers who protect institutionalised professionalism in organisational contexts (McGivern *et al.* 2015). This underlines that – despite the altruistic ideology of the profession – medical self-interests have not yet been firmly subordinated to the public interest in the increasingly commercialised environment of British society.

Conclusion: the medical profession in international perspective

This chapter has shown from a neo-Weberian and neo-institutionalist perspective that the medical profession in the United States and Britain has in different, but interconnected, ways operated in an enterprise context. Of course, medicine has primarily been the domain of professional groups rather than professional service firms as in accountancy and law (Brock and Saks 2016) – notwithstanding the involvement of groups like management consultants in evaluating medical performance outcomes and advising on health system reform on both sides of the Atlantic (Klein 2013; Light 2010). But this does not diminish the significance of the comparative case of medicine in the Anglo-American context in illuminating the interface between professionalism and enterprise, which particularly in the United States seems to have led to a substantial diminution of the standing of the medical profession. The comparison importantly too raises wider issues in its consideration of the public interest about the benefits or otherwise of the free market, both more generally and in this specific area (for counterposed views on this subject see, for example, Friedman 1962; Stiglitz 2010). In this respect, the analysis of medicine has also indicated at a helicopter level that, in the two liberal democratic settings examined, the altruism claims of doctors can often be challenged – even if at times the medical profession can be seen to have acted in the public interest. Although this chapter has necessarily been broad brush in focusing on the medical profession as a whole at a macro level, rather than breaking it down into smaller segments, it is clear that professional altruistic ideologies have at least in part served as rhetorical smokescreens masking professional self-interests in the enterprise environments in which they are embedded in both the private and public sectors.

Nonetheless, the issues raised about medicine in this chapter are not particular to the United States and Britain, but generalise to other modern neo-liberal societies. Of course, some commentators have argued that the concept of exclusionary professional closure in medicine is applicable primarily to the Anglo-American context because of the more limited autonomy of doctors and other professions in organisational bureaucracies elsewhere (see, for instance, Evetts 2006; Sciulli 2005). However, while full professional social closure is less prevalent in other modern societies, in many neo-liberal countries from Australia to Canada strong forms of exclusionary closure in medicine exist on a spectrum with various levels of independent regulation (Saks 2010). In this global framework, there is a range of international work which picks up the key contemporary professions and enterprise themes of this chapter. Thus Boyce (2008), for instance, examines the implications of the New Public Management reforms related to entrepreneurialism for professional cultures in health services in Australia. Allsop and Jones (2008) meanwhile consider arrangements for professional governance in medicine in enterprise contexts in a wider span of countries, including Canada and New Zealand. At another remove, Blomgren and Waks (2015) highlight the role of professional logic in the hybridisation of medical managers in Sweden where several institutional logics are at work – while Kirkpatrick and colleagues (2015) discuss more broadly in Europe the upshot of attempts to put doctors into hybrid clinical management roles. Further such research is necessary if the relationship between the medical profession, enterprise and the public interest in modern neo-liberal societies is to be better understood for the individual and collective good in the private and public sector on a global stage.

References

Abraham, J. (2009) 'The pharmaceutical industry, the state and the NHS', in Gabe, J. and Calnan, M. (eds) *The New Sociology of the Health Service*, Abingdon: Routledge.

Allhoff, F. and Hall, M. (eds) (2014) *The Affordable Care Act Decision: Philosophical and Legal Implications*, New York: Routledge.

Allsop, J. (1995) *Health Policy and the NHS*, London: Longman, 2nd edition.

Allsop, J. and Jones, K. (2008) 'Protecting patients: International trends in medical governance', in Kuhlmann, E. and Saks, M. (eds) *Rethinking Professional Governance: International Directions in Health Care*, Bristol: Policy Press.

Allsop, J. and Saks, M. (eds) (2002) *Regulating the Health Professions*, London: Sage.

Anderson, O. (1989) 'Issues in the health services of the United States', in Field, M. G. (ed.) *Success and Crisis in National Health Systems*, London: Routledge.

Arney, W. (1982) *Power and the Profession of Obstetrics*, Chicago, IL: University of Chicago Press.

Barber, B. (1963) 'Some problems in the sociology of professions', *Daedalus* 92: 669–88.

Barr, D. (2014) *Health Disparities in the United States: Social Class, Race, Ethnicity and Health*, Baltimore, MD: Johns Hopkins University Press, 2nd edition.

Becker, H. (1962) 'The nature of a profession', in National Society for the Study of Education (ed.) *Education for the Professions*, Chicago, IL: University of Chicago Press.

Berlant, J. L. (1975) *Profession and Monopoly: A Study of Medicine in the United States and Great Britain*, Berkeley, CA: University of California Press.

Blank, R. and Burau, V. (2010) *Comparative Health Policy*, Basingstoke: Palgrave Macmillan, 3rd edition.

Blomgren, M. and Waks, C. (2015) 'Coping with contradictions: Hybrid professionals managing institutional complexity', *Journal of Professions and Organization* 2(1): 78–102.

Boyce, R. (2008) 'Professionalism meets entrepreneurialism and managerialism', in Kuhlmann, E. and Saks, M. (eds) *Rethinking Professional Governance: International Directions in Healthcare*, Bristol: Polity Press.

Bradley, E. and Taylor, L. (2013) *The American Health Care Paradox: Why Spending More Is Getting Us Less*, New York: Public Affairs.

Brandt, A. and Gardner, M. (2000) 'The golden age of medicine?', in Cooter, R. and Pickstone, J. (eds) *Medicine in the Twentieth Century*, Amsterdam: Harwood Academic Publishers.

Braverman, H. (1998) *Labor and Monopoly Capital: The Degradation of Work in the Twentieth Century*, New York: Monthly Review Press, New edition.

Brock, D. and Saks, M. (2016) 'Professions and organizations in Europe', *European Management Journal* 34(1): 1–6.

Burrow, J. G. (1963) *AMA: Voice of American Medicine*, Baltimore, MD: Johns Hopkins Press.

Cacace, M. (2012) 'The US healthcare system: Hierarchization with and without the state', in Rothgang, H., Cacace, M., Frisina, L., Grimmeisen, S., Schmid, A. and Wendt, C. (eds) *The State and Healthcare: Comparing OECD Countries*, Basingstoke: Palgrave Macmillan.

Calnan, M. and Gabe, J. (2009) 'The restratification of primary care in England? A sociological analysis', in Gabe, J. and Calnan, M. (eds) *The New Sociology of the Health Service*, Abingdon: Routledge.

Cayleff, S. E. (2016) *Nature's Path: A History of Naturopathic Healing in America*, Baltimore, MD: Johns Hopkins University Press.

Chamberlain, J. M. (2015) *Medical Regulation, Fitness to Practise and Revalidation*, Bristol: Policy Press.

Coombs, J. (2005) *The Rise and Fall of HMOs: An American Health Revolution*, Madison, WI: University of Wisconsin Press.

Dent, M. (2015) 'Managing the medics in Britain', in Carvahlo, T. and Santiago, R. (eds) *Professionalism, Managerialism and Reform in Higher Education and the Health Services*, Basingstoke: Palgrave Macmillan.

Ehrenreich, B. and Ehrenreich, J. (1979) 'The Professional-Managerial Class', in Walker, P. (ed.) *Between Capital and Labour*, Brighton: Harvester Press.

Esland, G. (1980) 'Diagnosis and therapy', in Esland, G. and Salaman, G. (eds) *The Politics of Work and Occupations*, Milton Keynes: Open University Press.

Evetts, J. (2006) 'Organizational and occupational professionalism: The legacies of Weber and Durkheim for knowledge society', in Marcuello, C. and Fados, J. L. (eds) *Sociological Essays for a Global Society: Cultural Change, Social Problems and Knowledge Society*, Zaragoza: Prenas Universitarias de Zaragoza.

Foucault, M. (2001) *Madness and Civilization: A History of Insanity in the Age of Reason*, Abingdon: Routledge Classics.
Friedman, M. (1962) *Capitalism and Freedom*, Chicago, IL: University of Chicago Press.
Gabriel, J. (2014) *Medical Monopoly: Intellectual Property Rights and the Origins of the Modern Pharmaceutical Industry*, Chicago, IL: University of Chicago Press.
Goldacre, B. (2013) *Bad Pharma: How Drug Companies Mislead Doctors and Harm Patients*, New York: Farrar, Straus and Giroux.
Goode, W. (1960) 'Encroachment, charlatanism and the emerging profession: Psychology, sociology and medicine', *American Sociological Review* 25: 902–14.
Greenwood, E. (1957) 'The attributes of a profession', *Social Work* 2(3): 45–55.
Grimmeisen, S. and Frisina, L. (2010) 'The role of the state in the British healthcare system – between marketization and statism', in Rothgang, H., Cacace, M., Frisina, L., Grimmeisen, S., Schmid, A. and Wendt, C. (eds) *The State and Healthcare: Comparing OECD Countries*, Basingstoke: Palgrave Macmillan.
Haas-Wilson, D. (2003) *Managed Care and Monopoly Power: The Antitrust Challenge*, Boston, MA: Harvard University Press.
Hacker, J. (2001) 'Learning from defeat? Political analysis and the failure of health care reform in the United States', *British Journal of Political Science* 31: 61–94.
Ham, C. (2009) *Health Policy in Britain*, Basingstoke: Palgrave Macmillan, 6th edition.
Harrison, S. and Pollitt, C. (1994) *Controlling Health Professionals: The Future of Work and Organization in the National Health Service*, Buckingham: Open University Press.
Hughes, E. (1963) 'Professions', *Daedalus* 92: 655–68.
Johnston, R. (ed.) (2004) *The Politics of Healing: Histories of Alternative Medicine in Twentieth Century North America*, New York: Routledge.
Johnson, T. (1995) 'Governmentality and the institutionalization of expertise', in Johnson, T., Larkin, G. and Saks, M. (eds) *Health Professions and the State in Europe*, London: Routledge.
Jones, C. and Porter, R. (1994) 'Introduction', in Jones, C. and Porter, R. (eds) *Reassessing Foucault: Power, Medicine and the Body*, London: Routledge.
Kaufman, M. (1988) 'Homeopathy in America: The rise and fall and persistence of a medical heresy', in Gevitz, N. (ed.) *Other Healers: Unorthodox Medicine in America*, Baltimore, MD: Johns Hopkins University Press.
King, S. M. and Chilton, B. S. (2009) *Administration in the Public Interest: Principles, Policies, and Practices*, Durham, NC: University of Carolina Press.
Kirkpatrick, I., Hartley, K., Kuhlmann, E. and Veronesi, G. (2015) Clinical management and professionalism', in Kuhlmann, E., Blank, R., Bourgeault, I. and Wendt, C. (eds) *The Palgrave International Handbook of Healthcare Policy and Governance*, Basingstoke: Palgrave Macmillan.
Klein, R. (2013) *The New Politics of the NHS: From Creation to Reinvention*, London: Radcliffe Publishing, 7th edition.
Krause, E. A. (1996) *The Death of the Guilds: Professions, States and the Advance of Capitalism, 1930 to the Present*, New Haven: Yale University Press.
Levitt, R., Wall, A. and Appleby, J. (1999) *The Reorganized National Health Service*, London: Stanley Thornes Publishers, 6th edition.
Light, D. (2010) 'Health care professions, markets, and countervailing powers', in Bird, C., Conrad, P., Fremont, A. and Timmermans, S. (eds) *Handbook of Medical Sociology*, Nashville, TN: Vanderbilt University Press.
Lukes, S. (2005) *Power: A Radical View*, Basingstoke: Palgrave Macmillan, 2nd edition.

McGivern, G., Currie, G., Ferlie, E., Fitzgerald, L. and Waring, J. (2015) 'Hybrid manager-professionals' identity work: The maintenance and hybridization of medical professionalism in managerial contexts', *Public Administration* 93(2): 412–32.

McKinlay, J. and Arches, J. (1985) 'Towards the proletarianization of physicians', *International Journal of Health Services* 18: 161–95.

Malka, S. (2007) *Daring to Care: American Nursing and Second-Wave Feminism*, Chicago, IL: University of Illinois Press.

Moran, M. (1999) *Governing the Health Care State: A Comparative Study of the United Kingdom, the United States and Germany*, Manchester: Manchester University Press.

Muzio, D., Brock, D. and Suddaby, R. (2013) 'Professions and institutional change: Towards an institutionalist sociology of the professions', *Journal of Management Studies* 50(5): 699–721.

Navarro, V. (1986) *Crisis, Health and Medicine: A Social Critique*, London: Tavistock.

Nelson, H. and Fuller, R. (2017) *From Obamacare to Trumpcare: Why You Should Care*, Amazon Books: Kindle edition.

Nettleton, S. (1992) *Power, Pain and Dentistry*, Buckingham: Open University Press.

Newton, K. and van Deth, J. (2010) *Foundations of Comparative Politics*, Cambridge: Cambridge University Press, 2nd edition.

Ng, T., Harrington, C. and Kitchener, M. (2010) 'Medicare and Medicaid in long-term care', *Health Affairs* 29(1): 20–28.

Parkin, F. (1979) *Marxism and Class Theory: A Bourgeois Critique*, London: Tavistock.

Parry, N. and Parry, J. (1976) *The Rise of the Medical Profession*, London: Croom Helm.

Parsons, T. (1952) *The Social System*, London: Tavistock.

Peltz, M. (ed.) (2008) *Medicare and Medicaid: Critical Issues and Developments*, New York: Nova Science Publishers.

Porter, R. (2002) *Blood and Guts: A Short History of Medicine*, London: Allen Lane.

Potter, W. (2013) 'Producing public opinion: How the insurance system shaped US health care', in Watson, P. (ed.) *Health Care Reform and Globalisation: The US, China and Europe in Comparative Perspective*, Abingdon: Routledge.

Ramsden, E. (2013) 'Science and medicine in the United States of America', in Jackson, M. (ed.) *The Oxford Handbook of the History of Medicine*, Oxford: Oxford University Press.

Roberts, J. and Group, T. (2001) *Nursing, Physician Control and the Medical Monopoly: Historical Perspectives on Gendered Inequality in Roles, Rights and Range of Practice*, Bloomington, IN: Indiana University Press.

Rodwin, M. (2011) *Conflicts of Interest and the Future of Medicine: The United States, France and Japan*, New York: Oxford University Press.

Rosenthal, E. (2017) *An American Sickness: How Healthcare Became Big Business and How You Can Take It Back*, New York: Penguin Press.

Roszak, T. (1995) *The Making of a Counter Culture*, Berkeley, CA: University of California Press.

Roth, J. (1974) 'Professionalism: The Sociologists' Decoy', *Work and Occupations* 1: 6–23.

Saks, M. (1992) 'Introduction', in Saks, M. (ed.) *Alternative Medicine in Britain*, Oxford: Clarendon Press.

Saks, M. (1995) *Professions and the Public Interest: Medical Power, Altruism and Alternative Medicine*, London: Routledge.

Saks, M. (2000) 'Medicine and the counter culture', in Cooter, R. and Pickstone, J. (eds) *Medicine in the Twentieth Century*, Amsterdam: Harwood Academic Publishers.

Saks, M. (2002) 'Empowerment, participation and the rise of orthodox biomedicine', in Byrt, R. and Dooher, J. (eds) *Empowerment, and Participation: Power, Influence and Control in Contemporary Health Care*, Dinton: Quay Books.

Saks, M. (2010) 'Analyzing the professions: The case for a neo-Weberian approach', *Comparative Sociology* 9(6): 887–915.

Saks, M. (2012) 'Defining a profession: The role of knowledge and expertise', *Professions and Professionalism* 2: 1–10.

Saks, M. (2015a) 'Health policy and complementary and alternative medicine', in Kuhlmann, E., Blank, R., Bourgeault, I. and Wendt, C. (eds) *The Palgrave International Handbook of Healthcare Policy and Governance*, Basingstoke: Palgrave Macmillan.

Saks, M. (2015b) 'Power and professionalisation in CAM: A sociological approach', in Gale, N. and McHale, J. (eds) *The Routledge Handbook of Complementary Medicine in Social Science and Law*, Abingdon: Routledge.

Saks, M. (2015c) *Professions, State and the Market: Medicine in Britain, the United States and Russia*, Abingdon: Routledge.

Saks, M. (2016a) 'Professions and power', in Dent, M., Bourgeault, I., Dennis, J. and Kuhlmann, E. (eds) *The Routledge Companion on Professions and Professionalism*, Abingdon: Routledge.

Saks, M. (2016b) 'Review of theories of professions, organizations and society: Neo-Weberianism, neo-institutionalism and eclecticism', *Journal of Professions and Organization* 3(2): 170–87.

Saks, M. (2016c) 'The regulation of the English health professions: Zoos, circuses or safari parks?', in Liljegren, A. and Saks, M. (eds) *Professions and Metaphors: Understanding Professions in Society*, Abingdon: Routledge.

Saks, M. (2018 forthcoming) 'Professions, self-interests and the public interest: Theoretical and methodological challenges', in Pfadenhauer, M. and Schnell, C. (eds) *Handbook of the Sociology of Professions*, Berlin: Axel Springer.

Saunders, P. (2007) *Urban Politics: A Sociological Interpretation*, Abingdon: Routledge.

Sciulli, D. (2005) 'Continental sociology of professions today: Conceptual contributions', *Current Sociology* 53(6): 915–42.

Scott, W. R., Ruef, M., Mendel, P. J. and Caronna, C. A. (2000) *Institutional Change and Healthcare Organizations*, Chicago, IL: The University of Chicago Press.

Starr, P. (1982) *The Social Transformation of American Medicine*, New York: Basic Books.

Starr, P. (2013) *Remedy and Reaction: The Peculiar American Struggle over Health Care Reform*, New Haven, CT: Yale University Press, Revised edition.

Stevens, R. (1998) *American Medicine and the Public Interest*, Berkeley, CA: University of California Press.

Stiglitz, J. (2010) *Freefall: Free Markets and the Global Economy*, New York: W. W. Norton & Co.

Thomas, J., Pollard, K. C. and Sellman, D. (2014) *Interprofessional Working in Health and Social Care: Professional Perspectives*, Basingstoke: Palgrave Macmillan, 2nd edition.

Tritter, J., Koivusalo, M., Ollila, E. and Dorfman, P. (2010) *Globalisation, Markets and Healthcare Policy: Redrawing the Patient as Consumer*, Abingdon: Routledge.

Tulchinsky, T. and Varavikova, E. (2009) *The New Public Health*, Burlington, MA: Elsevier, 2nd edition.

Weber, M. (1968) *Economy and Society: An Outline of Interpretive Sociology*, New York: Bedminster Press.
Weisz, G. (2006) *Divide and Conquer: A Comparative History of Medical Specialization*, New York: Oxford University Press.
Wilensky, H. (1964) 'The professionalization of everyone?', *American Journal of Sociology* 70(2): 137–58.

Index

academic knowledge 111, 119–20
academics 86, 89, 90
accountability 35, 36, 94, 95
accountancy profession 3–4, 16, 31, 32, 36, 38, 94, 113, 124; Big Four/Five firms 36, 124, 161, 163, 165, 169; commercialised professionalism 73, 77, 78, 138, 139; differentiated markets 76, 77; gender issues *see* female lawyers/accountants and gender; and global financial crisis 17; green accounting 53; and lawyers, disputes over jurisdiction 29; long hours culture 142–4, 145, 148, 149, 150; multinational firms 139; outsourcing and offshoring 37; political identification of accountants 80; *see also* regulation and governance of accountancy profession
Accounting, Organizations and Society 1
accumulation, regimes of 75, 82
advertising agencies 112, 124
agency 78; and institutional entrepreneurship 123, 124; and new practice development 117
alliance governance 122, 126
allopathy versus homeopathy 29
alternative medicine 183, 184, 185
altruistic values 178; in medicine 4, 177, 179, 183, 187, 188
American Medical Association 181, 183, 185
American Psychological Association 29–30
anti-universalism 11
Apple 27, 88
apprenticeships 30
Arthur Andersen 36
articles 30
associate lawyers 33–4, 144

Association of Professional (Golf) Tour Caddies (APTC) 28
Association of Women Solicitors 147
attrition rates 140, 148, 149
audit 26
Australia: female professionals 137; medical profession 188
automation 90, 91
autonomy 13, 21, 32, 39, 69, 94, 110; and entrepreneurship 111, 117, 118; loss of 27

Baker & McKenzie 36–7
banking sector 54
Bar Council 79
BCCI (Bank of Commerce and Credit International) 79
Big Four/Five accounting firms 36, 124, 161, 163, 165, 169
billable hours targets 144, 145
Black, Asian, Minority Ethnic (BAME) female professionals 138
Blair, Tony 186
Blue Cross health insurance 182
Blue Shield health insurance 182
Bombardier (aircraft company) 88
bonuses, gender pay gap 137–8
Bourdieusianism 70–1, 142, 144, 149–50
bourgeoisie 70; *see also* middle class
Brexit vote 9, 10
Britain *see* United Kingdom
British Medical Association (BMA) 72, 79, 185
bureau-managerial-professional regimes 95
bureaucracy 26, 27, 29, 95

Canada: female accountants 137; medical profession 188

Canary Wharf development 37
capability, social and relational 105–6
capital: cultural 70–1, 72, 73, 79, 80, 81, 82, 87; economic 70, 71; human 142, 144, 148; social 116, 121, 125
capitalism 15, 91, 150, 179; financialised 150; global 138, 139, 140, 143, 145; patriarchal 141–5
Carnegie Commission 13
case treatment 106; inter- and multi-professional action in 102–3; multiple 103–4
Challenger disaster (1986) 35
China 87
church 28
citizen journalists 10
citizenship 73, 75
civil service 75, 77, 80; junior civil servants 79; senior civil servants 80
class 31, 87
classic professional service firms 112, 126
client relationship managers 33
client relationships 13, 33, 37, 104, 105, 106, 110, 114
clients, power of 139, 141, 143
Clifford Chance 32, 146
cloning 141, 146
co-presence 89, 90
codes of ethics 15, 19, 28, 178
cognitive dimension of social capital 121
cognitive science 27
collective justice 2, 11
collectivism 11
collegiality 13, 39, 102, 106
commercialised professionalism 73–4, 75, 77–8, 79, 81, 86, 87, 138, 139, 145
communication 12, 26, 114, 125
community 2, 11, 12
competency models 105
competition 15, 16, 33; price 15
competitiveness 139, 142; international 74, 75
complementors, in entrepreneurial ecosystems 119
complexity theory 4, 140, 141, 145, 149
conflicts between organisational and professional logics 93–107; coping responses 97–101 (combining professional and organisational logics 98, 99–100; interweaving multiple logics 98, 100–1; protecting professional logic 98–9; *see also* hybrid professionalism); as productive 96–7
conservatism, service class 67–8

Conservative Party, identification with 79–80
constructivist view of entrepreneurship 111
consumer choice 14, 18
consumer empowerment 40
consumer voice, in medicine 183
contests, framing 46, 57–8
cost effectiveness 3
counter culture 178, 183, 186
Cravath Swaine and Moore 31
Cravath system 33, 34
credentialing 13, 14, 15, 30, 70, 71, 112
cultural assets 71, 87; capital 70–1, 72, 73, 79, 80, 81, 82, 87; difference 11, 12; fragmentation 9, 11, 12, 19; homogenisation 11; individualism 111; politics 12

decoupling 49–50
democratic deficit 10
democratisation 138; of knowledge 10, 12, 26, 30
dentists/dentistry 79, 178
Dentons-Dacheng 32, 36
deprofessionalisation 32, 91, 150, 183
deregulation 16, 18, 139
deskilling 32, 88, 91
Diagnostic and Statistical Manual of Mental Disorders (DSM) 29–30
Diagnostic Related Groups 182
disaggregation 15
discretion 27, 94
disruptions, and framing strategies 46, 56–7
distributed firm ecosystems 122, 126
diversity policy 141, 147–9
division of labour: gendered 141, 142; new international 87
doctors 94, 95; political identification 79–80; *see also* medicine
donotpay.co.uk 40
Durkheim, Emile 9, 14

e-cigarettes debate 55, 56, 57–8, 59
e-discovery 40–1
earnings 28; inequality 13, 137–8
economic capital 70, 71
ecosystem view of entrepreneurship *see* entrepreneurial ecosystem
education 13, 28, 30, 70, 71, 75, 87, 99, 101; higher 13, 89–90, 138; remote 89–90; *see also* academics; universities
efficiency 3, 95; market 9, 13
elite class 87, 90, 91
embodiment, female versus male 145–6

Index

emergent service workers 87, 91–2
employment relationship, and service class 68, 71–2
energy debate *see* fracking debate
engineers/engineering 73, 77, 80, 94
Enron 9, 16, 36, 160, 161
entrepreneurial ecosystem 3, 114–22, 125, 126; actors in 118–20; dynamic 121; governance 121–2; network relations in 120–1; static 121
entrepreneurial firm 3, 115–18, 118–19, 125–6; governance 117–18, 126; new practice creation 116–17; new venture management 115–16; skills 73, 74, 86; team 3, 113–15, 125
entrepreneurialism 2–3, 103, 139
entrepreneurship 110–11; and autonomy 111, 117, 118; and change 111; constructivist view of 111; established networks as barriers to 110; institutional 122–5, 126; and opportunity 111; versus professionalism 111–13
epistemic arbiters 46, 54
epistemic arbitrage 46, 52–4
epistemic closure 59
equal opportunities policies 141
ethics, professional 13, 14, 15, 19, 28, 35, 178
ethnicity 138
European Commission 59
European Court of Justice 30
European Union 49, 55, 163
experience-based knowledge 114
expert citizen 10
expertise 26, 28; and new practice development 117; war on 9–11, 12, 18, 22

Federal Drugs Administration, United States 181
female lawyers/accountants 3–4, 137–56; associations and pressure groups 147; attrition rates 148, 149; Black, Asian, Minority Ethnic (BAME) 138; corporeality, as lack of professionalism 145–6; delaying childbirth 150; female-typed roles 137; foregoing of marriage/family 150; and long hours culture 142–4, 148; low-status roles 138, 140, 145, 150; misrecognition for specialisms 145; partnership positions 138; pay 137–8; sexualised roles 146, 150
field-level analysis *see* organisational fields

finance capital, multinational 11
financial scandals 9, 16, 17, 18, 79, 161
financialisation 27, 139, 149, 150
Finley Kumble 34
firm-level entrepreneurial processes; *see* entrepreneurial firm
Flexible Accumulation 75
flexible work initiatives 149
Flexner reforms (1910), United States 181
Flom, Joe 31
Fordism 73, 74, 75
Foucauldianism 178–9
fracking debate 55, 56–7, 58, 59
framing strategies 3, 46, 55–9, 60; contests 46, 57–8; disruptions 46, 56–7; normalisation 46, 58–9
free markets 13–16, 18, 69
Freshfields 37
functionalist approach to professions 28, 177–8

Gasland (documentary film) 57, 58
gender 3–4, 137–56; equality/inequality 116, 138, 141, 147, 148; and long hours culture 142–4, 145, 148, 149, 150; pay gap 137–8; and public–private sphere divide 142; segregation 137, 145; shift in law and accountancy 139–41; stereotypes 141, 148; and tournament system 141, 144–5, 146
gendered division of labour 141, 142
General Medical Council 184, 186
Glenn, John 35
global financial crisis (2008) 16–17, 86–7, 161
global value chain (GVC) 87, 88
globalisation 10, 11, 31, 33, 36–7, 49, 76, 87, 91, 149
Google translate 90
governance 4, 34, 35; alliance 122, 126; entrepreneurial 117–18, 121–2, 126; self- 14; transnational 48–9; *see also* regulation and governance of accountancy profession
governmentality 26, 34, 35, 178–9
grand narratives 9, 11
Great Recession (2008) 16, 17, 28, 33
Greek accounting profession 162, 163
green accounting 53
Greenberg Traurig LLP 117

health care 16, 53–4, 99, 101, 124; *see also* doctors; medicine

health insurance: United Kingdom 72, 184–5; United States 181, 182–3
Health Maintenance Organisations (HMOs), United States 182
Health and Social Care Act (2012), United Kingdom 187
higher education 13, 89–90, 138; women in 139
hive minds 27, 38
homeopathy versus allopathy 29
H&R Block Tax Preparers 90
hub-firm ecosystems 122, 126
human capital theory 142, 144, 148
hybrid professionalism 3, 98, 101–6, 187, 188

IBM 38, 40, 90
ideas 53
identities 96
ideological role of professionals 3, 21
ideologies 96
ignorant client thesis 74, 80
incentivisation 16
inclusion policy 141, 147–9
income inequality 13
individualism, cultural 111
individualistic professionalism 72
inequality, earnings/income 13, 137–8
information, interpretation of 3, 20, 22
innovation 95, 96, 110, 112–13, 114
Instagram 90
institutional change: divergent 123; professions as objects of 157, 166; professions as source of 21–2
institutional entrepreneurship 122–5, 126; in emerging fields 123–4; in mature and maturing fields 124–5, 126
institutional theory 50, 122–3; neo-institutionalism 177, 180
interactionism 28
interdependence 39
interest: and institutional entrepreneurship 123; *see also* self-interest
International Forum of Independent Audit Regulators (IFIAR) 160
International Monetary Fund (IMF) 51; Committee of Eminent Persons 54
internationality 47
intrapreneurship 111
Irish accountancy profession, regulation and governance of 158, 162, 164–5; Big Four/Five firms and 163, 165; delegated self-regulation 4, 159–60, 168; events leading to regulatory change 160–1; and fraud 159–60; oversight body 160–1, 164, 169; resistance to changes 164–5, 168, 169, 170
Irish Auditing and Accounting Supervisory Authority (IAASA) 160, 161

Journal of Professions and Organization 1
judges 79, 93, 94
junior civil servants 79
jurisdiction(s): disputes over 29, 39; in transnational space 48
justice, collective 2, 11

Kaiser Permanente 88, 182
Keynesian economics, crisis of 13, 16
Keynesian welfare state 18, 75
keystone model ecosystem 122
knowledge 26, 28, 29–31, 88; academic 111, 119–20; creation 113; democratisation of 10, 12, 26, 30; experience-based 114; hierarchies 52; integration 113, 114; local 11; movement of 87, 88; seeking 113–14; sharing 113–15; tacit 114
knowledge-based work 13, 17
knowledge strategies 3, 46, 60; epistemic arbiters 46, 54; epistemic arbitrage 46, 52–3; leveraging 46, 51–2, 54
Kodak Eastman 90
KPMG 36
Kushner, Jared 30

labour market: democratisation of 138; women's participation in 139
Labour Party 67, 80, 86
labour politics, decline of 67, 86
law/law firms/lawyers 3–4, 16, 17, 28, 30, 31, 32, 38, 80, 94, 101; and accountancy, disputes over jurisdiction 29; associates 33–4, 144; billable hours targets 144; commercialised professionalism 77, 78, 138, 139; Cravath system 33, 34; diamond model 34; gender issues in *see* female lawyers/accountants gender; and globalisation 36–7; lack of trust in 36; lockstep remuneration 34; long hours culture 142–4, 145, 148, 149, 150; meritocratic remuneration 34; multinational 139; outsourcing and offshoring 37, 39; political identification of professionals 79, 80; pyramid model 33; rainmakers 33, 34;

law/law firms/lawyers *continued*
  start-up management 116; and the state 75–6; technology use 40–1; tournament system 33–4, 141, 144–5, 146
Law Society 72–3, 75, 79; Gender Equality Scheme 148
lead clients, in entrepreneurial ecosystems 119
legacy students 30
Legal Aid Franchise Board 75
legal aid schemes 73, 75
Legal Services Act (2007), United Kingdom 34
LegalZoom 40
leveraging 46, 51–2, 54
licensing 14, 15
Lipton, Marty 31
local knowledge 11
lockstep remuneration 34
long hours culture 142–4, 145, 148, 149, 150

male breadwinner discourse 143
management consulting 16–17, 38, 76, 112, 113, 124, 125
managerial skill 73, 74, 86
managers 13
market efficiency 9, 13
marketisation 27; of the self 146–7
markets 29, 69, 86, 95; rising salience of 13–16, 18
Marxism 28, 179
Medicaid, United States 182
Medical Registration Act (1858), United Kingdom 184
Medicare, United States 182
medicine 28, 29, 30, 31, 91, 94; altruistic values 177, 179, 183, 187, 188; clinical guidelines in 102–3; codes of ethics 178; combining professional and organisational logics in 99, 100; devolution of work in 39; diagnostic 90; exclusionary professional closure in 188; public interest versus self-interest in 4, 177, 178–88; remote working in 39, 88; status and power in 177, 180, 182, 183, 184, 185, 187; *see also* doctors; health care; medicine in Britain; medicine in United States; New Zealand, medical profession; nurses; Sweden, medical profession
medicine in Britain 4, 177, 178, 179, 180, 183–7; alternative therapists 184, 185; code of conduct 178; general practitioners 185, 186; health insurance 72, 184–5; National Health Service (NHS) 16, 35, 72, 75, 76, 77, 80, 185–7; New Public Management principles 16, 35, 187; partnership concept 186; Patients' Charter 186; private sector 184, 185, 186; reforms (2010 onwards) 186–7; regulated self-regulation 186–7; specialist practitioners 185–6
medicine in the United States 4, 29, 177, 178, 179, 180–3, 187; alternative therapists 183; consumer voice in 183; health insurance 181, 182–3; Obama health reforms 182–3; private sector 180–1, 182; specialist practitioners 181–2, 183
mentoring 147
meritocratic remuneration 34
Mid-Staffordshire NHS Hospital Trust 39
middle class 87, 91, 142; *see also* bourgeoisie
midwifery 29, 185
modernisation 138
modernity 11, 74
monopoly 27, 28
mortgage market 17
motherhood, discourse of 140
multi-disciplinary practice 102, 124, 126
multinational firms 11, 139
myths and legends, professions' capacity to create 26, 27–8, 31

narratives 26, 27–8, 30–1
National Health Insurance Act (1911), United Kingdom 72, 184–5
National Health Service (NHS), United Kingdom 16, 35, 72, 75, 76, 77, 80, 185–7
National Union of Teachers 79
neo-colonial effects 52
neo-institutionalism 177, 180
neo-liberalism 2–3, 12–16, 17–18, 19, 22, 38, 50, 87, 93, 95, 138, 139, 140, 143, 149, 150
neo-professional service firms 112, 126
neo-Weberianism 177, 179–80; *see also* Weberian perspective
networks: in entrepreneurial ecosystems 120–1; established, as barriers to entrepreneurial activities 110; structural holes 48, 53; transnational 49, 50
new international division of labour 87
New Labour 186
new practice development 116–17

New Public Management 13, 15–16, 26, 34–5, 38–9, 93, 95, 96, 98; in health services 16, 187, 188
new venture creation 115–16
New Zealand, medical profession 188
normalisation, and framing strategies 46, 58–8
Norton Rose 32
nurses 39, 93, 94, 182, 185

Obamacare, United States 182–3
OECD (Organisation for Economic Co-operation and Development) 163
offshoring 37, 88, 89
opinion leaders 119
opportunity, and entrepreneurship 111
orchestra model ecosystem 122
organisational assets 70, 71, 87; fields 50–1; and institutional entrepreneurship 122–5, 126
organisational logic, conflict with professional logic *see* conflicts between organisational and professional logics
outsourcing 37, 39, 89, 91

paralegals 29, 39
paramedics 39
Parmalat 9, 16
partnership 41; concept of, in British health care policy 186; female 138; tournament for 33–4, 144–5, 146
paternalism 36
Patients' Charter, United Kingdom 186
patriarchal practices 140, 141–5, 150
patron–client relationships 141, 146
pay: female professionals 137–8; *see also* remuneration
performance: incentives 16; logic 95–6; measurement 95, 97, 99; responses to 98; review 32
pharmaceuticals 77
platform-based network model ecosystems 122
political identification, service class 79–80
portfolio careers 39
post-Fordism 74, 75, 86, 87
post-industrialism 13
post-modernism 2, 9–12, 17, 18, 22
post-truth world 10
power 4, 27, 30, 50, 51, 52, 126, 142, 150; of clients 139, 141, 143; in medicine 177, 180, 182, 183, 184, 185, 187
precariat 87, 92
presenteeism 143, 146

price competition 15
private sector service class 69–70, 81
private sphere: gendered division of labour in 141; versus public sphere 142
privilege 71
productive conflicts 96–7
professional associations 112, 120; erosion of power of 139; national 49; transnational 48
professional boundaries, permeability of 26
professional ethics 13, 14, 15, 19, 28, 35, 178
professional guidelines 102–3
professional logic, conflict with organisational logic *see* conflicts between organisational and professional logics
Professional Oversight Board (POB) 160
professionalism 3, 28–9, 32, 35–6, 38–9; commercialised 73–4, 75, 77–8, 79, 81, 86, 87, 138, 139, 145; individualistic 72; shifting nature of 68; social service 72–3, 74–5, 76, 78, 80, 81, 86, 87, 91; versus entrepreneurship 111–13
profit 19, 74, 75, 77, 139
proletariat 70
promotion 140, 141, 144; *see also* tournament system
property assets 71, 87
pseudo-expertise 10
psychiatry 30
Public Company Accounting Oversight Board (PCAOB) 160
public good 13, 28, 181, 183, 185
public health debates *see* e-cigarettes
public interest: and self-regulatory model for accounting profession 158–9, 164, 168; versus self-interest 178; versus self-interest in medicine 4, 177, 178–88
public sector service class 69–70
public sphere versus private sphere 142
public–private partnerships 35, 81
PwC 32, 90, 147

qualifications *see* credentialing
quality of services 104, 105, 106

radicalism, service class 78–80, 82
rational choice theory 142
rationality 11, 12, 142
reciprocity 39, 121
reflective reframing 113, 114

regulation 46, 120; external 26, 94; medical profession, United Kingdom 186–7
regulation and governance: of accountancy profession 4, 157–76; and Big Four/Five firms 161, 163, 165, 169; enforcement policing work 170; institutional work underpinning the dismantling of self-regulation 158, 166–70, 171; oversight bodies 157–8, 158–9, 166, 167, 168–9, 170, 171; translating global governance trends to local level 161–2, 170; *see also* Irish accountancy profession; self-regulation of accountancy profession
relational dimension of social capital 121
remote working: in education 89–90; in medicine 39, 88
remuneration: lockstep 34; meritocratic 34; *see also* pay
Review Group on Auditing (RGA), Ireland 160
reward systems 33
right politics 18
risk management 3, 19–20
robotics 90, 91
Royal College of Physicians 31
Royal College of Surgeons 31
Royal Dutch Ahold 16

Sage Edge 89
Samsung 27
science 11, 12, 26, 31, 120
scientific professionals 12, 76, 77, 79
security forces 80
self-governance 14
self-interest: versus public interest 178; versus public interest in medicine 4, 177, 178–88
self-promotion 146–7
self-regulation 26, 27, 34
self-regulation of accountancy profession 157, 158, 161–2; delegated 4, 159–60, 168; public interest, underpinnings of 158–9, 168
senior civil servants 80
service class 3, 67, 67–85; assets establishing membership of 70–1; co-ordination/control of labour process 70; conservative nature of 67–8; cultural capital 70–1, 72, 73, 79, 80, 81, 82; economic capital 70, 71; and employment relationship 68, 71–2; fragmentation of 68, 69–71, 80, 81; political identification 79–80; public–private sector divide 69–70, 81; radicalism 78–80, 82; and trust 68, 69, 71–5, 74, 82, 86, 91
sexism 147
sexualisation 146, 150
shadow banking 54
Shipman, Dr Harold 39, 186
Skadden Arps 31, 34
social activities, participation in 146, 150
social capital 116, 121, 125
social ecology 28–9
social reproduction 142–3, 150; women and 141
social service professionalism 72–3, 74–5, 76, 78, 80, 81, 86, 87, 91
social workers 79, 93, 94, 179
socialisation 14, 112
Solicitors from Hell website 36
start-up management 115–16
state 12, 21, 26, 29, 69, 75–6, 79, 80, 86, 120, 179
status 4, 27, 31, 150; in medicine 177, 180, 182, 183, 184, 185
structural dimension of social capital 121
structural holes 48, 53
Sun Microsystems 124
Sweden, medical profession 188

tacit knowledge 95, 114
taxation, epistemic arbitrage 53
teachers 79, 93, 94
team-level entrepreneurial processes 3, 113–15, 125
technical ability 73, 74, 86
Technical and Computer Graphics (TCG) 122
technical middle class 87
technological change 13
technology: disruptive 27; increased use of 40–1, 139
tele-presence 89, 90, 91
tele-robotics 90, 91
Tesla 27
Thatcherism 69
tobacco control *see* e-cigarettes debate
total commitment requirement 141, 143
tournament system 33–4, 141, 144–5, 146
training 14, 26, 28; unconscious bias 148
trait approach to professions 28, 177–8
transnational governance 48–9
transnational professional associations 48; professional projects 3, 46–64; decoupling 49–50; framing strategies 3, 46, 55–9, 60; knowledge strategies 3,

46, 51–4, 60; organisational fields 50–1; transnationality 47–9
transnational social space: structural holes 48; thinness of 48, 49, 51
transparency 36, 38, 95
Trump, President Donald 9, 10, 30, 183
trust 28, 35–6, 38, 89, 121; loss of 26, 34, 35; reinvigoration of 38, 39; and service class 68, 69, 71–5, 74, 82, 86, 91
Tyco International 16

Uniqlo 88
United Kingdom: Brexit vote 9, 10; female accountants 137; medicine in *see* medicine in Britain; political party identification 67, 79–80
United States 16, 17, 19, 87; female accountants 137, 138; medicine in *see* medicine in the United States
universities 86, 88–9, 89–90; in entrepreneurial ecosystems 119–20

values 3, 14, 18, 21, 33, 34, 35, 39, 68, 96, 100, 102, 118, 144, 177, 180
virtual reality 40, 41
vocation 32

wealth, redistribution of 73
Weberian perspective 28, 29, 177, 179–80
welfare state 18, 73, 74, 75, 86, 95
Wiggin media law firm 38
women: higher education 139; labour market participation 139; social reproductive role 141; *see also* female lawyers/accountants
work flows 101, 102, 106; multiple 106; organising as part of 104–5
work intensification 139, 141, 143–4
working class 87
World Health Organisation 57
World Trade Organisation 49, 163
WorldCom 160, 161
wormhole effects 49
WPP 117

Taylor & Francis eBooks

Helping you to choose the right eBooks for your Library

Add Routledge titles to your library's digital collection today. Taylor and Francis ebooks contains over 50,000 titles in the Humanities, Social Sciences, Behavioural Sciences, Built Environment and Law.

Choose from a range of subject packages or create your own!

Benefits for you

- Free MARC records
- COUNTER-compliant usage statistics
- Flexible purchase and pricing options
- All titles DRM-free.

Benefits for your user

- Off-site, anytime access via Athens or referring URL
- Print or copy pages or chapters
- Full content search
- Bookmark, highlight and annotate text
- Access to thousands of pages of quality research at the click of a button.

REQUEST YOUR FREE INSTITUTIONAL TRIAL TODAY

Free Trials Available
We offer free trials to qualifying academic, corporate and government customers.

eCollections – Choose from over 30 subject eCollections, including:

Archaeology	Language Learning
Architecture	Law
Asian Studies	Literature
Business & Management	Media & Communication
Classical Studies	Middle East Studies
Construction	Music
Creative & Media Arts	Philosophy
Criminology & Criminal Justice	Planning
Economics	Politics
Education	Psychology & Mental Health
Energy	Religion
Engineering	Security
English Language & Linguistics	Social Work
Environment & Sustainability	Sociology
Geography	Sport
Health Studies	Theatre & Performance
History	Tourism, Hospitality & Events

For more information, pricing enquiries or to order a free trial, please contact your local sales team:
www.tandfebooks.com/page/sales

Routledge
Taylor & Francis Group

The home of Routledge books

www.tandfebooks.com